"THE FAR LEFT"

By

Billy James Hargis, Founder-Director

CHRISTIAN CRUSADE
Christian Crusade Publication
Box 977
Tulsa 2, Oklahoma

First Edition, 50,000

Copyright, 1964 Christian Crusade

This book was published by Christian Crusade, Tulsa 2, Oklahoma, as a part of a "mass distribution of anti-communist literature" campaign. Write for full listings of books, booklets and other printed anti-communist material written by Billy James Hargis, designed for mass circulation at economical prices.

ABOUT THE AUTHOR

"This Is My Story"
by Billy James Hargis

I am a minister of the gospel of Christ. I was ordained by the Rose Hill Christian Church, Texarkana, Texas, May 30, 1943. My church membership is still there. I served for a while as a Christian Church evangelist. Also, I pastored three churches as a full-time minister — First Christian Church, Sallisaw, Oklahoma; First Christian Church, Granby, Missouri; and First Christian Church, Sapulpa, Oklahoma.

It was while pastor of the First Christian Church, Sapulpa, Oklahoma, that I became aware of the threat of Communism internally. In the fall of 1947, I organized Christian Crusade, as a Christian weapon against Communism and its godless allies.

Christian Crusade publishes two periodicals — *Christian Crusade* monthly magazine (36 pages) and *Weekly Crusader* (8-page anti-Communist intelligence report). My daily broadcasts are carried by radio stations across the nation. These programs are called "Christian Crusade." Also we make available to television stations a Christian Crusade television series and additional educational films produced by our movement. In February every year we conduct an Annual Anti-Communist Leadership School somewhere in America; in August each year we conduct an Annual Convention of Christian Crusade somewhere in America; during the summer months — June, July and August — we conduct the Christian Crusade Anti-Communist Youth University at the Summit Hotel, Manitou Springs, Colorado.

This is my fourth full-length book, the others being *Communist America . . . Must It Be? The Facts About Communism And Our Churches,* and *Communism, The Total Lie.* These books have enjoyed a combined printing of over 300,000.

I suppose I have spoken in as many anti-Communist rallies as anyone. For seventeen years, we have been conducting Christian Crusade Anti-Communist Rallies throughout the United States and the free world, regularly.

My wife is the former Betty Jane Secrest of Portsmouth, Ohio. We have four wonderful children — Bonnie Jane, Billy James II, Becky Jean, and Brenda Jo. Betty Jane and I thank God daily for these four precious children whose freedom and welfare mean so much to us.

That's about all I can say for myself. I am a minister doing a minister's job. I thank God for the opportunity to influence people for righteousness and truth.

— Billy James Hargis

DEDICATION

While writing this book, I made up my mind to dedicate it to that person in America who, I feel, is most sincerely anti-communist—sort of a "man of the year" in the anti-communist ranks. Since this book was prompted by the assassination of President Kennedy by the Communist Lee Harvey Oswald, and since this same assassin had attempted to take the life of General Edwin A. Walker in his Dallas home last April 10, I feel that no one is more worthy of this "Dedication" than General Walker himself.

So, to General Edwin A. Walker we dedicate this volume because he has been willing to give up everything of material value to pursue his sincere anti-Communist goals. Few Americans would be willing to make the sacrifice that he has made. Even in the face of death, he seemed resigned to give his life joyfully for the cause of Freedom, Liberty and Christian Americanism.

TABLE OF CONTENTS

CHAPTER I
COMMUNISM IS UN-CHRISTIAN, UN-AMERICAN

I believe in Jesus Christ as the promised Messiah, the Saviour of all believers, whether they are Jew or Gentile, and in His divinely authorized Church, the body of believers. I believe in America, her freedoms, her ideals and in her traditions. To me, America is one of the greatest gifts that God has ever given man, outside of the gift of His only begotten Son and His divinely-inspired Bible. The spiritual traditions and ideals of freedom of Americanism are, I believe, the greatest of any nation in history.

I believe in the Constitution of the United States, and in the Constitutions of the fifty Republics that make up these United States. I believe that Communism violates all of our freedoms that we have enjoyed as Americans. I believe that Communism is opposed to our American ideals, transgresses our traditions, is weakening our nation's unity, and is wrecking our American way of life. To me, it is an inevitable fact that if Communism triumphs, Americanism will die.

My sole objective in writing this book on the "Far Left" is to help save America from a godless, despotic dictatorship which is based on bloodshed, barbarism, suppression, and slavery, all of which are un-Christian, un-American and unpalatable to freedom-loving men. I am convinced that every real American, if he but knew the truth, would strive to defend his nation from Communists who, utilizing their weapons of intrigue and infamy, are imposing upon our country their profane pattern of serfdom.

Jesus Christ said, "Ye shall know the truth, and the truth shall make ye free." It is my firm faith that the first step in defense of American safety and the preservation of Constitutional Government is to break the conspiracy of silence enveloping and endangering her. What I will state in this book about Communism internally and its left-wing allies is not known to me alone, nor is it news to many in high places and in lesser positions. But most of those who know these facts speak them in fearful whispers, dreading the intimidation of a powerful left-wing press. This "fear hysteria" will not cure the creeping paralysis of inertia attacking America, nor will it arouse Americans to the actual menace of Communism.

Up until the assassination of John F. Kennedy on the streets of Dallas, Friday, November 22, most Americans said of the threat of Communism, "It cannot happen here." Now, all Americans, with any loyalty and patriotism, know that it can happen here and, indeed, it did happen here. Communism internally has been responsible for the assassination of the President of the United States.

The power of Communism and/or fear of Communism was so rampant in the land that, rather than a ground-swell against left-wing and pro-Communist men and movements in the United States, demanding justice from the godless cause that took the life of the President of the United States, there has instead been a vain attempt by men, motivated either by love of Communism or by fear of Communism, to equate Communism with other so-called "extremists" such as conservatives, outspoken anti-Communists, etc.

Furthermore, those who did not attempt to equate Communism with anti-Communism sought to blame *all*

6

Americans for the death of the President. As former Congressman Hamilton Fish of New York City, who was the Chairman of the first Congressional Committee ever to investigate Communism in the United States, wrote after the assassination of President Kennedy, "Why should patriotic Americans absorb the blame and the stigma for the criminal act of a Communist? The American people, including the citizens of Dallas, are no more responsible than the Mexican people were for the murder of Trotsky by another Marxist Communist. Lenin once said, "Destroying all opposition by invective, slander, smear and blackmail is one of the techniques of Communism." The top Commissars in the Kremlin must be laughing up their sleeves watching professional "liberals" and political opportunists smearing patriotic Americans for exposing and combating the Communist menace to freedom everywhere, particularly in Latin America. Let us stop playing Russian Roulette, or flirting with world Communism that seeks to destroy and bury us. Let us unite in preventing Communist smear propaganda from dividing the American people and undermining our prestige throughout the world."

Robert Morris, former chief investigator for the Senate Internal Security Subcommittee investigating Communism and, more recently, President of the University of Dallas, said in an editorial following the assassination of President Kennedy: "Moscow, American Communists, and their allies are waging a sustained campaign against the verdict that a Communist shot the President. Communist pamphleteers are passing out leaflets in New York City in a campaign that has no precedent, and charging the responsibility for the assassi-

7

tion of the President to J. Edgar Hoover and other anti-Communists. We have too often seen these campaigns succeed in the past. This is the framework for the struggle ahead. A powerful Communist-originated campaign will be leveled now, with emotional cover, to equate all criticism and dissent with 'hatred that generates assassination'. The Communists and their allies will now be working day and night to associate resistance to their aggression with 'hateful right-wing activity'. Let us hope that the new religious spirit that prevails now across the land will help the American people see through this sophistry."

This, then, is the purpose of this book. Not only will we attempt to expose Communists, the Communist fronts, and the Communist conspiracy internally, but we will also focus a spotlight of truth upon those organizations and men who have aided and abetted the cause of Communism by word or deed, whether intentionally or unintentionally.

The entire left-wing movement is of the devil. As Christians, the first way in which we can recognize the devil and his presence is that he is a liar. He speaks lies, he uses lies, his conspiracy is built on lies. Hear the words of Jesus and His controversy with the Jews: "Why do you not understand my speech? Even because you cannot hear my word. Ye are of your father, the devil, and the lusts of your father ye will do. He was a murderer from the beginning and abode not in the truth because there is no truth in him. When he speaketh a lie, he speaketh of his own, for he is a liar and the father of it, and because I tell you the truth, ye believe me not." What are the lies that are confronting the American people today as a result of this internal Communist conspiracy, and in connection with this murder of the President of the United States?

The first lie is that there is no conspiracy, that the Communist conspiracy does not exist, and there are not thousands upon thousands of trained Communist agents in this country today, some of them trained, as Lee Harvey Oswald obviously, was, to be expert killers. The murder of the President of the United States was one of the most skillful acts of killing imaginable and could have been accomplished only by great training, and now the facts show that Oswald received such training inside the Soviet Union, while he lived there as a citizen.

It is a lie hatched in hell that the so-called "right-wing extremists" are guilty of the murder of the President of the United States. That lie was put out as official Communist Party propaganda in the first flash of Tass News Agency in Moscow as reported in this country within minutes after the President was killed. Tass, the Russian Communist News Agency, said it was believed that "right-wing extremists" were responsible for the murder of the President, and specifically branded General Edwin A. Walker as being one of those guilty. (Tass was strangely quiet in later days when the Federal Bureau of Investigation revealed that evidence indicated that Lee Harvey Oswald also had tried to take the life of General Edwin A. Walker in his Dallas home on the previous April 10.)

When you hear these lies of the Communists, you know they are lies. You know,therefore, that the devil is at work in the person who speaks them and you know

9

that the Communist conspiracy is operating in that person. You have no need to look any further. You have no need to look for a connection with the Communist Party, for a Communist Party card, or for an organization which has been branded as a "Communist front" with which the person might be affiliated, because the conspiracy is a spiritual frame of mind, a satanically spiritual thing, and its presence is betrayed by its nature.

Not only does the devil, in his followers, lie, but the devil is an accuser. In Revelations 12:10-11 we read of the vision of John exiled on Patmos: "I heard a loud voice saying in Heaven, Now is come salvation, and strength, and the kingdom of our God, and the power of his Christ: for the accuser of our brethren is cast down, which accused them before our God day and night. And they overcame him by the Blood of the Lamb, and by the word of their testimony; and they loved not their lives unto the death."

The devil is an accuser and he will appear, accusing you and accusing me. He will accuse good Americans of feeling hate if they oppose Communism. And when we hear over and over again that everybody who opposes Communism or evil is a monger of hatred, we begin to get frightened, but we shouldn't. As Christians, we know the reality and the power of the satanic accuser.

We must live in love and it is because of love that we take a stand for liberty and freedom throughout the Scriptures, we are taught that love is the keeping of the law. "Love thy neighbor as thyself" is the summary of the second table of God's law. If you love God, then you will keep His Commandments. And to keep God's law does not simply mean you obey it, it means you enforce it. You are the keeper, you and I. To us, God has entrusted the whole of His law and if we break it in one point, we break it in all.

How do we show our love of God? By a silly, sentimental affection for murders and thieves and killers and conspirators? Heaven forbid. We show it by an enforcement of God's law and a punishment of those who willfully and maliciously break God's law and teach the breaking of God's law. That is love and no man can exercise it without a heroic effort. One must love God to punish a criminal just as a man must love his child in order to punish him.

Yes, it has happened here. Even the death of the President of the United States at the hands of a Communist assassin has not stirred the masses of the American people or the leadership of America sufficiently to resist Communism internally and to enforce our laws against the Communist conspiracy within.

In America, the seeds of confusion and disunion are spawning and spreading, and Communism is growing. In their efforts to wean Americans from Americanism, Communists devilishly revile and defile everyone whose opinions and convictions differ in any way from their own. Their subtle, sinister schemings sway and mislead many Americans who in ignorance or weakness yield or submit to Communism their previous loyalty to God, to country, and to their fellow men. We have no right to give up our country to the Communist conspiracy without a battle. We are the beneficiaries of the sacrifices of countless American soldiers who, throughout our life as a Republic, have fought for our God-given rights, our religious, industrial, educational, and social freedoms, freedom of speech and of the press; and we, their heirs, must never surrender them.

Hatred has no place in the heart of any Christian, but love of country should be in every Christian's heart to inspire him to defend America against any system of government that would wrench our rights from us and destroy our freedom.

J. Edgar Hoover, head of the Federal Bureau of Investigation, tried to warn the American people in a speech entitled "Communism Is A Menace" at the close of World War II, saying that Communists were liars and that Communism was a system based on lies and deception, and that no American citizen could believe in the promises, goals, or objectives of this deceptive, satanic international conspiracy. Hoover was concerned over the inroads that Communism was making in the United States immediately following World War II, and said in his speech:

"During the past five years, American Communists have made their deepest inroads upon our national life. In our vaunted tolerance for all peoples, the Communists have found our Achilles' heel. The godless, truthless way of life that American Communists would force upon America can mean only tyranny and oppression if they succeed. When they raise their false cry of unity, remember there can be no unity with the enemies of our way of life who are attempting to undermine our democratic institutions. The Fascist-minded tyrant whom we conquered on the battlefields is no different from the American communistic corruptionist who now uses the tricks of the confidence man until his forces are

12

sufficiently strong to rise with arms in revolt. When they preach unity, let us not forget that when we were struggling to prepare for defense of the United States, the Communists preached pacifism and fought American efforts to aid our allies and to build our common defenses. For true Americans, there can be no unity with the enemy within and no compromise with those who would destroy all that we fight for. When it comes to governmental systems, we prefer our own American way, and we do not want the Communists in this country attempting to undermine our democracy or any of our institutions.

"Americanism is on trial. Its real test lies in the ability of red-blooded Americans to meet and defeat the fifth column of destruction. A knowledge of the lurking menace is necessary. We are rapidly reaching the time when loyal Americans must be willing to stand up and be counted. If we would protect America, we must determine that no group of espionage agents or subverters, and no coalition of paid anti-American propagandists shall sway us from our American way of life. To allow America to become infected with the malignant growth of Communism is a breach of our trust to those who gave their lives for American principles."

The Communists themselves boast that for every party member, there are ten others ready to do the party's work. These include their satellites, their fellow travelers, and their so-called progressive and phony liberal allies.

In recent years, we have seen the growth of a far-reaching patriotic movement of average Americans called "conservatism." These conservatives represent all classes of American life, especially those of the middle class Americans who are motivated by love of God and country and freedom, and are willing to risk persecution in their local communities, misunderstanding, and, in some instances, prosecution, because of their fearless stand for traditional American concepts and Christian principles. As a result of the patriotic actions of these people and their willingness to sacrifice for the cause that they believe in, more and more Congressmen, Senators, and other elected officials reflect the conservative philosophy.

There is no doubt in my mind that the Communist assassin, Lee Oswald, intended to kill the President of the United States and disappear in the confused crowd, thus letting the conservative, anti-Communist element of Dallas take the blame. But it didn't work. God is on the throne. He saw to it that Lee Harvey Oswald was apprehended by a courageous Dallas policeman, Officer Tippit, who, in turn, gave his life for the cause of freedom in attempting to arrest the Communist assassin of the President.

To understand Communism and its so-called "sophisticated intellectual allies" in the United States, comprised of left-wing or pro-Communist elements, we must understand that, by nature, these groups are godless. Communism and most adherents of "liberal intellectualism" have a common motivation, a defiance of God's dominion over mankind. However, the defiance of God and His supernatural word by the liberals and Communists, is not new to mankind.

Long ago at the very dawn of the human race, the divine rights of Heaven were called into question. In the Garden of Eden, Adam and Eve violated God's com-

14

mand. It was the first revolt of the human race against Divine authority. It was the first attempt of frail humanity to "grapple with the Lord God" and to "vanquish Him in His Heaven". This first revolt was a dismal failure as will be all similar revolts in history, including the one inspired by Marx, Lenin, Stalin, and Khrushchev. From the very moment of the first revolt of the human race against Divine authority, man needed God to right the wrong brought by the sin of Adam and Eve; for God it was who was offended and God alone it was who could forgive the offense. Man had been destined for eternal life, but sin robbed him of that Divine inheritance. Thus, in order to regain what he had lost, man felt his need of God and realized that he was absolutely dependent upon God. Deep in the heart of all of God's creation was an eternal yearning to bow and worship before One whom he looked upon as a Diety, One who would satisfy the eternal cry of the creature for the Creator. When man turned away from the true God, we find him creating for himself a false god to worship. One generation created the golden calf, others bowed to false images of various descriptions; but their worship of these lifeless, energyless creatures was hollow and vain.

Time and again, down through the centuries, man has sought to put God out of his life, but whenever and wherever he has done so, his very being has demanded that he worship some false deity. Man's very religious nature demands that he do so. Today the Communists worship at the altar of atheism. Today the liberals worship at the altar of blind internationalism and ever-failing socialism. The great need of this hour is to forsake the false gods created by vain men in their attempt to make a better world without the Prince of Peace. Man need not dwell alone. God is at hand with all His help. Christ, His Son, is our leader and companion-in-arms. Let the conflict be fierce. Man is not alone. The promised Redeemer is at hand to save the human race and to wage war against the powers of darkness. In the person of His Divine Son, the Eternal Father has descended into the arena to take part in that struggle which began in the Garden of Eden. The God-man has come to cross swords with the enemy of the human race.

In every generation, the adversary of Christ and His church has relentlessly fought God's dominion over the earth. The father of liars, Satan's occupation is warfare; and faithful to that pursuit, he battles ceaselessly against the Church of Jesus Christ. The strategy of the Evil One appears to change with the succeeding centuries, but its objective is always the same — the destruction of the Church of Jesus Christ. The Apostle Peter, looking down through the centuries, prophesied, "Your adversary, the devil, is a roaring lion going about seeking whom he may devour." Today we find Satan incarnate in international Communism, and in its offshoots in the United States, the "Far Left". These American adherents of socialism in one form or another, blind to the fearful realities of godless, despotic Communism, consider the "orthodox" Church of Jesus Christ to be the only international force that is capable of blocking the growth of world Communism and socialism. With all the diabolical hatred that characterized earlier persecutions against the body of Christ, communistic propaganda is at present leaving nothing undone to uproot from the minds and hearts of the human race a belief in the teachings and doctrines of Christ. Diabolical hatred is the motivation and force behind communistic activities. Satan, clothed in Communist garb, is waging bitter war against the Kingdom of Christ.

Let there be no doubt that this satanic hatred which we see today aimed at the anti-Communist conservative ranks is directed in reality against the Church of Jesus Christ. She is the only organization strong enough to withstand the organized plans of Communism. Communists themselves realize this fact.

History has a way of repeating itself, and the 20th Century persecution of Christians behind the Iron Curtain is a challenge to every loyal Bible-believing child of God to rally to the banner of Christ. Leaders are needed who are imbued with courage and motivated by zeal for Christ's Kingdom, as were the apostles and the martyrs of centuries ago.

On November 16, 1963, just one week before the assassination of the late President Kennedy, J. Edgar Hoover, head of the Federal Bureau of Investigation, identified these satanic Communist forces at work in America as "hate mongers." He said:

"These lethal influences are at work, constantly undermining the sense of personal responsibility and self-discipline so essential to our nation's welfare. Who are these enemies of our Republic? They are the crime syndicates, the narcotics peddlers, the labor racketeers, the unscrupulous businessmen, the corrupt politicians, and all others who blatantly defy the laws of the land. They are the hate mongers and the false liberals who would subvert our Constitution and undermine our democratic processes in furtherance of their selfish aims. They are the Communists and other subversive elements who wave false banners of legitimacy and patriotism while relentlessly plotting to destroy our heritage of freedom. Communism — and all its forms and all its variations — is the avowed enemy of liberty and of justice and of God. The Communists fear free and independent thought. They fear truth. They fear God, even though they deny Him. They fear the inherent courage and dignity of man created in His image."

We are not so much concerned in this volume with Communism internationally as we are Communism in the United States. We leave to other authors a detailed analysis of Communism internationally and confine our major observations to Communist activities in the United States and the support they are receiving from the "Far Left."

Communist objectives widely publicized in their own literature were briefly summarized by a Congressional Committee in 1931, which, I feel, is still the best short definition of Communism: "Hatred of God and all forms of religion. Destruction of private property and inheritance. Promotion of class hatred. Revolutionary propaganda through the Communist International. Stirring up Communist activities in foreign countries in order to cause strikes, riots, sabotage, bloodshed, and civil war. Destruction of all forms of representative or democratic governments including civil liberties, such as freedom of speech, of the press, of assembly, and trial by jury. The ultimate and final objective is by means of world revolution to establish the dictatorship of the so-called proletariat into one world Union of Soviet Socialist Republics with the capital at Moscow." (This is from report 2290, U. S. House of Representatives, by Fish Committee, 1931.)

The unfortunate thing is, as this volume will prove, millions of Americans who would greatly resent being charged with pronounced communistic leanings are actually promoting its apostolate through membership in various organizations and other associations.

When you talk of Communism internally, one of the first challenges from the liberals invariably is, "But the Communists represent so few Americans. There are probably less than 25,000 of them." We must understand in dealing with Communism internally that the size of the Communist Party itself is not important. It will never be large. Even in Soviet Russia slightly more than one per cent of the people belong to it. Outside of the Soviet Union, the Communist Party wants trained men who will seek to get into every sort of organization, interest themselves in it and work themselves toward the top so that they may steer it into the direction of Communist sympathy. There are many such agents in the United States.

The present Communist strength in the United States is not to be gauged by the small number of people that the party leadership admits belongs to the Party. While our uninformed liberals insist that Communism is not a threat internally, we must remind our readers that the present Communist strength in the United States is not to be gauged, either, by the small vote it polls during an election. If there are so few Communists, how is it that in San Francisco, California, in the 1959 City-County elections, Archie Brown, number two Communist in California and one of the ringleaders of the infamous riots at the 1960 San Francisco hearings of the House Committee on Un-American Activities, while seeking a seat in the Board of Supervisors, received 33,500 votes from the people in that county? The Communists had every reason to be encouraged by this result.

In a headline article in the *San Francisco Examiner* on Monday, September 25, 1961, entitled "U. S .Reds Come Out In Open," there was a news story saying that there were "Communists from nineteen states in the largest open-party gathering since the Rosenberg execution protests of almost ten years ago." In a rally at the St. Nicholas Arena in New York City, over 3,000 people heard the former professor of Union Theological Seminary, retired Methodist clergyman, the Rev. Dr. Harry F. Ward, pledge his support of Communist objectives.

If the present strength of the American Communist Party is limited to less than 10,000, as the liberals insist, how can they garner such a tremendous vote in San Francisco County and do so well in their New York City rally?

Far from being on the decrease, American Communism is on the increase. In the "Annual Report for the Year of 1961 of the House Committee on Un-American Activities," page five, the Committee reported there are indications that, at the present time, the distribution and readership of Communist literature is increasing rather than decreasing. Circulation of the official Communist Party newspaper, *The Worker*, has risen steadily since 1957.

It is not difficult to believe these charges by the House Committee on Un-American Activities when you read the May 6, 1962, issue of the *Sunday Worker*, in which the Communist boasted that "7,000 men, women, and youths attended the Communist May Day Rally in New York City." In *The Worker* of May 7, 1963, the Communists boasted, "5,000 people braved forty-four degree weather and a brisk wind on Union Square to hear Gus Hall, Scott Nearing, William L. Patterson, Joseph North, and other speakers sound the May Day keynotes of 'peace, civil rights, and job security.'"

In the annual report of the House Committee on Un-American Activities for 1957, the Committee revealed that the Kremlin "has succeeded in enlisting more than a million Americans into a nation-wide campaign of political subversion. Their participation has ranged from membership in the far-flung network of Communist-front organizations to the signing of Communist-sponsored petitions and has included substantial financial contributions."

For someone to say that Communism internally represents *no* threat in the United States today, especially in the view of recent events when a Communist assassin took the life of the President of the United States, is to show gross ignorance and unconcern for truth and for America.

However, in all fairness, the thing that should concern Americans most is not the number of Americans who vote for Communist candidates in an election or who support the Communist Party or join Communist fronts, but is the countless number of Americans who are being influenced by the seed of Soviet philosophy which is sown by columnists of the daily papers, by clever writers in magazine articles, by thousands of school teachers in the classroom, by many a college and university professor, by ultra-left clergymen, by the movies, by the television networks, by the radio networks, and, more particularly, through organizations with high-sounding, deceptive, and even appealing names. If it were not for the manner in which the left-wing press has misled people, Communism would have no possible appeal except perhaps to the destitute, to the indolent, to those who can be so easily emotionally aroused against the rich. Having nothing to lose and being promised much under the new order, such people readily listen to the Communist promoter. But the cleverness of Comintern propaganda has made Communism look good even to many men of wealth and to men of culture. As Senate Document No. 14 stated, "The Bolshevik movement in the United States would have sapped its own energies and disintegrated or have degenerated into pure anarchy if it had not been for the support and assistance it has constantly received from the so-called parlor Bolsheviks and pink revolutionists in America. They have served the function of keeping it alive and on an active footing, when otherwise the efforts of Lenin and the Communist International would have failed."

The great American author, Howard E. Kershner, in an address delivered at Harding College, Searcy, Arkansas, on April 7, 1961, gave a fitting illustration:

"At the close . . . (of my visit) . . . in Moscow at the end of September, 1960, a top official of the Communist

Government said to me: 'We'll be over to finish the take-over of America sooner than you think.' Upon my return with these startling words still ringing in my ears, I began to search to see if he was telling the truth. It took me some time to comprehend the extent to which Communists and their sympathizers and dupes have influenced the economic, fiscal, military, and foreign policy of our government during the past twenty-five years. The official that I was referring to presides over a whole floor of a large government building in Moscow. Three hundred scholars work under his direction, studying all the important newspapers, journals, and books published throughout the civilized world. They work on projects he assigns to them and their reports become the basis of the policies of the U. S. S. R. I saw there all the leading papers and periodicals published in America and other advanced countries. At one point this man said to me: 'You know as well as I that a mixed economy is not permanent and you have already mixed so much socialism with your formerly free economy that you cannot now avoid complete socialization. We do not have to urge you or fight you. We only have to sit here and wait until you voluntarily walk into our camp.' I have said as much on many occasions myself, but I was surprised to see this Communist leader accept the rapid socialization of America as indicating beyond doubt that we are headed toward Communism. He smiled at me self-assuredly as though he was perfectly confident that we were already in the trap. When I argued strongly for free enterprise and limited government, he would turn to a bookcase behind his chair, take down a book written by some left-wing American author, such as J. Kenneth Galbraith, Arthur Meier Schlesinger, Jr., or Alvin Harvey Hansen, and from the mouths of many of my compatriots would prove his socialist theories correct. It was shocking to me to learn that the closest advisors of the President of the United States are also among the 'authorities' that are diligently consulted and cited by the leaders of the U.S.S.R."

One of the greatest patriots it has ever been my privilege to meet was Matt Cvetic, former counterspy for the FBI. Mr. Cvetic died on January 26,1962. However, before his death he wrote an editorial for our Christian Crusade magazine entitled "One Communist." Mr. Cvetic's article should be a challenge to every American today to get into this fight against Communism internally:

"Why worry about the Communists? Why worry about a few Red crackpots? What possible harm can one Communist do? There are only 25,000 Communists in the United States; they wouldn't have a chance against us ... or would they?

"These and many similiar questions have been asked me many times since I left my post as a Communist for the FBI in 1950 to testify in Washington.

"Many clergymen, educators, business men, bankers, political leaders, diplomats and others try to delude themselves into believing that 'Killer' Khrushchev really doesn't mean it when he repeats over and over again his threat to communize America and bury us. Frankly, for nine years, while posing as a Communist, I sat in hundreds of secret Communist meetings where the overthrow of our country was plotted; meetings in which the mass murder or enslavement of many of the above mentioned Americans was discussed.

"Contrary to what many think, the numerical strength of the Communist Party is relatively unimportant in their plot to conquer the world. What is important to the Reds is getting their agents, sympathizers and dupes into strategic posts in all sections of American society as well as in our government.

"The numerical strength of the Communist conspiracy in the country is not actually known. It can only be approximated from available intelligence sources and Congressional reports. These sources place the number of Soviet Agents operating in the United States at some 15,000 at any given time. They operate with immunity, thanks to our gullibility in extending diplomatic recognition to Soviet Russia in 1933, and later to her satellite co-conspirators. While posing as a Communist for the FBI, every Soviet agent I met operated from the Red embassies and consulates; the Red-organized United Nations; through cultural exchanges; in the trade, travel and agriculture missions; and in Scientific and Educational expeditions from the Soviet Union and the satellite countries. In addition, literally hundreds of other Soviet agents find haven in Communist front organizations, many of which have had the support of such American personalities as Mrs. Eleanor Roosevelt and Nobel Prize Winner, Chemist Linus Pauling.

"As for the number of Red quislings in the American Communist Party, they number some 25,000 hardcore and dedicated conspirators. On top of this, the Communists have been able to count some quarter of a million fronters, sympathizers, defenders, and dupes in our churches, educational institutions, political bodies, unions, social, civic and welfare groups to aid and abet them in their plot against our country.

"Let me illustrate by my experience as a Communist for the FBI how dangerous *one* Communist can be.

"In 1941 the FBI requested me to infiltrate the Communist Party for the purpose of securing intelligence information for our government. At that time I was employed by the United States Employment Service in Pittsburgh. My job was placing men and women in government employment and basic industries. As soon as I led the Reds to believe I was sympathetic to their cause, they began sending their Communist agents to me to put to work in government and industry. Remember, at this stage of my 'Red masquerade,' I was supposedly only a sympathizer, not a full-fledged Communist. True, I reported every move of the Reds to the FBI, but assume the harm I could have done, were I really a Red sympathizer being used by the Communists.

"After being recruited into the Communist Party, my first Party assignment was in the Professional Branch. My co-conspirators in this branch numbered some 200 Reds in various professions. Their Party assignment was to infiltrate our government, our educational system, the motion picture industry, communications, chemical laboratories, the legal profession, engineering, and any other place into which they could weasel their way. Once on the inside, needless to say, the Communist was to use his position to further the

Communist conspiracy.

"From the Professional Branch I was assigned to the Clergical Commission of the Communist Party. The objective of this Red unit was, and still is, the infiltration of church organizations for the purpose of promoting the Communist line in our Churches.

"My next post in the Communist Party was on their Finance Committee. My job on this committee was to raise finances from dupes, fronters, sympathizers and Party members to keep the Red machinery moving in high gear.

"From this 'exalted office' I was placed on the Reds' Educational Commission. As a member of this conspiratorial group, my job was to plot the infiltration of American universities, colleges and high schools. Ironically one of the more than 400 Reds I named in my sworn testimony, when I unmasked as an FBI undercover agent in 1950, was an English professor in an Eastern university where one of my sons, Matt, Junior, was studying for his Master's degree. This Red professor's last act, before the university fired him as a result of my sworn testimony, was to flunk my son in English as retaliation for my exposure of his Communist connections.

"Another of my Communist posts was on the Political Commission of the Party. This is the outfit which set up the ill-fated Progressive Party in the late 40's. Currently it is actively infiltrating both major political parties.

"Along with all these assignments, I was appointed to the Yugoslav Bureau of the Communist Party, where I worked with Tito's Red Agents in America.

Later as a member of the Communist's Trade Union Commission, I helped direct the infiltration of many unions in steel, coal and electrical industries, and sat in on strategy meetings of Reds which directed the infiltration of the unions in the Rocky Mountain States and the Farm Organization in the Midwest and on the West Coast.

"As one 'Communist', even tho' a pseudo one, I had many other Party assignments in those nine years. I have listed some of the most outstanding to prove to the reader by my own experiences how dangerous one sympathizer, fronter or Communist in the wrong spot can be.

"Bear one thing in mind. THERE ARE NO HARMLESS COMMUNISTS, FRONTERS OR SYMPATHIZERS. It takes only one 'harmless' Red to blow up a dam, waterworks or a plant. It takes only one Communist, fronter, sympathizer or Red dupe in our universities, colleges or high schools to poison the minds of many of our children. It takes only one dedicated Communist in a strategic position in our church organization to mislead many into supporting Communist causes and objectives. Yes, ONE COMMUNIST IS DANGEROUS!

"Remember . . . hateful Karl Marx was only one Red, and he founded the devilish Communist scheme for World Slavery.

"Ostensibly, I too was one Red, but thank heaven my allegiance was to God and my country which I was trying in my small way to serve."

Mr. Cvetic's words were a prophecy. Had they been heeded and had the Justice Department enforced the laws that are on the books against Communism internally, John F. Kennedy would probably be alive today.

No longer can we say, "Can it happen here?" It *is* happening here. Only an aroused, alert citizenry, motivated by love of God, can save this country now.

Dr. Charles Malik, the great Lebanese leader and former President General of the United Nations General Assembly, has said, "The civilization which has been blessed and transformed by Christ needs only a mighty hand to shake it out of its slumber, and once shaken, once really awakened to its world responsibilities which it and it alone can shoulder, there is nothing it cannot bear and do."

Surely the assassination of the President of the United States by Communists would be enough to shake America "out of its slumber." As my good friend, Ezra Taft Benson, said, "God and our children will judge us for what we do with our land and our liberties. With God's help, the light of high-resolve in the eyes of the American people must never be dimmed. Our freedom must — and will be preserved. May God give us the wisdom to recognize the threat to our freedom and the strength to meet this danger courageously. We should all remember that we have the best government under the best Constitution in the world, therefore let us preserve them in their present form by combating every un-American influence in our midst, especially that which, based on pure materialism, is calculated to rob our nation of its attachment to religion and eternal spiritual values, of its faith in God and its trust in man."

In this struggle, we are not alone; for the battle

is but a renewal of ancient hostilities between the Kingdom of Jesus Christ and the Kingdom of Satan. In the 20th Century, as in the first century, Christ is still our Leader and Captain, even as He said, "I am with you always, even to the consummation of the world." He prophesied that persecution would pursue the church; but He also promised that the gates of hell would not prevail against Her. And so today, loyal followers of Jesus Christ who make up the Church of Christ have every reason to believe that they are not alone as atheistic Communism launches its bitter attack against the Church, Christ, and God Himself.

CHAPTER II

THE HISTORY OF THE COMMUNIST PARTY IN THE UNITED STATES

Edward Hunter, the famous expert on psychological warfare, frequently a friendly witness in government investigations into Communism internally and internationally, said, following the assassination of Mr. Kennedy: "President Kennedy was deluded by the line that Communism is no menace here in America. He paid for this illusion with his life. His horrible death should warn us against a similar 'assassination' of our nation by a Red sniper in space. The effort to divert attention from the pro-Communist, Marxian motivation of the killer could make this warning vain. If we as a people come to believe that Communism is not a deadly peril right here or anywhere else it exists, our country will pay the same price as President Kennedy did. We already were being successfully conditioned into acceptance of this delusion. The consequences could be immensely more tragic than what happened at Dallas."

That there is a threat from internal Communism, no thinking American, loyal to our traditions and concepts, can deny. Only the self-deluded liberal with his sophisticated dreams of world government, predicated on peaceful co-existence with international Communism, can ignore the ignoble fact that Communism is a threat internally.

If Communism were but a godless philosophy, there would be less cause for concern. But the Communists are organized into action and into political parties in the majority of the countries of the world. And it must be kept in mind that the Communist Party in any land is not merely a political party, but it is an "action organization," which has as its principal goal and objective the subjection of the entire world to its rule, and the re-making of man and all human institutions to conform to the Communist distortion of reality. The Communist Party in the United States is a conspiracy. It is, as Dr. James D. Bales of Harding College, Searcy, Arkansas, suggested in his book, *Communism — Its Faith and Fallacies,* a "combat party." Even the left-leaning United States Supreme Court decided on June 5, 1961, that the Communist Party, U.S.A., was not a genuine American political party, but was, in effect, directed by Moscow.

Nikita Khrushchev and other leaders of the Communist conspiracy have repeatedly made it clear that world Communism is subservient to the Soviet Union. The Communist Party in America still considers itself a mere branch of an international movement with head-

31

quarters in Moscow. The American Party accepts the Communist Manifesto, which states that Communism is an international movement, not a national movement, and that Communists must work for the welfare of the *world* Communist movement.

Americans must remember that there are two ways that individual Communists in the United States get their orders from Moscow. One, directly; second, through the Communist publications. Communists read their publications, such as *People's World, World Marxist Review, The Worker, Political Affairs,* etc., for guidance and for party directions.

That the Communist Party and its members are a conspiracy within is more than a theory. It is a fact. Gus Hall is the present General Secretary of the Communist Party with headquarters in New York City. Back in 1934, while on trial, he stated that he was willing "when the time comes" to take up arms and overthrow the Government of the United States of America.

The Communist Party, U.S.A., does not try to be a party of the masses, but a party of the revolutionary elite. It is the general staff of the revolution inside the United States. It is, as they say, the "vanguard of the working class, the most class-conscious section of the working class." Stalin called the Communist Party the "political leader of the working class," and, the "general staff of the proletariat."

J. Edgar Hoover explains, "The Communist Party in this country remains an inseparable arm of the treacherous, atheistic international conspiracy which is being directed against the free world from Moscow."

As was suggested in the first chapter of this book,

the fact that the Party is not large in number does not mean that it is not dangerous. As Dr. Bales pointed out in his book, "A conspiracy, although but a small minority, which is well organized and part of an international movement, does not need *many* members in order to be exceedingly dangerous. They were a small minority when they took over Russia." To this fact, J. Edgar Hoover added, "...numbers mean nothing and those nations which have attempted to assess the threat of Communism on the basis of numerical strength alone are eating the bitter bread of slavery for their short-sightedness."

The seeds of Communism had been sown in the United States long before the Bolshevik Revolution, which took place in Russia in 1917. There was a left-wing faction of the Socialist Party in the United States at the turn of the century. For years, the Socialists had been trying to get the United States Government to take over all major industries and socialize our economy, but this attempt at peaceful legislative reform had failed. Then the American left-wingers heard of the successful revolution in the Soviet Union in November 1917, and how the Communists had used revolutionary violence to seize power and had thereafter socialized, by force, Russia overnight. This was promptly accepted by the left-wing Socialists as the formula for America. Many of the leading lights of the Socialist cause in America immediately began to form a Communist Party for the U.S.A., determined to use violent revolutionary activity to Sovietize America at the earliest possible date. Their greatest encouragement in this attempt to overthrow the Government of the United States by force and violence, if necessary, came from one John Reed, a journalist, who had recently returned from Russia with glowing enthusiasm for the revolution and world Communism.

The group of left-wing Socialists in the United States, determined to organize the Communist Party, U.S.A., made contact with the leaders of the Russian Communist conspiracy and were invited to send delegates to the Soviet Union in March 1919 to help form the Third International, which had been copied after Karl Marx's First International, for more world Communist revolution. When these American left wingers returned home, they began their campaign.

John Reed used newspaper columns in New York City to agitate the workers to revolt. Members of the old I.W.W. (International Workers of the World) joined the Communist ranks, bringing with them their tried and proven techniques of sabotage and violence which the I.W.W. had successfully employed during World War I. The actual organization of the Communist Party, U.S.A., was aided by an official representative of the Government of the Soviet Union, C.A. Martens, who was sent over to this country from Russia, bringing along with him substantial quantities of money to set up Communist cells in all walks of American life, especially in the American labor unions and the U.S. Armed Forces. Whenever "Comrade" Martens spoke, he assured his audience that his mission from Moscow was to free the "downtrodden workers of capitalistic America." As the movement progressed, American Communists went to the Soviet Union to be trained to set up the "Communist Labor Party of the United

States" as a branch of the Russian-sponsored Communist International. Later the word "labor" was dropped.

The officers of the new Communist Party signed the "twenty-one conditions of admission," which would embarrass them many years later when the Communist Party war ordered to register in 1952 as an agency under the direct control of the Soviet Union. Among the commitments which the officers of the American Communist Party signed were: "The program of the U. S. Communist Party must be sanctioned by the regular Congress of the Communist International. All decisions of the Communist International . . . are binding upon all parties belonging to the Communist International (which would include the U. S. Communist Party)" It was these obvious ties between the American Communist Party and the international Communist conspiracy headquartered in Moscow that led the U. S. Subversive Activities Control Board to make the following statement in 1953 after extended hearings: "We find upon the whole record that the evidence preponderantly establishes that Respondent's Leaders, (leaders of the Communist Party, U.S.A.) and its members consider the allegiance they owe the United States as subordinate to their loyalty and obligations to the Soviet Union."

With the organization of the Communist Party in the United Sates in 1919, the American people saw first hand the Communist weapon of terror, murder, violence, force, and anarchy abroad in the land, inspired and directed by the international Communists. Beginning April 28, 1919, a series of thirty-six bombs were discovered in the mails addressed to such persons as the Attorney General, Justice Holmes of the Supreme Court,

J. P. Morgan, John D. Rockefeller, and other prominent Americans. One of the bombs actually reached the home of Senator Hardwick, who had been trying to prevent the migration of Communists from the Soviet Union to the United States. A servant opened the package and the bomb exploded, blowing off her hands. On September 16, 1920, a large bomb was carried in a horse-drawn carriage to the corner of Broad and Wall Streets in New York City, the headquarters of American capitalism. The vehicle was parked across the street from the three-story limestone building occupied by the firm of J. P. Morgan & Company. Suddenly a great roar went up from the carriage, blue-white flames shooting into the sky, resulting in the death of thirty people and in the injuring of hundreds more. It wrecked the interior of the Morgan offices, smashed windows for blocks around, and caused general havoc, resulting in the hospitalization of hundreds and hundreds of people. These acts of murder and violence created a ground swell against Communism in every part of the United States. Actually, the ground swell resulted in the Attorney General of the United States demanding that a whole shipload of Communist aliens and Communist leaders be deported to the Soviet Union via Finland on the S.S. BUFORD.

It is no surprise that the Communists will use assassination or murder as a part of their plan to overthrow the free nations of the world. After all, the use of terrorism was advocated by Nikolai Lenin, the number one hero of the Communist world. Communists around the earth are warned against any deviations from the policies of Lenin. Lenin informed the Communists of the world in Volume II, Page 17, of *The Selected Works of Lenin* published by International Publishers (one of Communist conspiracy's publishing houses in the United States): "We have never rejected terror on principle, nor can we do so. Terror is a form of military operation that may be usefully applied, or may even be essential in certain moments of the battle, under certain conditions, and when the troops are in a certain condition. The point is, however, that terror is now advocated, not as one of the operations the army in the field must carry out in close connection and in complete harmony with the whole system of fighting, but as an individual attack, completely separated from any army whatever."

From the days of Nikolai Lenin until today, the Communists have lived up to Lenin's instructions to use terror as a "form of military operation" in harmony with "the whole system of fighting" and also as "an individual attack, completely separated from any army whatever." Any refugee from a Communist country who has suffered at the hands of these inhuman tyrants can give specific facts regarding the continuing use of terror in Communist countries as a matter of "principle."

It is indeed tragic that the United States news media system, in reporting the assassination of the President of the United States on November 22, 1963, overlooked in all of its coverage the fact that murder is a vital and inseparable part of the very basic philosophy of the International Communist conspiracy. A point to remember is that the Communist conspirators will murder whenever they feel that murder serves their purpose. History records when Communism takes over a country, they murder, imprison, or send to slave camps, thousands of national leaders at all levels of government and millions of the nation's citizens. Countless human beings are murdered as a matter of political expediency. Any man or woman will be murdered or imprisoned whom the Communists think may show any potential leadership for a subsequent "freedom uprising" against the Communist dictatorship.

In dealing with the Communist Party, U.S.A., or with individual members of the Communist conspiracy, such as the President's assassin, Lee Harvey Oswald, it must be remembered that the Communist conspirators have no principles. The Communist meaning of morality is that anything is moral which serves the Communist cause. It matters not whether it is lying, breaking treaties and agreements, or murdering.

Few names among Communist leaders in the United States are better known to the American people generally than the name of William Z. Foster. He was a charter member of the Communist Party, U.S.A., and was the person designated by the party leaders to take over the United States labor unions. Over one million dollars was sent into the United States from the Soviet Union to be used by William Z. Foster to help spread Communism in the labor unions. Foster's initial effort to infiltrate American labor unions and take over places of leadership began soon after the Armistice, when the workers were already in a state of emotion resulting from World War I. No single American Communist was ever as successful in his conspiratorial activities as William Z. Foster. However, not once did he ever really conceal his fundamental ambition to overthrow the United States Government by force and violence and to subordinate the American laborer as well as other Americans to the mandates of a Communist dictatorship patterned after and loyal to the Soviet Union. In fact, William Z. Foster undoubtedly thought of himself as the coming dictator of the "Soviet United States." He ran for the presidency of the United States on two occasions and wrote a book called *Toward Soviet America*, telling just how the Communists would take over.

After the ground swell against Communism in 1920, from 1921 to 1924 members of the Communist Party sought to avoid arrest by operating underground. But when the Wartime Emergency Acts were repealed, the Communist leaders came to the surface again and continued their campaign openly for a revolution to overthrow the United States Government.

Unable to make substantial advances among the masses, the Communists turned to the so-called intellectuals in the early 1930's. The appeal of Communism to the sophisticated intellectual coincided with the age of daring debunking. This was a time when men and women began to question the existence of God. Litigations were being filed in courts across the land trying to outlaw any recognition of God in public schools and in government life. This was the age of evolution, when the seeds of doubt were first planted in America's educational system concerning the creation of the world by a Merciful Father. Furthermore, the intellectuals reasoned, there was something wrong with the American system; or why the depression? Even today, the United States is reaping the harvest of the intellectual revolt of the 1930's, which resulted in agents of Communism infiltrating every echelon of American society, including some of the highest offices of the United States Government.

Among the most famous Communists who were to become top officials in the United States Government was Alger Hiss. Hiss started out in the Department of Agriculture, then served on the Special Senate Committee Investigating the Munitions Industry. For a while, he served in the Department of Justice, then went to the State Department. There he made a phenomenal rise, serving as Director of the highly important Office of Political Affairs. He served as advisor to President Franklin Delano Roosevelt at the Yalta Conference, and as the first Secretary General of the United Nations when it met in San Francisco. Every visitor's pass to the U. N. Assembly in San Francisco had to be signed by Alger Hiss for admission.

Another top Communist was Harry Dexter White, who became the Assistant Secretary of the United States Treasury and author of The Morganthau Plan.

John J. Abt served in the Department of Agriculture, the W.P.A., the Senate Committee on Education and Labor, and was then made a Special Assistant to the Attorney General in charge of the trial section.

It is interesting to note that while Lee Harvey Oswald, the assassin of President Kennedy, was being held in the Dallas jail, he requested that "John J. Abt be his counsel." John Abt is not merely a Communist lawyer from out of the 30's, he has held several positions in the Communist-controlled Progressive Party and also in the Civil Rights' Conference, a cited Communist front. He was an early supporter of the National Lawyers Guild (the foremost legal bulwark of the Communist Party) and of the Guild's Committee

On Civil Rights And Liberties. Another of Abt's long associations is with the American Committee for Protection of Foreign Born (one of the oldest Communist Party auxilaries).

On August 3, 1948, Whitaker Chambers testified that John Abt had been a member of the so-called Ware-Abt-Witt group, a Communist cell operating in high circles in the United States Government in Washing, D. C.

Not long after Harold Ware — the son of Ella Reeve "Mother" Bloor — was killed in an auto accident in 1935, John Abt married his widow, Jessica Smith. She has been identified under oath as a Communist. Under Ware's tutelage, she founded in the late 20's *Soviet Russia Today* a party organ which later became *New World Review*. She remains the editor. On several occasions, Abt has written for his wife's magazine on such subjects, for instance, as his recollections of a Congress of the Kremlin-controlled World Federation of Trade Unions, which he attended.

It is interesting to note at this point that the *New York Times*, which would like to be known for its "fairness," said in its columns of November 24, 1963: "Oswald's only utterance directed to outsiders today was — 'I want to talk to Mr. — in New York.' The name sounded like Abt or Apt. (In New York, John J. Abt, who has represented the Communist Party in a number of litigations, said he had never heard of Oswald)." It's amazing how some of these newspapers on the left can soft-pedal anti-Communist news stories when they want to.

Another Communist who infiltrated government

circles was Henry H. Collins who served in the N.R.A., the Department of Agriculture, the Department of Labor, and the Department of State. During World War II, he became a Major in the Army and in 1948 became executive director of the American Russian Institute "cited by the Attorney General as a Communist-front organization." Other "famed" personages from members of Russia's most important spy cell in Washington, D. C., directed by Whitaker Chambers, who were able to rise to top places in government included Charles Kramer, who served on the National Labor Relations Board, in the Office of Price Administration and, in 1943, joined the staff of the Senate Sub-Committee on War Mobilization; Nathan Witt, who served in the Department of Agriculture and then became the Secretary of the National Labor Relations Board; Harold Ware, who served in the Department of Agriculture; Victor Perlo, who served in the Office of Price Administration, the War Production Board, and the Treasury; Henry Julian Wadleigh, who became a prominent official in the Treasury Department.

As W. Cleon Skousen pointed out in his book, *The Naked Communist*: "In later years when Chambers was asked to give his explanation as to why so many well-educated Americans were duped into committing acts of subversion against their native country, he explained that once a person has been converted to the ideology of Communism, he will consider espionage to be a moral act — a duty — committed in the name of humanity for the good of future society. The unbelievable extent to which Americans participated in Russian-directed espionage against the United States during the depression and during World War II has only recently become generally recognized. Many complete books have now been written which summarize the evidence unearthed by the FBI, the courts, and Congress." It is fitting to remember at this point that Whitaker Chambers, one of the top Communists in the United States, became editor of *Time* magazine and co-editor of other Luce publications, broke with Communism in the late 1930's and, because of his sensational testimony before the House Committee on Un-American Activities, exposed Alger Hiss. No greater volume is available anywhere on the Communist conspiracy in the United States than Chambers' autobiography, *Witness*. Unfortunately, Mr. Chambers died about two years ago.

Another top Communist who headed the Russian espionage system in the United States at one point was Elizabeth Bentley. In the early 1940's, Miss Bentley was used by the Russian espionage apparatus to collect secret material from Communists in high government circles in Washington, D.C. Miss Bentley said she first became the courier for the Silvermaster spy group which was extracting information from Communist contacts in the Pentagon and other top-secret governmental agencies. According to sworn testimony of Elizabeth Bentley, she worked with three major spy cells in the American Government — the Ware cell, the same group Whitaker Chambers had handled, the Silvermaster cell, and the Perlo cell. The Silvermaster cell consisted of such well-known left-wingers as: Nathan Gregory Silvermaster, who had served as Director of the Labor Division of the Farm Security Administration; Solomon Adler, a Treasury Department representative in China; Norman Bursler, special assistant to the Department of Justice; Frank Coe, who held many important government jobs, including Assistant Director of the Division of Monetary Research, Treasury Department, special assistant to the United States Ambassador in London, assistant to the Executive Director of the Board of Economic Warfare, and Assistant Administrator of Foreign Economic Administration; and William Gold, known also as Bela Gold, who worked as assistant head of the Division of Program Surveys, Bureau of Agricultural Economics, Department of Agriculture, with the Senate Subcommittee on War Mobilization, and in the Office of Economic Programs and Foreign Economic Administration.

Others who were connected with the Silvermaster cell were: Mrs. William (Sonia) Gold, who has been with the Division of Monetary Research, Treasury Department; Abraham George Silverman, who had been Economic Advisor and Chief of Analysis and Plans, Assistant Chief of Air Staff, Materiel and Services, U. S. Air Corps; William Taylor of the Treasury Department; and William Ludwig Ullman, also associated with the Division of Monetary Research in the United States Treasury Department and with the Air Corps Materiel and Services Division in the Pentagon.

The Perlo Cell was headed by Victor Perlo, head of a branch in the Research Section in the Office of Price Administration, and who also served on the War Productions Board handling problems relating to military aircraft production. Other top government officials in the Perlo cell included Edward J. Fitzgerald of the War Production Board; Harold Glasser, Treasury Department; Charles Kramer, National Labor Relations Board; Solomon Leshinsky, United States Relief and Rehabilitation Administration; Harry Magdoff, Statistical Division of the War Production Board in the Office of Emergency Management; Allen Rosenberg of the Foreign Economic Administration; and Donald Niven Wheeler of the Office of Strategic Services. Other names revealed by Elizabeth Bentley, people who obtained secret information from government files for her, although they were not tied to any particular Communist cell in government circles, were Michael Greenberg, Joseph Gregg, Maurice Halperin, J. Julius Joseph Duncan Chaplin Lee, Robert T. Miller, William Z. Park, Bernard Redmont, and Helen Tenney. These names help our readers to understand the remarkable sources of information which the late Elizabeth Bentley said the Soviet underground tapped in Washington, D. C., during the time she served with the Russian Secret Police as the Russian Secret Police paymaster and courier in the nation's capital. Miss Bentley worked doggedly for the Soviets until 1944. After becoming disillusioned with Communism in 1944, she walked into the FBI headquarters in Washington, D. C., stating she was willing and ready to reveal all that she knew about the Communist conspiracy in the nation's capital and to make amends to her native country. After her sensational break with Communism, the so-called liberal press of the United States began to accuse her of being everything from a degenerate to a psychopathic liar or a victim of insanity. She found herself, like Whitaker Chambers, after his break with Communism, cast away and alone. It can now be told that the great patriot, Alfred Kohlberg, devised ways and means to quietly help Miss Bentley. Miss Bentley died the week following the assassination of President Kennedy, at the age of 55. In recent years she had been employed as a school teacher.

No book dealing with the history of the Communist Party, U.S.A., would be complete without some mention of the alliance between Communism and Nazism. To understand this phenomenon, we must go back in history to the fall of the German Kaiser in 1918. Upon the capitulation of the Kaiser, the Communists tried to take over Germany. Immediately, anti-Communist political groups sprung up throughout Germany and through a frantic political coalition, they prevented the Communists from seizing power. It was in this atmosphere that Adolf Hitler began his infamous political career. He joined the National Socialists (Nazi) Party which was strongly anti-Bolshevik, although socialistic and by 1921 had become its leader. Hitler organized his notorious Nazi Stormtroopers to retaliate against the spreading rash of Communist violence. He had his Brownshirts trained in street fighting, rioting, and the suppression of political opponents by "direct physical attack." Failing to take over the German province of Bavaria in 1923 with his 10,000 Stormtroopers, Hitler wrote his satanic manuscript entitled *Mein Kampf* or *My Battle,* while imprisoned after the abortive Bavarian Revolution. In this book, Hitler told quite candidly his plans to overthrow every nation bordering on Germany. He furthermore declared that the natural course of German expansion would eventually carry the Nazi conquest into the fertilee Ukrainian agricultural region which had been conquered by the Soviet

Union and then into the rich Russian oil fields.

In 1933, Stalin secretly tried to negotiate a "deal with Hitler to get him "off his back." One of Stalin's leading secret agents, General W. G. Krivitsky wrote in his book, *In Stalin's Secret Service*, of these efforts. According to General Krivitsky, Hitler rejected Stalin's overture to friendship. Therefore, Stalin knew that the German Fuehrer could be dealt with only as an outright enemy of the Soviet Union. Then in one of the smartest tricks of his career, Stalin hastened to gain the sympathies of the free world for his anti-Hitler and anti-Nazi policies. He not only attempted, but succeeded in identifying Russia's policies with the political and economical welfare of all freedom-loving people of the world. He called this campaign to make his slave state policies popular, THE POPULAR FRONT.

At the Seventh World Congress of the Communist International, meeting in Moscow in 1935, he instructed Communists from every country in the world to form a "united front" with any national political group which opposed Hitler and his allies, even right-wing parties which the Communists had previously attacked. Again, history records that this POPULAR FRONT was the most successful tactic ever adopted by Communist strategists. It permitted Communists to associate openly with the most conservative, highly-respected political groups and even formerly anti-Communist groups in capitalist countries throughout the world.

In 1938, Hitler occupied Austria. In 1939, he seized Memelland and Lithuania and then prepared to march into Poland. However, Stalin wanted Poland, too, so Hitler hesitated, not wanting an all-out war with the Western Powers unless he had some assurance that Stalin would not interfere. Therefore, in 1939, Hitler made his overture to Stalin to sign a non-aggression pact and, to everyone's astonishment, Stalin accepted. This meant that Hitler could go to war against Poland or any other country outside of the Soviet Union and its satellites with the assurance that Russia would not interfere. In the United States, this caught the Communist Party completely off guard. For years Red Propaganda had portrayed Stalin as the number one Anti-Nazi and Anti-Fascist of the world. Now there was a coalition between Stalin and Hitler which necessitated that the Communists get their propaganda in reverse. Some American Communists, according to Whitaker Chambers, openly complained of this alliance between Stalin and his greatest enemy, Hitler, but it was General W.G. Krivitsky who explained to Chambers the "why" of the alliance. He explained that the alliance was merely proof of Stalin's genius as a strategist, that Stalin knew this pact would turn Hitler loose on Europe, but that he also knew that as the war progressed, it was likely that the Western nations would fight themselves into utter exhaustion. At this point, the Soviet Union would step in. Almost without a blow or a shot fired, the Soviet Union would be able to take over all of Europe in the name of the "dictatorship of the proletariat." The pact between Hitler and Stalin was signed August 23, 1939. On September 1, 1939, the German Panzers were crushing the helpless Polish nation. Also, as Stalin had anticipated, England and France were immediately dragged into the war because of their commitments to Poland. In victory after victory over the British and French, the Nazis seemed unbeatable as they expanded their occupation into Denmark, Norway, Holland and Belgium.

Again, the master strategist was at work, moving the leaders of the world around like chessmen on a chess board. Stalin now encouraged the Japanese war lords to attack the United States. On April 13, 1941, Stalin signed a pact of non-aggression with Japan which permitted the Japanese war lords to launch their Pan-Asiatic campaign in the Pacific and the Far East.

Stalin's philosophy was simple. The nation that stayed out of World War II the longest would win the war. That nation, of course, must be Russia. However, here Stalin made his big mistake. He had not evaluated Adolf Hitler correctly. In fact, at the very moment Stalin was promoting his "neutrality pact" with Japan, Hitler was secretly announcing to his military staff: "The German Armed Forces must be prepared to crush Soviet Russia in a quick campaign." And the quick campaign started on June 22, 1941. Ignoring the pact with Stalin, Hitler attacked Russia on a two thousand-mile front with 121 divisions and 3,000 planes just as he said he would in his book *Mein Kampf*, written years before. This shattered all the plans of Stalin and he found himself in the midst of World War II. Within six months after the beginning of the war, the Germans has occupied 580,000 square miles of the richest land of the U.S.S.R., penetrating to a point only sixty miles from Moscow. All of this shocked the rest of the world into the stark reality that the Nazi Empire might extend itself from England to Alaska. Instinctively, the American Government began cheering for the underdog, the Soviet Union.

Then the fatal dawn of Sunday, December 7, 1941 brought the devastating attack of the Japanese on Pearl Harbor and the United States found herself in the middle of World War II. America in the war, observing the defeat of Russia at the hands of the Nazi Fuehrer, resulted in the alliance between the United States and the U.S.S.R. Immediately, the American policy of generosity and benevolence began to manifest itself. President Roosevelt undoubtedly felt that he could convert the Communist leaders to the American way of thinking by showering them with overwhelming generosity. It was assumed by the American officials that the Soviet Union would be so appreciative of this help and aid in whipping our mutual enemy, that they would become permanently and sympathetically allied with the United States and the Western democracies in building a world of peace and prosperity.

In June, 1942, Molotov came to Washington, D. C., and was the guest of Mr. Roosevelt in the White House. After his departure, the American people were told of the new U. S. aid policy to the Soviet Union. On June 22 of that year (the anniversary of Hitler's attack on the U.S.S.R.) a Russian Aid Rally was held in New York City's Madison Square Garden.

Billions and billions of dollars of Russian lend-lease was authorized by the United States Government. It has only been in recent years, since the close of World War II, that the American people have gradually learned the infamous details concerning the flood of goods and American treasure which went to the Soviet Union under our lend-lease. Over eleven billion dollars in aid, ranging in everything from war materiel to cigarette cases, phonograph records, ladies' compacts, sheet music, pianos, antique furniture, jewelry, novelties, household furnishings, fishing tackle, lipsticks, perfume, dolls, bank vaults, playground equipment, gold-mining equipment, and quantities of many other types of illegal, "non-military merchandise" were shipped to the Soviet Union. Eleven billion dollars worth of aid went to the Soviet Union from the United States as a "loan" never to be repaid, including $3,040,423,000 worth of "non-military merchandise" such as we have listed above.

The awful truth about our give-away to the Soviet Union was revealed by an American officer, Major George Racey Jordan, who was the official U. S. expediter for Russian lend-lease at the Great Falls Air Base in Montana. In Major Jordan's book, *Gold Swindle*, he speaks of our gifts of gold-mining equipment to the Soviet Union:

"During the war, the War Production Board issued an order No. L-208, closing all gold mines because, it said, the machinery was needed for mining copper for the war effort. That strange order was drafted by Harry Dexter White, Assistant Secretary of the Treasury, who advised our government on so many policies which strengthened the Soviet Union and weakened the United States. None of the gold-mining machinery was of any use to any military operation. Some — if not all — of this specialized equipment was shipped from Seattle to Vladivostok in the Soviet Union to be operated by unskilled political prisoners. I knew of this because the orders passed through the lend-lease depot at the Great Falls, Montana, Air Base when I was in charge. I saw proof of vast shipments of gold mining machinery."

Now in 1964, as a result of this equipment shipped to the Soviet Union during World War II, the Soviet Union potentially is the Number One supplier of the world's gold needs. Russian gold is now flooding the markets of the world, the sale of which can only enhance the economic situation in the Soviet Union. Can the Americans match Russian gold sales on the world market? Absolutely not. For twenty years we have been recklessly giving away American dollars to foreigners, thus depleting our own gold reserves. Surely, we should have known that we could not recoup our war spendings or gifts to other nations. Dollars spent for foreign materials, construction, and services have remained as a claim against our economy for goods or services for which nothing has been received in exchange. As Major Jordan points out in his book:

"We are just beginning to realize the dollars we gave to foreign nations or their citizens, or to our Americans abroad, can return as a demand on our stockpile of gold — a demand the American Government cannot refuse. If enough foreign claimants exercised their present rights to demand such redemption, our entire financial system could crack and fall apart as did Germany's after World War I."

In an Associated Press article in October of 1963, the American people were informed:

"The Commerce Department reports the U. S. balance of payments' deficit in the second quarter of 1963 was about $1,300,000,000, a $500,000,000 increase over the first three months of the year. If projected for the remainder of 1963, the loss of dollars would shatter the record $3,900,000,00 outflow of 1959 and 1960. The mounting deficit — the widening difference between the amount of money leaving the country and the lesser amount coming in — augurs possible further losses in the U. S. gold stockpile."

Our gold reserves are now down to a little over fifteen billion dollars from the original twenty-seven billion dollar high mark at our gold depository at Fort Knox, Louisville, Kentucky. Immediately, the uninformed will ask why we don't replenish our depleted stockpile by mining our own gold. The answer is that United States Government action prohibits it. In an action in the mid-30's, the United States Government decreed all mined gold must be sold to the United States Treasury or licensed dealer at its 1934 fixed price of thirty-five dollars per ounce. But the cost of mining gold has increased several hundred per cent. Obviously, mine owners cannot hire labor, buy machinery, and meet other costs if they must sell at 1934 prices. Since the gold mines have been closed these nearly thirty years, they have filled up with water. Machinery — that which was left after the Russian steal — grows rusty. Skilled gold miners moved to other jobs and no new men were taught gold-mining techniques.

Why are we so crippled? Let Major Jordan answer that question: "Because back in 1942, a little group of government officials headed by a clever, far-sighted Soviet agent, Harry Dexter White, instituted an ingenious series of moves which put an end to gold-mining as a necessary prerequisite to a managed money system.

Domestic gold production was ended, yet our dollars were allowed to flow abroad like water. The mines are still closed. The mining machinery the government seized is now producing uranium in the Jachymov, Dobris, and Marianske Lazne mines of Czechoslovakia and gold in the wastes of Siberia."

Are the Communists still in business in the United States? Unfortunately, they are. Still obedient to the Soviet Union and the cause of international Communism, they carry on their conspiratorial activities in this country seemingly unharassed. Volume after volume of Congressional Reports on the Communist conspiracy *internally* are printed at the taxpayers' expense, but their message goes unread and unheeded by a majority of America's liberal leaders in politics, education, and religion, and by the American people as a whole. Only small vocal anti-Communist militants known as "conservatives" have shown any interest in recent years in the Congressional Reports on the Communist conspiracy internally.

Members of the Communist Party, U.S.A., National Committee, as of 1961, included the following "members at large": James S. Allen, New York; Herbert Aptheker, New York; Philip Bart, New York; Erik Bert, New York; Jesus Colon, New York; Benjamin J. Davis, Jr., New York; Elizabeth Gurley Flynn, New York; Simon W. Gerson, New York; Gus Hall, New York; Clarence A. Hathaway, New York; James E. Jackson, New York; Arnold Johnson, New York; Geraldine Lightfoot, Illinois; Hyman Lumer, New York; Mildred McAdory, New York; George A. Meyers, Maryland; William L. Patterson, New York; Pettis Perry, Southern

California; Irving Potash, New York; Danny Queen, Illinois; Al Richmond, Northern California; Mortimer Daniel Rubin, New York; Jacob (Jack) Stachel, New York; William Weinstone, New York; Helen Allison Winter, Michigan, and Henry Winston, New York. These are just a few of the admitted "heads of the Communist apparatus in the United States." Under the National Committee, there are twenty-one District Organizations of the Communist Party, U.S.A., each with its own officers and leaders — all paid conspirators.

There are Federal laws that would eliminate the Communist Party and would thus do away with the Communist threat internally, if enforced. Had these laws been enforced during the Kennedy Administration by the Justice Department under the Attorney General, Robert Kennedy, President Kennedy would probably be alive today. The Justice Department failed to enforce "the law of the land," i.e. to arrest those Communists who had refused to register as agents of the Soviet Union and put them on trial for treason. Under the law, according to a decision of the United States Supreme Court, Communist Party members were supposed to register as agents of the Soviet Union by November 20, 1961. The officers of the Communist Party were supposed to register by December 1, 1961, and all the ordinary members of the Communist Party were supposed to register by December 20, 1961. Although their deadline ran out two years ago, the Justice Department made no arrests or individual indictments of Communist Party members across the country. In fact, on August 24, 1962, the Associated Press carried a report that "a Justice Department official said today 'No

Communists have registered with the department under the Internal Security Act of 1960.' Thomas K. Hall, executive assistant in the Department's Internal Security Division, said only one or two requests for the registration forms had been received and even those may have been from curiosity collectors." This led Texas Senator John Tower to address a letter to the Justice Department on February 26, 1962, in which he asked why the Department of Justice had failed to prosecute "known Communists who did not register in compliance with the Subversive Activities Control Act of 1950."

It bears repeating: If this law had been enforced by the Department of Justice, Mr. Kennedy might still be alive today. Since there is no doubt in anyone's mind that the assassin, Lee Harvey Oswald, was a Communist, having lived in Russia, having renounced his American citizenship, and having been arrested for Communist activities upon his return to the United States later, he would have been arrested, tried, and, by this time, jailed, and would not have been free to assassinate the President of the United States. So, then, the failure of government officials, whoever has the responsibility to enforce the law, is responsible, in part, for the death of the President of the United States.

Because of the tremendous influence of Communism internally and its liberal allies, the American leaders in the realm of religion, politics, and education have not adequately backed the Federal Government's investigations into Communism. Since the Federal Government cannot operate in any field where there is no public support, the failure of educators, clergymen, and government officials to back internal investigations into

Communism and to take action as a result of these investigations has made it possible for a Communist assassin to take the life of an American President. In fact, investigations into Communism and the prosecution of Communists have been discouraged by many leaders of the American community for the last ten years.

The Washington, D. C., affiliate of the National Council of Churches, which is called the National Council of Churches' Capitol Area, whose offices are located at 1751 North Street, Northwest, Washington 6, D. C., *lobbied* in the nation's capital early in 1963 to abolish the House Committee on Un-American Activities and to kill the financial appropriation for the Committee from Congress. Each Congressman received a letter from the Reverend David Colwell, Chairman of this ministerial association, on their official letterhead, dated January 3, 1963, urging the Congressmen to "vote for a change of the rules to abolish this committee which we feel has long outlived its usefulness and that if a proposal for an appropriation for the committee comes before the House that you will vote against such an appropriation."

Finally on Wednesday, February 27, 1963, Congress gave its Committee on Un-American Activities a vote of endorsement, 385 to 20. Members also approved a $360,000 appropriation for the committee on a roll-call ballot. The United Press International on that day pointed out that "the effort to trim the committee's funds attracted fourteen more votes than did a similar move two years ago." Representatives William Fitts Ryan (Democrat-New York), Thomas L. Ashley (Democrat-Ohio), and James Roosevelt (Democrat-California) joined in protesting that the committee spent too much for what it produced. Ryan said that the committee's methods tended to violate constitutional freedoms.

How long Americans will sit back in selfish and smug complacency and belittle the danger of Communism in the U.S.A. is hard to foretell. How long Americans will be deceived by the relatively small number of Communist votes cast and be unmindful of the tactics of the "united front" and of European history is a rather depressing prospect to face. America today more than ever, needs men who are neither Fascist nor Communist — men who are of the character of whom the bard of the Yukon writes when he says:

"Send me men girt for the combat,
    Men who are grit to the core.
Send me the best of your breeding,
    Send me your chosen ones.
These will I clasp to my bosom,
    And these will I call my sons.
For I will not be won by weaklings,
    Subtle and suave and mild,
But men with the heart of a viking
    And the simple faith of a child."

Have you the courage of the Vikings of old? Have you the faith of your younger years in God, your home, your personal and political liberties? The answer can be given not in words, but in deeds; first by intensive study of the problems we are presenting in this book; secondly, in carrying knowledge into action — and soon.

58

CHAPTER III
COMMUNIST FRONTS IN THE UNITED STATES

Article Three, Section One of the Constitution of the Communist Party of the United States of America states: "Any resident of the United States, eighteen years of age or over, regardless of race, color, national origin, sex or religious belief, who subscribes to the principles and purposes of the Communist Party, shall be eligible for membership." Article Three, Section Four states that members who are behind six months with their dues to the Communist Party "shall be dropped from party membership." These *actual* members of the Communist Party represent one of the greatest threats to the United States internally. However, in my opinion a far greater threat than an actual member of the Communist Party is an American — be he Democrat or Republican, Protestant, Catholic or Jew — who supports a Communist front organization intentionally or unintentionally and spreads Communist poison in the name of religion and freedom.

Several types of Americans serve the Communist cause. In addition to the open Communists who join the party unashamedly are the "secret Communists," sometimes referred to as "sacred cows," or "crypto-Communists." Lee Pressman, Nathan Witt, John Abt, and Alger Hiss were secret Communists. Undoubtedly there are many others in high places in government, education, and religion of whom we are unaware, as yet.

The American Government had warning of the crypto-Communists through no less an authority than J. Peters, Russian head of a Communist spy ring in the United States, who said, "The Communist Party is like a submerged submarine; the part that you see above water is the real Communist organization; that is, the conspiratorial apparatus." These crypto-Communists are under orders from Moscow to have no dealings with members of the Communist Party. They carry no membership card; do not attend open party meetings. Often the high party officials of the Communist Party do not even know who the secret Communists are in their district. These crypto-Communists probably never say anything which is openly in favor of Communism. In fact, occasionally they will say mildly critical things about Communism to detract suspicion. Alger Hiss was guilty of this. Consequently, it is extremely hard to prove a case on a secret or crypto-Communist.

The Communists have also used three other types of Americans who are not Communist Party members to serve their evil purposes under disguise. These are: (1) fellow travelers — Americans who join Communist-front groups and lend their time, money, and influence to the Communist cause; (2) Communist sympathizers — Americans who sympathize with the Communist cause, but do not belong to the party or Communist-front groups; (3) naive, innocent, misguided Americans who accept the Communist Party line, all the while insisting that they are anti-Communist.

Victor Kravchenko, former Soviet official who renounced Communism in 1944, said that he considered fellow travelers in America "to be a much more dangerous force than the official Communist Party." Most Communist fronts are organizations operating under Communist control to achieve some specific Communist objective. Some of the fronts are originated by the Communists and others are captured. The term "united fronts" refers to Communists and non-Communists working together against some foe or for some specific objective which the Communists favor. A "united front operation" is not necessarily controlled by the Communists. Many Americans have been deceived into thinking that Communist-front organizations are just harmless groups for the expression of "Far Left" opinions. This naive conception of the uninformed is the farthest from the truth. The Communist front is just as essential to the Communist conspiracy as are their training schools, espionage cells, or their official party press. Most of the Communist fronts in America are led by hard-core Communist conspirators, and veteran sympathizers.

At this point, I think we should go into detail concerning Communism's "united-front technique," because it is directly aimed at you, the average American. This is perhaps the most important and successful technique of the Communist conspiracy in the United States. The united front is the Communist tactic of working with non-Communists, often anti-Communists, on specific issues where there is ideological agreement. Usually the non-Communists are completely unaware that they are working with Communists to accomplish an important Communist conspiracy objective which will move us closer to nightmarish horror under Communist tyranny. So, the united-front tactic becomes the means by which the Communists recruit large numbers of American citizens into supporting pro-Communist objectives.

In one of the resolutions coming out of the Seventeenth National Convention of The Communist Party held in New York during December 1959, the Communists said that their united-front policy was "the key to progress on all fronts." Now just who do the Communists plan to recruit for these united-front activities which they feel are so important to their plot to enslave all Americans? The answer is "You," Communism's intended victim. Gus Hall, general secretary of the Communist Party told his fellow-conspirators in his keynote address at this Seventeenth Communist Party Convention: "We want to participate in, organize and lead the broadest of united-front movements — on every level — in a thousand ways, in ten thousand places, on one hundred thousand issues — if possible, with one hundred eighty million people. Obviously, we cannot make an understanding of the anti-monopoly character of these struggles on the part of others a condition for a united front, but we ourselves must at all times under stand that this is their basic nature." Here, Gus Hall told the Communists that each and every American citizen is a potential dupe of the Communist Party. Furthermore, he told the Communist delegates that it was obvious that the dupes would not know that they were helping to promote a Communist objective or aiding and abetting the cause of Communism, but they, the Communist leaders, would always know that the united-front cause was a Communist cause and the result would be the same as if it was carried out by Communists altogether. The desired results would be the weakening of America internally, the spreading of Communist poison, and the eventual overthrow of our government. At the 1959 Communist Party Convention, one of the Resolutions passed had to do with "mastering the united front." The Resolution contained the following: "Mastery of the theory and practice of the united-front policies is a key task for the whole party — before every organization, every member, the united front is the basic style and method of our mass work. This encompasses Comrades in the labor and mass organizations, as well as those Comrades able to function publicly as Communists — all party organizations can and must play a role in winning this biggest unwon battle, whether on a large scale by helping to move many organizations into concert on one or more issues or on a small scale by moving small numbers of people on single issues." In short, the resolution means that the Communists were to work to bring the vast majority of American citizens around to Communist thinking and cooperating with Communist objectives although the people would not know they were helping the Communist cause. And, as all thinking Americans know, thus far the American people have swallowed enough of the Communist lies to allow these conspirators fabulous success within our country.

The *one* thing the Communists must make sure of is that the American people remain ignorant of the Communist conspiracy internally. Here, the "Far Left" aids and abets the cause of Communism by constantly stressing the numerical smallness of the Communist Party and in the insistence that there is no threat from Communism internally.

"Go after the labor members," seems to be the national cry of the Communist Party as a result of their Seventeenth National Convention. They spoke of "concentrating our action to basic, decisive sections of the working class." By this, they mean they hope to dupe certain sections of American workers. The Communists think nothing of sending Communist conspirators with college degrees and even some with Master's and Doctor's Degrees, into ordinary factories to work at regular laboring jobs to influence their fellow union members. Of course, these highly educated conspirators conceal their educational backgrounds to employers and fellow union members. Once into these jobs, they work at achieving key union positions and with their higher level of education, they attempt to influence union members along the line of thinking what Communist leaders want them to think.

FBI Director J. Edgar Hoover, and the House Committee on Un-American Activities, have constantly warned of this program of agitating the laboring American which the Communists refer to as "colonization of basic industries."

William Z. Foster, former Communist Party Chairman, realized the importance of this tactic, for in his book, *Toward Soviet America*, he said that the Communist goal in the factories was "to make every shop a fortress for Communism."

It is apparent then that through their united-front activity, Communist conspirators plan to recruit the masses of American workers into a program of self-destruction. The classic example of the united front in acttion was a rally conducted in 1960 at the Madison Square Garden in New York City, sponsored by an organization known as The Committee for Sane Nuclear Policy. At this meeting, speeches were given by the late Mrs. Eleanor Roosevelt, Walter Reuther, singer Harry Belafonte, socialist leader Norman Thomas, and the 1936 Republican presidential candidate, Alf M. Landon.

About 17,000 people were reported to be present at this meeting. After the speeches, about 4,000 men, women, and children, chanting and singing "Ban The Bomb," marched through the heart of Manhattan and demonstrated in front of the United Nations Headquarters against nuclear testing. The Communist *Worker* in New York City worked diligently to help build the crowd for this rally in Madison Square Garden. In the Communist *Worker* of May 15, 1960, there was a huge headline across the front page which read: "For Sanity in Foreign Policy: All Out to Madison Square Garden, Thursday, 7:45 p.m." It is amazing that these famous Americans who participated in this rally as "headliners" did not disavow the Communist support on the night of the rally.

Here is a prime example of the united front operating very successfully. You may rest assured that at rallies such as this there will be little or no criticism of the godless, Kremlin mass murderers who make nuclear tests necessary in the first place because of their threat of world conflagration. These organizations usually leave the impression that world tensions are all the fault of the United States, and Communism's determined plot to enslave all free men is completely ignored.

While many liberals, including the leadership of the National Council of Churches, are urging unilateral disarmament, the Soviet Union pushes full speed ahead, arming its satellites, creating a war machine second to none in the world, with their eye constantly on the subjugation of the world to the Communist dictators. If the United States were to enter into "unilateral disarmament," this would be tantamount to surrender to

International Communism. Unilateral disarmament is the "better-Red-than-dead" theory in reality.

This insane theory of unilateral disarmament has received the all-out support from the liberal clergymen affiliated with the National Council of Churches and the World Council of Churches. In a meeting of the Central Committee of the World Council of Churches, the ruling body of clergymen of this world ecumenical group, at Nybork, Denmark, August 23, 1958, a resolution was passed which, according to an Associated Press release of that date, "stirred minor criticism." The resolution simply stated, "If all-out war should occur, Christians should urge a cease fire, if necessary on the enemy's terms and resort to non-violent resistance." This is like saying to the Soviet Union, "Come ahead. Invade our country. We will surrender without a fight." Some of the clergymen go along with this satanic philosophy because of sincere feelings of pacifism. Others go along with it because of sympathy with Communism. Still others advocate peace at any price, unilateral disarmament, piece-meal surrender because of fear of the atom bomb or a nuclear holocaust.

One of America's most celebrated comedians, Steve Allen, has added his support of the "Committee for a Sane Nuclear Policy." In the January 13, 1961, issue of our *Weekly Crusader*, we reported on "Steve Allen's misguided fight for peace." We reported that Allen made an appearance at Denver's East High School Auditorium that year, sponsored by the Colorado Committee for a Sane Nuclear Policy, where he was greeted by fifteen pickets carrying placards which, according to Denver newspapers, read, "We Don't Want Him, You Can

Have Him, He's Too Red For Us," and "Send Khrushchev's Water Boy Back to New York And Hollywood."
Other of the picket signs said, "We'd Rather Be Dead
Than Red" and another, "To Weaken Our Defense Is
Treason." The Denver papers reported, "Allen entered
the building through a rear door and, thus, did not meet
with the pickets out front. When told about them, he
flushed and appeared to take the incident as a personal
affront. He said in emotional tones: These people break
the laws of God and man! The law of God is—*Thou
Shalt Not Bear False Witness Against Thy Neighbor.
The laws of the State of Colorado prohibit libel. These
people are misguided and uninformed. There are no
Communists in the National Sane Committee or in the
Colorado Sane Committee.*'" When Allen says that there
are no Communists in the Colorado or National Sane
Committees, he admits that he has little or no conception of the "united-front technique" of the Communist
conspiracy. Senator Dodd (Democrat-Conneticut), in a
speech delivered before the United States Senate on
May 25, 1960, revealed: "Because I esteem the sincerity
of the original founders of the Committee for a Sane
Nuclear Policy and the sincerity of the speakers who
appeared at the May 19, 1960, rally at Madison Square
Garden (mentioned above), it is for me an unpleasant
duty to have to notify them that the unpublicized chief
organizer of the Madison Square Garden Rally was a
veteran member of the Communist Party; that there
was also evidence of serious Communist infiltration at
chapter level throughout the Committee for a Sane Nuclear Policy; that the Communist Party and its front organizations had done their utmost to promote the meet-

ing; that Communists provided much of the organizing machinery for the meeting because they planned to use it as a pressure instrument in support of Soviet nuclear diplomacy. This information was confirmed by the Subcommittee on Internal Security only several days before the Madison Square Garden Meeting was scheduled to take place. The name of the Communist Party member who served as chief organizer of the Madison Square Garden meeting is Henry H. Abrams.. The Subcommittee has received evidence, much of it still of a classified nature, that Henry Abrams is not a lone infiltrator, but there exists, in fact, a serious Communist infiltration in the Committee for a Sane Nuclear Policy. The Communist purpose in supporting the test-ban agitation and in going all out to make the Madison Square Garden meeting a success is to exert pressure on the Administration to make still further concessions to the Soviet viewpoint in order to arrive at a test-ban agreement; to create a climate of public opinion which will make it impossible for the Administration to resume small underground tests, even though there may be every reason to believe that the Kremlin is conducting such tests; to enervate the free world so that it becomes incapable of responding with appropriate measures to challenges at Berlin and other points."

Considering the united-front technique, the most tragic thing is that many well-meaning Americans like Steve Allen, G. Mennen Williams, and other famed names such as Linus Pauling and Norman Thomas, in their support of SANE and in their participation at their public rallies, fail to see that Soviet Russia which, at the end of World War II, had only 190,000,000 people and was outnumbered eight-to-one by the free peoples of the world, now has over 900,000,000 under her domination, one-third of the world's population. What they choose to ignore is the fact that the Communist aim is to control the world including, and predominately, the United States.

Gullible, unthinking Americans have been used by the Communist conspirators for years and their intensified united-front campaign seems to go unabated, even after the assassination of the President of the United States by a Communist assassin. Our only hope is to encourage all Americans to study and learn the facts about godless Communism and its numerous united fronts. If a substantial number of Americans had a basic understanding of the nature, methods, and objectives of international and internal Communism, the Communist conspiracy's united-front technique would get nowhere. But Communists depend upon the apathy and ignorance of the American people.

Communist conspirators are not long, shaggy-haired revolutionists who stand on soap boxes and yell openly for the violent overthrow of our United States Government, while a Communist Party "dogtag" dangles around their necks. This is a picture that most Americans seem to have of Communists and, consequently, they think that Communists are almost nonexistent in our land. Communists are very clever operators who seem to be masterminded by Satan. They operate within every area of American life. In most instances, their Communist connections are kept secret except for the few admitted Communists and sympathizers whom the Red leaders keep above ground for propaganda purposes and to transmit the "party line" to the underground apparatus.

Communist conspirators get down to the grass roots level and work among the masses of our people who have no idea as to who or what Communists are. They work inside labor unions, business associations, men's clubs, women's clubs, schools, colleges, and churches.

While many anti-Communists waste their time in various idealistic activities which accomplish little or nothing toward stemming the Red tide, Communist conspirators are busily engaged in improving their united-front technique. Their intensified attention to this activity may mislead millions more innocent Americans into thinking and acting as the Soviet Union desires. The only effective opposition will come through grass roots education on basic issues concerning the internal threat of Communism, and through increased spiritual and political activity by the dedicated individual.

In a report issued by the Special Committee on Un-American Activities on March 29, 1944, Communist-front organizations are identified:

"Communist-front organizations are characterized by their common origin. The rigid conformity of these organizations to the Communist pattern, their interlocking personnel and their methods generally used to deceive the American public, being part of a conspiratorial movement, their essence is deception.

"For the guidance of the American people in detecting Communist-front organizations, we present the following criteria:

(1) Does the organization have Communist Party members or those trusted by the Communist Party in its posts of real power — or its executive board, as sec-

retary, organizer, educational director, editor, office staff?

(2) Are meetings of the organization addressed by Communists or their trusted agents? Does its publication include articles by such persons?

(3) Does the organization follow the Communist Party line?

(4) Does the organization cooperate with campaigns, activities, publications of the Communist party or other front organizations?

(5) Is the address of the organization in the same building with other front organizations, or within the cooperating vicinity?

(6) Does the organization cooperate with Communist-controlled unions?

(7) Does the organization's official publication reflect the line of the Communist Party, publish articles by pro-Communists, advertise Communist activities, or those of other front organizations or of Communist vacation resorts?

(8) Are questions injected in the meetings or in official publications which have more to do with current policy of the Communist Party than with the professed purposes of the organization?

(9) Are funds kicked back directly or indirectly to the Communist Party or to other front organizations?

(10) Is printing done at a Communist printing house?

(11) Does the organization use entertainers associated with pro-Communist organizations or entertainments?

(12) Does the organization receive favorable pub-

licity in the Communist press?

(13) Is the organization uniformly loyal to the Soviet Union?"

In addition to these thirteen rules on how to identify a Communist front, J. Edgar Hoover, head of the FBI, in testimony before the House Committee on Un-American Activities on March 26, 1947, added additional questions: "Does the organization denounce American and British foreign policy while always lauding Soviet policy; and does the organization utilize Communist double talk by referring to Soviet-dominated countries as democracies, complaining that the United States is imperialistic or capitalistic and constantly denouncing monopoly capital?"

The value to the Communist Party of these various front organizations is described by J. Edgar Hoover in his book, *Masters of Deceit*, as follows:

"Through these fronts, the Communist Party is able to influence thousands of non-Communists, collect large sums of money, and reach the minds, pens, and tongues of many high-ranking, distinguished individuals. Moreover, fronts are excellent fields for party recruitment. Thousands of party members were recruited through the many fronts operating in the 1930's and 1940's. The party has operated hundreds of major fronts in practically every field of party agitation: 'Peace'; Civil Rights; Protection of the Foreign Born; Support for Smith Act 'Victims'; Abolition of H-Bomb Tests; Exploitation of Nationality and Minority groups.

"We must not think of fronts in terms of legitimate organizations. A few fronts collect dues, issue a newspaper, or sponsor organized activities, such as a sports program or cultural affairs. Most, however, exist only on paper . . . their assets usually consist of a few office supplies, a second-hand mimeograph machine and a mailing list. The danger of a Communist Party front rests not on its physical appearance or size, but on its ability to deceive."

One source says there have been 20,000 Communist fronts organized in the United States since the Communist Party set up headquarters on the East Coast in 1919. In 1957 alone the House Committee on Un-American Activities listed a total of 663 Communist front organizations in operation in the United States that year, plus 122 publications cited as Communist or Communist fronts by Federal Agencies. In addition to these fronts and publications, there were 155 organizations and 25 publications cited as Communist or Communist fronts by state or territorial investigating committees.

At this point, consider this interesting fact relating to the recent assassination of Mr. Kennedy. Through an act of the United States Supreme Court headed by Earl Warren (case of Steve Nelson vs. Pennsylvania), individual states of the union were denied the right to make or enforce laws governing subversion and treason. The grossest wrong possible is for any American to charge Dallas, Texas, or the State of Texas for not having apprehended Lee Harvey Oswald, the Communist assassin, before the death of Mr. Kennedy, since the Supreme Court, through this action, denied the states the power to do just that. In one sweeping decision, the Supreme Court ruled that no state could either create anti-subversive laws or enforce them. Consequently, Steve Nelson, the head of the Pennsylvania Communist Party, was freed from a Federal Penitentiary because of the decision.

The number of Communist fronts in existence in the United States today is entirely too great to list in this book. However, from the book, *Guide to Subversive Organizations and Publications, And Appendixes,* published December 1, 1961, we list just a few of the "organizations cited as Communist or Communist front by federal authorities:"

Abraham Lincoln Brigade or Battalion
Abraham Lincoln School, Chicago
Almanac Singers
The American Committee for a Free Yugoslavia
American Committee for Democracy and Intellectual Freedom
American Committee for Friendship with the Soviet Union
American Committee for Protection of Foreign Born
American Committee for Spanish Freedom
American Council on Soviet Relations
American Jewish Labor Council
American League Against War and Fascism
American League for Peace and Democracy
American Negro Labor Congress
American Peace Crusade
American Peace Mobilization
American Russian Trading Corp. (AMTORG)
American Slav Congress
American Student Union
American Veterans for Peace
American Women for Peace

American Writers' Congress

American Youth Congress

American Youth for Democracy

Briehl's Farm, near Wallkill, New York

California Emergency Defense Committee

California Labor School, San Francisco

Citizens' Committee for Constitutional Liberties, New York City

Citizens' Committee to Preserve American Freedoms

Civil Rights Congress

Colorado Committee to Protect Civil Liberties

Colorado Peace Council

Committee for the Protection of Oregon's Foreign Born

Community Unitarian Fellowship, San Diego

Denver Peace Council

Downtown Club, Los Angeles

Emergency Civil Liberties Committee

Independent Progressive Party

Independent Voters' League, Pittsburgh

Information Bureau of the Communist and Workers Parties (Cominform)

Institute of Pacific Relations

International Book Store, Inc., San Francisco

International Labor Defense

International Publishers

International Union of Student (World Student Congress)

Intourist, Inc.

Jefferson School of Social Science, New York City

Jewish Peoples' Committee

Labor Youth League
Los Angeles Committee for Protection of Foreign
   Born
Minute Women for Peace
Modern Bookstore, Chicago, Illinois
National Committee to Abolish the Un-American
   Activities Committee
National Council of American-Soviet Friendship
National Lawyers' Guild
National Negro Congress
New Century Publishers
New England Citizens' Concern for Peace
People's Institute of Applied Religion
Progressive Party
Socialist Workers' Party
Southern Negro Youth Conference
World Peace Congress
Young Communists League

The report of the House Committee on Un-American
Activities for the year 1961 lists some of the main English language publications which are cited by the Committee as Communist or pro-Communist. Among the
Communist publications are:

   The Worker
   People's World
   Political Affairs
   Main Stream
   National Guardian
   New World Review
   Jewish Currents

Also, a group of Union publications are listed by the Committee as Communist, including:

The Dispatcher (International Longshoremen's and Warehousemen's Union)

U.E. News (Radio and Machine Workers of America)

Mine, Mill Union (Mine, Mill and Smelter Workers' Union)

New York Teacher News (Teachers Union)

A. C. A. News (American Communications Association)

The average paid circulation of all the Communist publications in the United States per issue is over 263,000. The Committee points out that the readership total is no more an accurate guide to Communist strength in the United States than is the figure of 10,000 party members. Also not included in the tabulation are publications such as the following, which are the official organs of cited Communist front groups:

The Social Question Bulletin. (Official organ of the Methodist Federation for Social Action)

Rights. (The official organ of the Emergency Civil Liberties Union)

Abolition. (Publication of the New York Council to Abolish the House Un-American Activities Committee and Youth To Abolish HUAC, etc.)

As was stated in the first chapter of this book, circulation of the Communist publications has risen steadily since 1957. These periodicals are but a small part of the weapons in the U.S. Communist Party's propaganda arsenal. In addition to them, the party prepares and distributes each year millions of handbills, pamphlets, reprints of magazine articles, and speeches, and similar items which carry its line to non-Communist American citizens. The Communist fronts play a key role in the distribution of this propaganda, although they are not the only vehicles used for its dissemination.

It should also be noted here that Communist propaganda publications published by the Communist Party and its Fronts within the United States do not by any means account for all the Communist literature distributed and read in this country. On September 11, 1961, the Chairman of the House Committee on Un-American Activities pointed out that in 1960 the U.S. Bureau of Customs had processed over fourteen million packages of Communist propaganda mail entering this country from abroad and that these packages contained in excess of twenty-one million items, such as newspapers, magazines, books, posters, and pictures. This was an increase of 137 per cent over the year 1959. He also pointed out that in the two months of February and March, 1961, over 162,000 packages of magazines and 11,000 packages of newspapers were addressed to the United States from Communist Cuba alone. This propaganda was delivered in the United States by American mail, postage free, under an international postal agreement with allies.

In an issue of the *Weekly Crusader*, November 17, 1961, the postal propaganda problem was pointed out. It was stated at that time that Communist propaganda printed in China was coming into the United States by the millions of pieces to be delivered, postage free, to gullible Americans. One such document printed in Communist China in 1958 which had a mass distribution in this country, postage free, was entitled "Data on Atrocities of U.S. Army in South Korea." Here are some excerpts from this Communist treatise: "From the very first day of their occupation, the American imperialists have been trying had to convert South Korea into a project for squeezing out maximum profit for the millionaires of Wall Street and an outpost for their aggression of the Asian continent. The American imperialists since 1950 have committed atrocities unprecedented in the history of mankind in their aggressive war on Korea. They have massacred, at random, innocent people in Korea. They have destroyed and pillaged more than 5,000 schools, 1,000 hospitals and clinics. The American soldiers arrested Kim Bu Ing, a dock worker in Inchon, for the only reason that she was a member of the Women's Union. After violating and torturing her by every means, they stripped her naked, burned her with a heated iron poker, then killed her." This type of lying propaganda is both unsolicited and unwanted by the great bulk of patriotic Americans who receive it.

Just how extensive is this Communist flooding of the U.S. mails? According to a "Washington Report" supplement by Congressman Glenn Cunningham, member of the Post Office Committee of the House of Representatives: "The United States Customs Bureau at New Orleans counted at least 30,000 packages of Communist propaganda destined for schools and colleges in the U.S. during a recent twelve-month period. Each package contained five to fifteen different publications on youth leadership for Communism, and this was only one of forty ports at which such materials enter the U.S. In one recent year, seven million pieces of such Communist literature appeared through New York City. It is significant that the Deputy Director of Customs in the Port of New York said in June (1961) that Communist propaganda is 'really flooding this country' since the Kennedy Administration order of March 17." Now what was Congressman Cunningham referring to when he mentioned "the Kennedy Administration order of March 17?"

Under the Eisenhower Administration, the President of the United States instigated a policy that all "suspect mail" from Communist countries arriving in the United States be forwarded to an Inspection Investigation Division to determine if it was subversive. However, at the insistence of the Secretary of State, Dean Rusk, on April 6, 1961, shortly after Mr. Kennedy's inauguration, an official order No. 20247 was issued by President Kennedy stating that this practice of investigating "suspect mail" was to be abolished. Thus, as Congressmen Cunningham said, permitting "Communist propaganda to really flood this country."

It is hoped that President Johnson will rescind the Kennedy order and will return to the practice advocated by President Dwight David Eisenhower in this matter. Unless President Johnson does take such executive action, the Government, Congress, the Postal Service, and Federal Customs can do nothing about the flood of Communist propaganda into the United States because: (1) the United States is obligated under an International Postal Agreement to deliver or transship all foreign-postage mail arriving at its sea and air terminals, and

(2) constitutional law and the so-called sanctity of the mails prohibits opening much of this mail or stopping its delivery unless requested by the addressee. On August 12, 1961, according to an article in the Long Beach, California *Independent,* a "local postal spokesman confirmed that massive quantities of Communist literature and political propaganda were being landed at the Ports of Long Beach and Los Angeles ... that Los Angeles alone picks up between 5,000 and 10,000 bags of mail each month from ships arriving at the Ports of Long Beach and Los Angeles containing such material."

On August 23, 1962, the White House took action against the Amendment proposed by Congressman Glenn Cunningham (Republican-Nebraska) which had been aimed at stopping the mail delivery of Communist propaganda from overseas in the United States. The White House came out in firm opposition to this attempt to stop the flow of Communist propaganda into this country. Edward R. Murrow, who personally announced President Kennedy's decision, said that the Amendment of Congressman Cunningham would have only "blocked receipt of materials from behind the Iron Curtain which is vital to research and analysis of what's going on in Communist countries." As if we do not have spies and informers in every country behind the Iron Curtain that could give us this information, without opening our mails to the flow of Communist material, most of which reaches gullible youth.

Congressman Gordon Scherer, for ten years a member of the House Committee on Un-American Activities, now living in Cincinnati, Ohio, said in a speech before Congress on September 8, 1961: "Of the more than 1,000 different types of these periodicals which come to our shores each year, the great mass is printed in English and goes to native-born Americans; to our libraries, colleges, seminaries, and to people with extreme left-wing propensities who are in positions to mould American opinion." It is little wonder then why Congressman Cunningham asked Congress one day: "How in the world can we go to the American people and ask and compel them to pay increased postal rates when this huge volume of Communist propaganda is coming to this country and is delivered free? We know that, as a result of that, this is adding a terrific burden on the financial position of the Postal Department and is contributing immensely to the deficit that we have."

No consideration of the extent to which Communist propaganda is disseminated among the American people can be complete without consideration of its distribution through media which are considered completely respectable, non-Communist, and even anti-Communist. Unfortunately, from a statistical viewpoint, it is impossible to gauge even approximately the extent to which this goes on.

The former head of the Central Intelligence Agency, Allen W. Dulles, on a "Meet the Press" program on December 21, 1961, stated that Communists have tried to sell their propaganda and unfortunately they have succeeded in many cases. They have placed their propaganda in their own publications, then it is picked up by leftist journals, and then it gets more and more respectability until people are quoting Communist propaganda, sometimes maybe without knowing what they are doing.

An Assistant Director of the FBI addressed the Virginia Press Association on June 18, 1961, on the subject of "The Fourth Estate vs. The Fifth Column." In the course of his address, he indicated very clearly that there is Communist infiltration in the press in this country and said: "The Communists seldom miss an opportunity to exploit our free press. They are definitely interested in infiltrating the newspaper field and placing members or sympathizers in strategic positions. This is one of the party's prize objectives. By successfully infiltrating non-Communist publications, Communists gain far wider dissemination of their views than is possible through their own press since their thinly-veiled propaganda is camouflaged by the fact that it appears in a respectable publication. Moreover, the appearance of Communist views in non-Communist publications goes far toward substantiating the spurious claim of the Communist Party, U.S.A., that it is a liberal and progressive political party."

To conclude this condensed review of the Communist-front movement in the United States, a quote from the House Committee on Un-American Activities' Annual Report for 1961 is most appropriate: "The Communist Party is always creating new Communist fronts — so many in fact that this committee and other official agencies could not possibly investigate and formally cite all of them. For this reason, no listing of officially-cited organizations and publications has ever been complete. Today, as in the past, there are a considerable number of organizations which are under Communist control and which are very obviously promoting Communist objectives although they have not been officially cited as Communist fronts."

Therefore, as the Committee concluded in this report: "The number of members of the Communist Party would be an accurate gauge of Communist strength in the United States IF all Communists were members of the Communist Party, IF there were no Communist fronts, no Communist-dominated unions, no Communist-infiltrated organizations, and no non-Communist organizations and individuals cooperating with the Communist Party and its fronts. It would be an accurate gauge of the internal Communist danger IF the Communist party received no help from abroad, IF it was not reaching hundreds of thousands of Americans with its propaganda, and IF there were not groups in this country composed of fanatical extremists who, though not Communists, constantly agitate for the adoption of policies and actions which the Communists also demand because Moscow deems them vital to the final victory of the world Communist movement. Because none of the above conditions hold, however, the bare figure of 10,000 Communist Party members has little relevance to the question of the strength of the Communist movement in this country and the degree of danger it represents. To the contrary, this figure — 10,000 — tends to be misleading rather than informative."

In his excellent book, *Martin Dies' Story*, former Congressman Martin Dies of Lufkin, Texas wrote: "Let us remember it doesn't matter whether a person is a Communist or not. Is he advancing any of the Communist purposes? If he is, that is all that Moscow wants. A Communist could not do more. In fact, Georgi Dimitroff told the Lenin School of Political Warfare, 'Let us be friends.' It is obvious that not only have Communist successes in the United States not been halted, but they are actually increasing at an accelerated rate. The ignorance of the average American on this subject is appalling and the liberals are determined that he shall not have the facts. The powers and pressures of bureaucracy are influencing, if they are not forcing, the American businessman into a socialistic economic structure which is a Communist-approved stem on the road to Communism. This is not my argument. It is what the Communists say.

"They are still here — those who advance Communist purposes — the question is 'what are the American people going to do about it?' "

"Am I therefore become your enemy, because I tell you the truth?" (Galatians 4:16.)

CHAPTER IV

ALLIES OF THE COMMUNISTS — NAZIS, FASCISTS, AND THE SPLINTER-GROUPS

To understand the international and internal threat of Communism, all Americans should take a second look at the leaders of the world Communist conspiracy. We have mentioned in this book something about the Communists who lead the Communist Party, U.S.A.

I counted it a privilege to know personally Congressman Francis E. Walter, Democrat of Pennsylvania, who served as Chairman of the House Committee on Un-American Activities until his death in 1963. In a speech which appeared in the *Philadelphia Inquirer* in

March of 1958, Chairman Walter gave an excellent resume of the leaders of the *international* Communist conspiracy in an article entitled, "Comradeship Is Fatal." Because of the importance of this material, we are reprinting it:

COMRADESHIP IS FATAL

"Present-day leaders of the international Communist empire, in the course of their careers of murder and terror, have deliberately destroyed more men, women, and children than populate the eastern United States. Despite the long history of Soviet treachery and deceit which lies in full view of the civilized world, we find ourselves being subjected once more to the sweet persuasion which seeks to lead us into comradeship with men whose real intents are best observed in their broken promises and lust for power.

"In recent months the emphasis has been on 'coexistence' and 'disarmament' conferences. Now the demand is for a 'summit meeting' at which our President and the heads of the governments of the free world would sit down with the bosses of the Iron Curtain countries to end the cold war.

"We may well wonder what new and bitter hoax awaits us. The plausibility of Nikita Khrushchev and his colleagues, coupled with the eager willingness of many quarters of the free world to believe them, appear to have rebutted common-sense and our own experience.

"Who are these Communist leaders with whom our representatives would meet at the 'summit'? The Committee on Un-American Activities has examined their careers searchingly. We believe a study of these men will demonstrate beyond doubt the character of Communism's masters and the hopelessness of attempting to negotiate with them as if they were men of good faith. Here they are:

NIKITA KHRUSHCHEV

"As First Secretary of the Communist Party of the Soviet Union, Khrushchev two years ago denounced the dead Josef Stalin as a vicious murderer and terrorist. A few years earlier, Khrushchev was hailed as 'the faithful disciple and companion-in-arms of Comrade Stalin.'

"Khrushchev's rise to power in the party coincided with the notorious purge of the mid-1930's. He actually played a leading role in the mass terror of that period. Stalin sent him to the Ukraine to carry out the party purge there. He is, as a result, one of the most hated men in the Soviet Ukraine today.

"In carrying out his assignment, he was as systematic as he was ruthless. He openly boasted that 'we have destroyed a considerable number of enemies, though not all.'

"A salient feature of his record is his relentless onslaught against independent farmers. His rise to power was accompanied by the betrayal and the physical destruction of his closest associates. At the helm of the party, he lost no time in undermining and finally ousting Georgi Malenkov and Vyacheslav M. Molotov, his political rivals in the collective leadership, and in establishing himself in Stalin's fashion as the master of the Soviet.

"Khrushchev is the sworn enemy of the democratic form of government. He reviles the United States as being devoid of political freedom and economic stability and ruled by a handful of greedy capitalists who enslave the working people.

"His fanatical belief in the superiority of the Communist system leaves no doubt in his mind that, whether there be peace or war, the ultimate communization of the world is certain.

"To obtain this objective, Khrushchev displays versatility and flexibility in selecting the device he considers most effective and promising at the moment: nuclear blackmail, subversion, propaganda, interference in the domestic affairs of other states, or exploitation of anticolonial and nationalist feelings in Asia and Africa. All these expedients serve the single-minded goal of Soviet aggrandizement and of accelerating the march of Communism.

"On March 27, 1958, all pretense at a 'collective leadership' in the Soviet Union came to an end when Khrushchev, already First Secretary of the Soviet Communist Party, took over Bulganin's post as Premiere of the Soviet Union. Thus, Khrushchev has emerged from the power struggles as undisputed dictator of the Soviet Union. It remains to be seen whether the new dictator can make his position as secure as Stalin's was, or whether he will in turn become a victim of new power struggles in the Soviet political volcano.

WALTER ULBRICHT

"Exerting practically unlimited power as head of the Communist Party in East Germany, Walter Ulbricht also holds the title of First Deputy Premier in that Soviet puppet government. He represents a dangerous and relentless enemy of America and all it stands for.

"A founder of the German Communist Party in 1918, he managed to survive Hitler, the purges under Stalin, the postwar executions of East European leaders, and Khrushchev's anti-Stalinist campaign.

"His hour of triumph came in April 1945, while Berlin was in flames and the battle of the city was raging. Ulbricht was flown in from Moscow to set up the German civilian government.

"There are few fields of life in East Germany in which Ulbricht has not imposed subservience to the Soviet Union. He has ordered servile imitations of Russia in the fields of science, linguistics and education, the theater, architecture, and sports. He has made the organization of the East German state a miniature replica of the Soviet Union.

"The magnitude of discontent with his regime became evident with the revolt of East Berlin in June 1953. Ulbricht suppressed it ruthlessly with Soviet armed power.

"His pro-Sovietism is surpassed only by his anti-Americanism. He has distorted history to paint America as the villain on the world stage. Regardless of talk of 'peace' and 'peaceful coexistence,' Ulbricht's goal remains unchanged: the communization of all of Germany as a decisive step toward the communization of the whole world.

JANOS KADAR

"Communist Party head in Hungary and, until recently, Premier of that country, Janos Kadar is a Communist Quisling for the Kremlin and a master of the doublecross.

"He is a man of ambition but no integrity; of a personal drive but no character; of natural political skill but devoid of high intelligence. So loyal is he to Communism that after 32 months of imprisonment and torture under one Red regime, he became the willing servant of the Kremlin in the reconquest of Hungary in November 1956.

"In November 1956, when Hungary attempted to throw off the Soviet yoke, Kadar set up a Soviet puppet government and 'invited' Russian tanks into Budapest. Some 32,000 persons were killed and parts of the capital reduced to rubble in smashing Hungary's bid for freedom. At the height of the counterrevolution, Kadar justified the brutal treatment of his countrymen:

" 'A tiger cannot be tamed by bait. It can be tamed and forced to peace only by beating it to death.'

WLADYSLAW GOMULKA

"First Secretary of the Communist Party in Poland, he has managed, by making a few concessions to workers, peasants, and the Catholic Church, to head off a Polish repetition of events in Hungary.

"But while his 'road to socialism' may differ slightly from the Russian road, it is still communistic. Gomulka has made that point abundantly clear.

"He denies being a 'national Communist', a term he calls an American invention. As proof, he notes that his program includes the main aims of every Communist Party:

1. Seizure of power by Communist;
2. Establishment of a Communist dictatorship;

3. Nationalization of industry; and

4. The promotion of international Communism in 1956 foreign affairs.

"His present power dates to 1956 when he staged a comeback after falling into disfavor in 1948. Stubborn, relentless, he is fanatically devoted to Communism, although it has brought his country insoluble problems. He is struggling with opponents within his own party; whether he will survive as Poland's leader, only time will tell.

MAO TSE-TUNG

"Chairman of the People's Republic of China, less than a year ago he announced a new freedom of Communist China:

" 'Let a hundred flowers bloom and let a hundred schools of thought contend,' he suggested generously. Some Chinese took him seriously — and faced a new wave of terror.

"It was Mao who proclaimed the People's Republic in October 1949. The fiction of China's 'disassociation' from Russia was shattered with his signing of the Sino-Soviet Friendship Pact in 1950 in Moscow.

"He never makes a speech in which he does not pay tribute to the U.S.S.R. At Stalin's order, Mao sent vast Chinese armies to fight Americans who were resisting Communist aggression in Korea.

"To crush resistance at home, Mao ordered what he called 'mass shock,' in which 12,000,000 Chinese— according to Communist figures — were wiped out.

"He has conducted a 'hate America' campaign for years and still refuses to account for American soldiers missing in the Korean War. As part of his drive, he has endorsed defiance of the United Nations, atrocities against prisoners of war, violation of the Korean truce, and subversion throughout Southeast Asia.

CHOU EN-LAI

"Premier, and until recently, Foreign Minister of Communist China, Chou appears affable in his personal relations. In this he resembles his boss, Mao Tsetung. His past has been that of a fanatic and dedicated Communist and the basic pattern of his policy — a combination of force and deceit — has been evident for years.

"In foreign policy, where Mao has given him a relatively free hand, Chou has operated with the same combination. His record in Korea is particularly sordid.

"Defying the United Nations, which branded Red China as an 'aggressor', Communist China fought against the American and U.N. armies for nearly three years. When Communism lost the war, Chou became one of the instigators of the false accusation that the United States had used 'bacteriological warfare' in Korea.

"Under the armistice terms, Red China promised to return captured prisoners of war; instead Chou used them in an insidious game to barter American lives for United States concessions. His promise not to increase armaments in North Korea was violated almost from the beginning of the truce.

"Lately, he has switched again to deceit. At the Afro-Asian Conference in Bandung, Chou made a dramatic offer to negotiate a peaceful settlement of the Formosa question with the United States. But it soon developed that the only basis on which he would negotiate was the immediate surrender of the island to the Communists.

"There we have some of the leaders with whom we are asked to negotiate a peace. We must remember we are not dealing with partners but with adversaries dedicated to accomplish our destruction with every ruse and subterfuge which they have used successfully in enslaving almost half the world."

Most thinking conservatives are convinced that the present controversy between Khrushchev and Mao Tse-tung is as fictitious as the so-called split between Tito of Yugoslavia and Stalin of the Soviet Union in years past. The history of the entire international Communist conspiracy, as well as the Communist Party, U.S.A., is replete with constant bickerings, recriminations, denunciations, charges, and countercharges. However, the Communist forces of the world seem always able to pull their ranks together to accomplish their singular goal — the communization of the world.

In recent years we have seen the differences between American Communists dissolved and a closer cooperation between the splinter groups of the conspiracy develop. The Trotskyite Communists, who have been feuding with the Stalinist Communists since the 1920's, compose the largest of the splinter organizations. In the past their relations with the Communist Party had been marked by extreme bitterness; however, Khrushchev's speech attacking and denouncing Stalin at the Twentieth Congress of the Soviet Communist Party in 1956 has done much to heal the breach between these two groups. Following the Twentieth Congress, the world

Communist conspiracy, through a Cominform publication, called upon the orthodox Communists of the world to work for united action between themselves and other Communist groups. Since that time, the U.S. Communist Party, following Moscow's orders, has made a deliberate effort to heal the breach between itself and the Socialist Workers (Trotskyites Communist) Party in the United States. There has been increasing evidence of success in this endeavor. On numerous occasions, representatives of the Socialist Workers Party, who some years ago would have nothing to do with the orthodox party, have been appearing on the same platform with the Communist Party leaders. A good illustration of this is the September 1961 protest rally against the use of nuclear weapons which was held in Los Angeles. Among the speakers were John T. McTernan, Chairman for the Unitarian Fellowship for Social Justice (a man who has been identified as a member of the Communist Party by several witnesses); Theodore Edwards, Chairman of the Southern California Socialist Workers (Trotskyites) Party; and also Dr. A. J. Lewis, Executive Secretary of the Los Angeles Fair Play for Cuba Committee. (The President's assassin, Lee Harvey Oswald, was a member of the Fair Play for Cuba Committee.)

We should make mention here of the main splits within the Communist Party since 1920. Perhaps the first group to split from the Communist Party was the Proletarian Party of America formed in 1920. Like most splinter groups, the Proletarian Party, founded by one John Keracher, claims to be the real Marxist Party in the United States and that all other so-called Communists are imposters. This organization is still active in a few states, including Illinois and Michigan.

The expulsion of Trotsky by the Russian Communists in the fall of 1927 had its effect on the Communist movement in the United States. Campaigns to tear down the Trotsky image were demanded by Moscow with the implied threat of reprisals against any national group failing to take a position against the expulsion of Trotsky. On May 17, 1929, Communists who had been expelled from the American Communist Party because of their friendship with Trotsky formed the Communist League of America, left-wing opposition of the Communist Party. This group of Communists are often called the Trotskyites and their history has been a stormy one. In December 1934 the Communist League of America merged with the American Workers Party. In March 1936 the American Workers Party merged with the Socialist Party and in June 1938 the Socialist Party began a series of wholesale expulsions of the Trotskyites. On New Year's Day 1938 James P. Cannon, who was one of the first Communists to be expelled from the party for Trotsky loyalty, and his followers formed the Socialist Workers Party. In December 1941 with seventeen of his followers, Cannon was convicted in Minneapolis on charges of conspiracy to create insubordination in the Armed Forces of the Government — the first conviction under the Smith Act.

The Socialist Workers Party is still active today, but is not a large organization and is very limited in its activities. Its program rests on the principles of Marxism as expounded by Marx, Engels, Lenin, and Trotsky. Another one of the Communists to be expelled at the same time as Cannon, was Albert Weisbord. Although he was an ardent admirer of Trotsky, he wanted to be the grand dictator of the American Communist movement, so he broke with Cannon and formed his own organization called the Communist League of Struggle.

Another splinter group of the Communist Party is the American Workers Party. This was formed at a Conference for Progressive Labor Action meeting held in Pittsburgh, Pennsylvania in December 1933. The leaders of this Communist splinter group, the American Workers Party, were a "minister" by the name of A. J. Muste and another would-be dictator by the name of J. B. Slutsky, alias J. B. S. Hardman. A unity convention was held in December 1934 when the members of the Communist League of America were taken into the American Workers Party and became known as Workers Party of the United States. In March 1936 the Workers Party of the United States merged with the Socialist Party and thus disappeared from the scene.

Another splinter of the Communist Party was the United Toilers, headed by Harry Wicks. It soon withered away.

Another split in the Communist Party was led by Jay Lovestone. He called his group Communist Party, U.S.A. (Opposition). Later this group was changed to the Independent Communist Labor League of America, and finally to the Independent Labor League of America. The organization was finally dissolved in January 1941 by a Declaration of Dissolution issued by Lovestone himself.

To understand the real success that the Communist conspiracy has had in brainwashing many American leaders to be anti-anti Communist and pro-Communist, the remarks of Communist Party leader Earl Browder are a case in point. In his book, *Socialism in America,* page 101, Browder said:

"The American Communist Party's role in the 1930's is perhaps the most complex factor most difficult to evaluate in retrospect and therefore a very controversial subject. A few characteristic features, however, seem to be indisputable. Entering the 1930's as a small ultra-left sect of some 7,000 members, remnant of the fratricidal factional struggle of the 1920's that had wiped out the old 'left-wing' of American Socialism, the Communist Party rose to become a national political influence far beyond its numbers (at its height, it never exceeded 100,000 members) on a scale never before reached by a Socialist movement claiming the Marxist tradition. It became a practical power in organized labor, its influence became strong in some state organizations of the Democratic Party (even dominant in a few for some years) and even some Republicans solicited its support. It guided the anti-Hitler movement of the American League for Peace and Democracy that united a cross-section of some five million organized Americans (A list of its sponsors and speakers would include almost the majority of Roosevelt's cabinet, the most prominent intellectuals, judges of all grades up to State Supreme Courts, church leaders, labor leaders, etc.). Right-wing intellectuals complained that it exercised an affective veto in almost all publishing houses against their books, and it is at least certain that those right-wingers had extreme difficulty getting published."

"THE FAR LEFT"

Understanding the conspiratorial aspect of international Communism, it is indeed strange that President Franklin D. Roosevelt recognized the Soviet Union in 1933. Four American presidents had refused to recognize the Communist Revolution in Russia because of its record of perfidy and broken agreements.

It was in 1920 that the United States Secretary of State, Bainbridge Colby, made the following important policy statement reflecting his attitude toward negotiation with the Communist leaders of the Kremlin:

"The existing regime in Russia is based upon the negation of every principle of honor and good faith ... of every principle upon which it is possible to base harmonious and trustful relations, whether of nations or of individuals. The responsible leaders of the regime have frequently and openly boasted that they are willing to sign agreements and undertakings with foreign powers while not having the slightest intention of observing such undertakings or carrying out such agreements ... we cannot recognize, hold official relations with, or give friendly reception to the agents of a government which is determined and bound to conspire against our institutions; whose diplomats will be the agitators of dangerous revolts; whose spokesmen say that they sign agreements with no intention of keeping them."

But in 1933, in spite of these many warnings and previous actions to the contrary by American presidents, Franklin D. Roosevelt made an agreement on November 16 of that year to grant diplomatic recognition to the Soviet Government. The stipulations in the agreement were that Communist leaders agreed to refrain from disseminating Communist propaganda in the United States, from interfering in United States internal affairs, and many other pledges. The ink was hardly dry on this agreement before the Communists began their internal subversion within the United States. This agreement meant nothing to the Communists.

Former Congressman Martin Dies has this to say about this agreement in his excellent book, *Martin Dies' Story*:

"At a meeting late in the evening of November 16, 1933 in the White House, President Franklin D. Roosevelt handed to Maxim Litvinoff, People's Commissar for Foreign Affairs of the U.S.S.R., a letter of recognition, in exchange for a letter of promises on which recognition was based. Litvinoff's letter pledged 'scrupulously' to refrain from interfering in the internal affairs of the United States, from any 'agitation or propaganda' and from any action aimed at the 'overthrow of the political or social order of the whole or any part of the United States.'"

It was on October 10, 1933 that Mr. Roosevelt wrote Michail Kalinin, who at that time was President of the Soviet Union, in Moscow, saying:

"Since the beginning of my Administration, I have contemplated the desirability of an effort to end the present abnormal relations between the hundred and twenty-five million people of the United States and the hundred and sixty million people of Russia.

"It is most regrettable that these great peoples, between whom a happy tradition of friendship existed for more than a century to their mutual advantage, should now be without a practical method of communicating directly with each other.

"The difficulties that have created this anomalous situation are serious but not, in my opinion, insoluble; and difficulties between great nations can be removed only by frank, friendly conversations. If you are of similar mind, I should be glad to receive any representatives you may designate to explore with me personally all questions outstanding between our countries."

To which Michail Kalinin replied on October 17, 1933:

"I gladly accept your proposal to send to the United States a representative of the Soviet Government to discuss with you the questions of interest to our countries. The Soviet government will be represented by Mr. M. M. Litvinoff, People's Commissar for Foreign Affairs, who will come to Washington at a time to be mutually agreed upon."

Because of the importance of the "agreement" with Litvinoff made by Mr. Roosevelt, we are reprinting here the entire letter signed by Maxim Litvinoff dated November 16, 1933, which was to be the basis for the recognition of the Soviet Union by the United States:

"I have the honor to inform you that coincident with the establishment of diplomatic relations between our two governments it will be the fixed policy of the Government of the Union of Soviet Socialist Republics:

"1. To respect scrupulously the indisputable right of the United States to order its own life within its own jurisdiction in its own way and to refrain from interfering in any manner in the internal affairs of the United States, its territories or possessions.

"2. To refrain, and to restrain all persons in government service and all organizations of the government or under its direct or indirect control, including organizations in receipt of any financial assistance from it, from any act overt or covert liable in any way whatsoever to injure the tranquillity, prosperity, order, or security of the whole or any part of the United States, its territories or possessions, and in particular, from any act tending to incite or encourage armed intervention, or any agitation or propaganda having as an aim, the violation of the territorial integrity of the United States, its territories or possessions, or the bringing about by force of a change in the political or social order of the whole or any part of the United States, its territories or possessions.

"3. Not to permit the formation or residence on its territory of any organization or group — and to prevent the activity on its territory of any organization or group, or of representatives or officials of any organization or group — which makes claim to be the government of, or makes attempt upon the territorial integrity of, the United States, its territories or possessions; not to form, subsidize, support or permit on its territory military organizations or groups having the aims of armed struggle against the United States, its territories or possessions, and to prevent any recruiting on behalf of such organizations and groups.

"4. Not to permit the formation or residence on its territory of any organization or group — and to prevent the activity on its territory of any organization or group, or of representatives or officials of any organization or group, which has as an aim the overthrow or the preparation for the overthrow of, or the bringing about by force of a change in, the political or social order of the whole or any part of the United States, its territories or possessions."

In exchange for recognition of the Soviets, you will notice that Litvinoff gave Roosevelt an assurance in this letter that no subversive group would be permitted in the United States. The American Communist leaders were worried about this promise but as Benjamin Gitlow, one of the original founders of the American Communist Party who later broke with Communism to become our Government's number one witness against the conspiracy, wrote in his book, *The Whole of Their Lives*: "At a special meeting, Litvinoff assured the frightened Communists that they had nothing to worry about. The Comintern is not restrained by the Soviet Government. 'After all, Comrades,' he concluded, 'you should by this time know how to handle the fiction of the tieup between the Comintern and the Soviet Government. Don't worry about the letter. It is a scrap of paper which will soon be forgotten in the realities of Soviet-American relations.'"

It is apparent that Franklin D. Roosevelt believed the Communists one hundred per cent which may have led to his death at the close of World War II, broken in body and spirit.

In 1943, before his first meeting with Stalin, Roosevelt told William C. Bullitt, our first Ambassador to the Soviet Union: "I have just a hunch that Stalin doesn't want anything but security for his country, and I think that if I give him everything I possibly can and ask for nothing from him in return, noblesse oblige, he won't try to annex anything and will work for world democracy and peace."

Winston Churchill, in his book *The Hinge of Fate*, quoted from a note which he received from Mr. Roosevelt, stating: "I know you will not mind my being brutally frank when I tell you that I think I can personally handle Stalin better than either your Foreign Office or my State Department. Stalin hates the guts of all your top people. He thinks he likes me better and I hope he will continue to do so."

It has been suggested that the President's enthusiasm for Stalin and his blindness of the threat of internal Communism was the result of the undue influence which Harry Hopkins had on him. Certainly Hopkins had a tremendous and, in my opinion, evil influence on the President of the United States. General John R. Deane, head of the United States Military Mission in Moscow during World War II, once wrote that Hopkins carried out the Russian lend-lease program "with a zeal which approached fanaticism." (Here it should be remembered that the eleven billion dollars worth of material which we sent to the Soviet Union including the gold-mining equipment was at the command of Harry Hopkins. Major George Racey Jordan worked as a liaison officer between the Soviet Government and Harry Hopkins.)

It is no wonder then, that Franklin Roosevelt and his New Deal opposed Congressional investigations into the Communist conspiracy led by a young Texas Congressman by the name of Martin Dies. President Roosevelt and the majority of his Administration were frankly, openly, and actively hostile to any investigations into the Communist conspiracy. In fact, Congressman Martin Dies and his committee reported to President Roosevelt the names of more than 5,000 employees at work in Roosevelt's Administration with subversive records. As Benjamin Gitlow states in his book *The Whole of Their Lives*: "The New Deal served as the American Kuomintang for the Communists, but with one important exception. The ruling group in the Kuomintang around Chaing Kai-shek had back of them years of training in the dark shadows of Oriental politics. They understood the crafty maneuvers of the Communists. The New Deal crowd were like innocent babes, who had a distorted and altogether wrong conception of Communists and Communist politics. The pro-Soviet New Deal crowd, from President Roosevelt down to the little bureaucrats holding unimportant desk jobs, accepted the Communists as honest idealists who were concerned primarily with the interests of the common people."

As we have stated elsewhere in this book, actually former Congressman Hamilton Fish (Democrat-New York), who is today serving on the National Advisory Board of Christian Crusade, headed the first committee to investigate Communism. In 1930 he introduced a resolution to the House of Representatives to investigate Communist propaganda, particularly in our educational institutions.

Martin Dies was sent to Congress as a result of the elections of November 5, 1930, from the same Texas district where his father had served as Congressman before him for a decade. While serving on the Committees on Immigration and Naturalization, Martin Dies learned first hand about Communism. Dies discovered that of approximately 10,000 admitted Communists in the United States, ninety-eight per cent were aliens. This fact was later admitted by William Z. Foster, Chairman of the Communist Party, U..S.A., in testimony before the committee. Martin Dies pushed his investigation of Communism as any good American would in spite of the fact that he was dubbed as a witch hunter by the "far-left."

In a speech before Congress in 1938, he said: "I regard Communism and Nazism and Fascism as having one underlying principle — dictatorship, the theory that government should have the right to control the lives, the fortunes, the happiness, the beliefs and every detail of the life of a human being and that man is a pawn of the government rather than the American conception that government is created for the benefit of mankind." In 1935, Martin Dies had attempted to get a bill passed by Congress which would exclude and deport Communist aliens. It was approved by both the State and Labor Departments, it passed the House, but Senate liberals under the leadership of Senator Robert M. LaFollette, Jr. (Progressive-Republican-Wisconsin) were able to prevent it from coming to a vote and it died. As Martin Dies later referred to this abortive attempt to kill Communism on the vine: "The consequences of this defeat were tragic. It had been a magnificent opportunity to strangle the infant monster of Communism in its cradle. Never again did we know this same opportunity because Communist aliens hastened to be naturalized while the influx of Communist aliens continued unabated."

The Martin Dies Committee and its successor, the permanent House Committee on Un-American Activities, have done a tremendous job in the fight against Communism internally. Also the Senate Internal Security Subcommittee has done a magnificent job protecting the internal security of the United States Government and both permanent committees should have the undying support of all liberty-and-freedom-loving Americans.

It should be remembered by all readers of this book that Fascism, Nazism, and Communism are ideological bedfellows. A quick check of the Webster's Dictionary will show that these three systems are the same. It is ironical, therefore, that the liberals would call conservatives or anti-Communists, Fascists. This is a clever way in which language is used as a Communist weapon. As Martin Dies pointed out: "Fascist is a term opprobrium misused to discourage and confuse anti-Communists. Virtually everyone to whom the derogatory label, Fascist, is allied stands firmly opposed to centralized, regimented, coercive government." The great challenge before every patriot today is to prove to the American people that Fascism and Communism are fundamentally alike and that the choice is not Communism or Fascism, but instead, is Marxism or Americanism.

The American people have been so brainwashed about the anti-semitic and race-supremacy traits of Hitler and Mussolini, that they have missed the welfare statism so central to Fascist rule. The American people have overlooked the fact that Fascism, like Socialism, is a halfway house to Communism. Peron of Argentina was a typical Fascist dictator. Undoubtedly he would have won the enthusiastic support of American liberals had it not been for his personal admiration for Mussolini and his worship of the Nazi military system. After all, under Peron the labor bosses got what they wanted:

government pressure upon all workers to join the unions, followed by huge pay increases, job security, bigger and earlier pensions, and other fringe benefits. Peron's philosophy was exactly the philosophy of American liberals today — up with the welfare state, down with incentives, productivity, and the like. Fascism is complete government control of property whose ownership is left for the most part in private hands. Control of this property affords to the dictatorship the opportunity to confer enormous favors upon their friends and to cause terrible vengence upon those they dislike.

History records that Hitler and Mussolini were both Socialists. Hitler, the Nazi, chose for his party the name "The National Socialist German Workers Party." He did so because, idcologically, he was a Socialist — a fanatical advocate of the government-planned economy. The attention of the American people was so riveted upon Hitler's goose-stepping pageantry and upon the Nazi claims of Aryan supremacy that his anti-free enterprise characteristics and his welfare state Socialistic program were overlooked. The astonishing truth is that, but for Hitler's anti-semitism and militarism, he might have become the idol of America's liberals, instead of their pet ape.

Mussolini, the Fascist dictator, was a dedicated Socialist all of his life. His promise to frighten Italian businessmen was that he would preserve the private ownership system by giving the masses enough — but only enough — Socialism to keep them from revolting. (Norman Thomas still insists that his so-called "Democratic Socialism" is entirely different from Mussolini's Democratic Socialism.) Mussolini was able to retain his power because of his "promises to the working class." Whenever he felt his popularity with the workers declining, he would add a "paid holiday." After two decades of Mussolini, Italy had more "paid holidays" than any other industrial country. The appeal of American liberalism today is the same appeal of Hitler's Nazism and Mussolini's Fascism. They all accomplish the same thing; (one) wage rates were raised regardless of productivity; (two) higher pensions were decreed and at an earlier age — the nation's capacity to support persons no longer productive bore no relationship to the size of the pensions; (three) the number of persons holding soft jobs on the government payroll was built up; (four) workers were required to become union members as a means of subjecting them to union discipline; and (five) union leaders were brought into the rulers' inner circle.

Because of the anti-business nature of Fascism, Nazism, and Communism, they have a special appeal to the "intellectuals." All of the so-called accomplishments of Nazism, Fascism, and Communism make perfect weapons for demagogues. There are other similarities between the American Socialists and the Nazis and Communists, including: They all believe the good things of life should come by government decrees and decisions. By using this technique, Hitler, Mussolini, or Khrushchev or an American Socialist could tell the people how much they — out of love for the people — have done for them. Another characteristic these left-wing groups hold in common is that Communists, Fascists, Nazis, and American-style Socialists want the people to feel a personal dependence upon their rulers for their happiness and welfare. Once the people feel that way, they will vote for those who will promise the biggest government benefits.

An example of the way the political opportunists use the label "Fascist" to smear any sincere conservative or anti-Communist is an article written by Sydney J. Harris which appeared in *The Tulsa World* December 4, 1963 and also in many other newspapers around our country that carry his syndicated column. The main object of this article seems to be to convince readers that Americans should be concerned about Fascism in our nation instead of Communism. In the first sentence, Harris observed:

"It's an interesting peculiarity of our social order that while the term 'Communist' is flung around frequently and often carelessly, its opposite number, 'Fascist' is hardly used at all." Harris went on to explain to his readers that in Europe, people had no hesitancy in calling right-wing radicals "Fascists". Mr. Harris contended that "this is what they are."

Sydney Harris contended that since the radical right in America were Fascists, it was a "foolish contradiction in terms" to speak of them as "extreme conservatives." He also contended that "there are many more Fascists and Fascist sympathizers in the United States than there are Communists and their sympathizers."

This column by Sydney J. Harris belabored the point further by stating that "year by year, one sees a Fascist spirit rising among the people" and then complained that this "Fascist movement ... has no business masquerading as 'Americanism' or 'conservatism' or 'patriotism' . . ."

In order to understand the vicious smear technique used by this syndicated columnist, we first need to further analyze and clear up some popular confusion which is widespread in our nation as to what constitutes the so-called extreme right. Generally, the term "extreme left" applies to Communists, Communist sympathizers and socialistic-minded people whose economic objectives are much the same as those of the Communists. The extreme right is supposed to be the opposite of this extreme left, but here is where the popular confusion arises.

There is a widespread fallacy throughout the nation that the extreme right, which is the opposite of the extreme left, is made up of people who believe in Fascism, Nazism or in the general principles of Fascism or Nazism. This is completely wrong because Fascism, Nazism and Communism, as we proved above, all stem from the same source. They all follow basically the ideology of Karl Marx. Communism is a system of government in which all power rests in the hands of the dictators. So are Fascism and Nazism. The only differences in Communism on one hand, and Fascism or Nazism on the other, are:

1. Communism is international socialism, while Fascism or Nazism is national socialism.

2. Under Communism, the government owns all of the means of production. Under Fascism or Nazism, private individuals own the means of production, but they are under the complete domination of the government dictatorship. The Fascist or Nazi government takes the power of making the vital decisions that are essential attributes of ownership. For purposes of this explanation,

we can say essentially that the Fascist and Nazi governments own the owners of the means of production.

Therefore, under any meaningful definition of these extremes, the extreme right would have to be something that is the opposite of Communism. This is definitely not Fascism or Nazism, as they are only *other* forms of Socialism. That fact places them on the extreme left. The opposite extreme of Communism, Fascism or Nazism is freedom — primarily the type of freedom established by our founding fathers.

The only way we can go to a bad extreme on the right is by carrying freedom beyond the point established by our founding fathers and have no law or order. This is anarchism and no genuine conservatives favor anything remotely resembling anarchism. Conservatives believe in Constitutional law under which the government protects the lives, liberties and property of the people and does not interfere with them otherwise. Actually, some of the anarchists helped form the Communist movement. In *Masters of Deceit*, J. Edgar Hoover explained that the First International of the Communists in 1864 consisted of "radicals, have-nots, socialists (and) anarchists."

In *The Techniques of Communism*, Louis Budenz, former Communist official, explained that in *State and Revolution*, Lenin blended "certain aspects of anarchism, syndicalism, and social democracy" into the theory and tactics of Communism.

In order to pursue this smear charge by Sydney J. Harris that "extreme conservatives" are really Fascists, let us further examine the true nature of Mussolini's Fascism in Italy and see if it was on the liberal left or the conservative right. In Mussolini's Italy, social security payments were increased so much that the taxes collected from employers and employees for it equalled about thirty per cent of their pay.

Mussolini used vast public works as a means of increasing his popularity with the masses. He put great numbers of people to work on large projects which had little economic value. (Who favors large public works projects in the United States — right-wing conservatives or ultra-left liberals?)

One of Mussolini's decrees made it almost impossible for employers to fire employees except by the payment of long severance pay. United States labor bosses are now demanding something similar in the United States. (Who favors this Fascist-type measure—conservative right-wingers or ultra-left liberals?)

In Mussolini's Italy, when a firm had troubles sustaining the huge government-required costs, the government invited applications for help. This aid might take the form of government orders or through other means. (Who favors a similar technique in America — right-wing conservatives or left-wing liberals?)

The very basic element of the appeal of Mussolini, Hitler and the other Fascists or Nazis to the people of their country was the appeal of "something for nothing." This is the exact opposite of extreme conservatism. Fascism and Nazism promised the "good things of life" from the goverment. They moved in every way possible to get people to depend upon the government powers-that-be for their needs. Shouldn't this throw a little more light on the question regarding to which extreme Fascism belongs? It quite obviously belongs on the extreme left, because Fascism and what is known as "extreme conservatism" in some American quarters today have nothing in common. However, the policies of Fascism and ultraleft liberalism have many points of similarity.

Turning back to the recent Sydney J. Harris column, we find him implying directly that "right-wing radicalism" and Hitler's Nazi movement were very similar and would lead to the same end. Mr. Harris deplored the support of movements which he considered to be masquerading as Americanism, conservatism or patriotism by "men who genuinely think of themselves as 'conservatives.'" He wrote that these "conservatives" do not "understand the implications of right-wing radicalism any more than the German industrialists understood what would happen to them when Hitler swept into power with their support."

Of course, we know that Hitler opposed Communnism until he and the Communist conspirators found it expedient to join hands and cooperate in their fight against freedom. Later, Hitler found it expedient to launch a military attack against the Reds. The opposition of Hitler to Communism was the opposition of one form of totalitarian socialism to another form of totalitarian socialism. Communism and Nazism were rival socialist systems.

Just as the Fascists did, Hitler left ownership of industrial property in private hands but usurped the power himself to make the decisions which are an essential element of ownership. He also owned the owners.

In establishing his totalitarian rule over Germany, Hitler allocated government orders to those firms which played ball with him. Harassment of and controls over industry are not trademarks of "extreme conservatives." These are trademarks of ultra-left liberals.

An article in the November 16, 1963, issue of *Human Events* by James L. Wick called attention to a speech of Hitler's which was made almost thirty years ago and which received little attention in America. Mr. Wick contended it should have been printed on the front page of every newspaper. In his speech, Hitler said:

"We shall banish want; we shall banish fear. The essence of National Socialism is human welfare ... National Socialism is the revolution of the common man. Rooted in a fuller life for every German from childhood to old age, National Socialism means a new day of abundance at home and a better world order abroad ..."

Does this sound like extreme conservatism? Anyone who has followed the affairs of our country during the past thirty or more years will recognize that it sounds quite similar to the promises of all good things by government on the part of the left-wing liberals.

Left-wing liberal smear artists often try to tie conservative, anti-Communist movements in with the American Nazi Party. In the American Nazi Party's printed program, we find them prescribing "a world police force;" laws to assure "every honest citizen . . . of education and training to the top level of his capacity ... (and) medical and hospital facilities . . . ;" government guarantee of "a decent level of family income" to all honest producers; and other government hand-outs and controls.

Just as in the case of Hitler, Mussolini and other socialistic dictators, we find that the American Nazi

Party's concept of government is one in which all good things come from a powerful central government.

The American Nazis profess strong opposition to the Communists, but once again, it is from the standpoint of a rival socialistic movement. The American Nazis picket conservative anti-Communist rallies just as they do Communist rallies. They have picketed Christian Crusade meetings.

We have in our files a letter dated July 13, 1962, from an American Nazi Party official in Chicago. In this letter, he was complaining about an anti-Nazi article by the late Matt Cvetic which we had published in our *Christian Crusade* magazine. He contended that the American Nazi Party was not a left-wing organization, but in the very next paragraph, this writer stated: "Nazism means NATIONAL SOCIALISM, not World Socialism."

This entire scheme of classing Anti-Communist conservatives into the same camp with Fascists or Nazis is utterly ridiculous. No thinking American who has the slightest knowledge of the basic elements of Socialism, Communism, Fascism, or Nazism should be deceived by such idiotic nonsense. However, many Americans are so deceived merely because they seldom, if ever, hear or read the truth on this matter.

The standard Red smear line is to class as Fascist anyone or any group that opposes Communism. In the twisted Communist mind, the term Fascist includes any individuals or organizations that effectively expose or oppose Communism. Just as in any other phase of their psychological warfare against freedom, the Communists attempt to pollute the minds of non-Communists with their nonsensical line that anti-Communist conservatives are really nothing but Fascists.

Another deceptive aspect of the December 4 Sydney J. Harris column is his contention that "Communist influence . . . is negligible" in our nation and that "there are many more Fascists and Fascist sympathizers in the United States than there are Communists and their sympathizers . . ."

Time after time, FBI Director J. Edgar Hoover has warned about the danger of minimizing the threat of Communism. In remarks made during 1957, he warned of "a terrifying apathy on the part of Americans toward the deadliest danger of our civilization." He said that some of this apathy was deliberately induced by "elements which desire you to believe that the Communist Party, U.S.A., no longer represents a threat to America . . ." He spoke of "the proclamation of well-meaning, uninformed individuals who, from their mountain of ignorance, maintain Americans are too worried over domestic Communism."

Mr. Hoover further warned Americans as follows:

"The Communist Party in the United States is NOT out of business. It is not dead. It is not even dormant. It IS, however, well on its way to achieving its current objective — which is to make you believe that it is shattered, ineffective and dying!" Mr. Hoover said that "those who try to minimize its (the Communist conspiracy's) danger either are uninformed or have a deadly axe to grind."

In testimony before the House Appropriations Subcommittee during March 1961, Mr. Hoover warned that the Communists "have infiltrated every conceivable sphere of activity: Youth groups; radio, television and motion picture industries; church, school, educational and cultural groups; the press; national minority groups and civil and political units."

On December 7, 1961, J. Edgar Hoover warned Americans in a speech: "The Communist threat from without must not blind us to the Communist threat from within. The latter is reaching into the very heart of America through its espionage agents and a cunning, defiant and lawless Communist Party, which is fanatically dedicated to the Marxist cause of world enslavement and destruction of the foundations of our Republic."

During July 1962, Mr. Hoover wrote in a newspaper article of "the Communist capacity to prevent our thinking and destroy the spiritual supports which form the foundations of our freedom."

In a speech to the National Catholic Youth Organization on November 16, 1963, J. Edgar Hoover warned these young people that "you have entered the world at a time when deadly forces challenge your right, and the right of every American, to live in freedom under God." In this speech, he told these young people of the "intensive campaign" by the Communists to "control the minds and win the allegiance of American youth."

Yet Mr. Sydney J. Harris deceives anyone who trusts his judgment and who reads his column which appeared in *The Tulsa World* of December 4, 1963, into believing that "Communist influence in this country... is negligible..."

In an article prepared for members of the National Strategy Seminar held in Washington, D. C., during

July 1959, J. Edgar Hoover stressed the importance of combating Communist mind warfare. He said, "...Our continued survival may well depend upon the action we take now to insure that all citizens, not only military personnel, are fortified against the continuous Communist ideological assault."

During December 1959, the late Francis E. Walter, Chairman of the House Committee on Un-American Activities, told Americans that "ignorance of Communism is our greatest weakness in today's total struggle with the Communist conspiracy..." Mr. Walter further warned, "Without a thorough knowledge of Communism, we can no more hope to survive and conquer it than we can hope to defeat cancer without authoritative and reliable knowledge of its nature."

Regardless of what their motives or intentions may be, suicidal nonsense such as that in the article on "Fascism" by Mr. Sydney J. Harris contributes in no small measure to putting Americans further and further into a deep sleep of apathy and complacency which will insure eventual Communist victory. It goes even further than that, by deceiving naive, uninformed Americans into believing that anti-Communists are their real enemies.

Of course, his column which appeared in *The Tulsa World* of December 4, 1963, is not the first time that Mr. Sydney J. Harris has written some confusing absurdity about the international Communist conspiracy. In a column published in the Evansville, Indiana, *Courier* of January 29, 1962, Mr. Harris contended:

"The basic conflict is not between the Communists and what we call the 'free world.' It is between those who understand the need for new approaches to our

118

universal problem, and those who cling to the old and obsolete methods ..." This is an example of a "far-left" thinker creating a dream conflict of his own to replace the real struggle with which Americans are faced.

In his column published in the Evansville, Indiana, *Courier* of January 13, 1962 (and in many other papers across the nation), Mr. Sydney J. Harris gave a unique explanation of his version of anti-Communist groups in America whom he contended proposed "extreme and fanatical measures for combating Communism."

In this column, Sydney Harris said that these anti-Communists were people with "a deep need to punish, and to find 'devils' who are responsible for the ills of society." He contended that these anti-Communists could not exist "without blaming some external agent for most of our woes." According to Mr. Harris, the "devil" in this generation happens to be Communism.

He went on to describe such people as "really psychiatric studies" and as "paranoiacs" who see "conspiracy" everywhere.

Then Mr. Harris came out with the same "Hitler" smear line which he used in his December 4, 1963, article. He wrote, "Actually, the sort of Americanism that the Birchers and their allies represent more closely resembles the 'Germanism' of Hitler than anything else. All superpatriotism is alike, no matter which flag it seems to hoist ..."

If our nation is to survive the determined drive of the international Communist conspiracy to enslave us, many more Americans are going to have to be aware of voices in the press, such as Sydney J. Harris, which attempt to mislead them into believing that Communism is not a clear and present danger to our nation. Many more Americans must cease to be victims of the smear line which identifies anti-Communist conservatives as a people with views similar to those of Fascists or Nazis. In this chapter we have thoroughly exposed this falsehood with factual information. Such information needs wide dissemination among uninformed Americans who may still be open-minded. We feel that there are many Americans in this category — who are open-minded but do not understand what is going on merely because they have not had the opportunity to read or hear documented, factual information exposing the suicidal propaganda of this day which has swept our nation.

One of the most important things for concerned Americans to keep in mind is that ignorance of the true nature, methods and objectives of the Communist enemy and of the successes already enjoyed by this enemy are essential prerequisites to a Communist takeover of the United States.

On pages 46 and 47 of the Annual Report of the House Committee on Un-American Activities for the Year 1961, there is an interesting question asked and answered which we desire to reprint here because of the import of this information:

"WHAT IF THE COMMUNISTS WERE NAZIS?"

"Certain individuals, publications, and groups in this country which cannot and never have been able to see any internal danger in Communism have, for many years, been expressing great fear of Nazism and Fascism.

"They have done this despite the fact that Nazism is today generally discredited throughout the world, that there is no international Nazi movement, nor any powerful Nazi party in any nation. Nazism in this country is represented by a small organization with an insignificant number of members who are generally considered crackpots, are shunned, and continually ridiculed, denounced, and exposed.

"During recent months, certain segments of the press — which have never done anything in the way of exposing the Communist Party or its fronts — have been packed with articles and exposes concerning both responsible and irresponsible anti-Communist groups in this country. These articles have often characterized, by implications or outright statements, all of these groups as constituting a very real danger to democracy, freedom, and our form of government. It is often hinted darkly — though no evidence is produced to substantiate the charge — that all of these groups are Fascist or neo-Fascist in their orientation.

"At the same time, the same newspapers and magazines are telling the American people, over and over again, that the Communist Party presents no danger at all to this country.

"But suppose Hitler were alive today! Suppose that he was the boss of an international Nazi machine comparable in size to the world Communist movement — a Nazi movement which had some 40 million members organized in secret, conspiratorial units in 87 nations of the world, which controlled one-fourth of the earth's surface, one-third of its population and 17 nations!

"Suppose that the American Nazi Party had the number of members, fellow travelers, collaborators, fronts, publications, cooperating non-Nazi groups that the U.S. Communist Party has today — and that Nazi propaganda publications emanating from the major centers of the movement abroad were pouring into the United States at the rate of many millions of packages annually, and a half-dozen or more publishing firms in the United States were turning out books extolling Nazism day after day!

"Would these same voices then be telling the Congress and the American people that there was no need to worry about the U.S. Nazi Party?

"The answer is obvious. Their publications would be filled, day after day, with denunciations and exposures of the American Nazi Party and all its fronts, collaborators, and fellow travelers. The airwaves would feature numerous similar items by commentators who can today see no danger in internal Communism. There would be demands that this committee's appropriations be increased tremendously, its staff enlarged, and its activities greatly expanded — and that every State in the Union set up a committee to fight the Nazi menace within its boundaries.

"The anti-Communists of today who are denounced as 'right-wing extremists' would be made to look like ineffective 'babes in the woods' in the art of propagandizing and agitating against those they believed to be a real danger to the Nation. Anti-Nazism would be the biggest thing in the country."

Every true Christian conservative that I have ever met detests Nazism, Fascism, Communism, and Socialism with equal contemptuousness.

The FBI counterspy, Matt Cvetic, wrote for our *Christian Crusade* magazine shortly before his death on the subject of the "Resurgence of Nazism — a Communist Booby Trap."

"Once again the American people are being made the target of a tremendous left-wing propaganda campaign in order to create confusion and discredit the patriotic forces in our nation. We are being warned by the Communists, Fabian Socialists, and ADA, the assorted professional liberals, to beware of the 'resurgence of Nazism.'

"Opportunistic politicians and editorial writers, ready to grab at any bits of cheap sensationalism, hastened to spread this phony 'Nazi' masquerade.

"Some motion picture and television studios, quick to smell a 'good thing' for the box-office, rushed to take out of moth-balls any old films depicting the now defunct Nazi and Fascist movement. With typical Hollywood fanfare, the Nazi 'Dodo' is being promoted to a fare-thee-well.

"While these reminders of past Nazi atrocities are being fed to the American public, the Communists, Fabian Socialists and their allies are busy with their propaganda machinery. By clever innuendo, these 'peddlers of World Socialism' are striving to create the illusion that this 'resurgence of Nazism' is a part of the patriotic, conservative, and anti-Communist movement. Nothing could be further from the truth! The Nazi-Fascist ruse, often used by the international Communists to discredit and destroy all opposition, has absolutely nothing in common with patriotism, conservatism and freedom. On the contrary, Nazism and Fascism means National Socialism, and belongs in the Leftist camp. They have one thing in common with Communism, Trotskyism and Fabian Socialism — they are all for World Socialism.

"By branding people and organizations Fascist or Nazi, the Communists and their witting and unwitting dupes are able to keep the sharp eye of scrutiny from their own murderous and anti-religious conspiracy. By shouting loud and long, the Communists are able to distract people's attention from the fact that Communism, Nazism and Fascism destroy all opposition by mass-murder and build a society of state-owned state-controlled slaves.

"I am frequently asked: 'Would the Communists actually murder someone who opposes their plot for world conquest?' My answer is very definitely — yes. And why not? The Communists have murdered tens of millions since they came to power. One human life, more or less, would make little difference to these calloused mass murderers. They are particularly clever enough to make murder appear as a suicide.

"Let us not be misled by the Communist Booby Trap. Resurrecting a defunct Nazi movement, and branding their opposition with the Fascist brush is a shop-worn Red gimmick. In the future, when cries of 'Fascism' are tossed at us by Communists and their illiberal liberal allies, let us remind them that Nazism and Fascism belong in the camp of Communism and World Socialism and not in the 'Camp of Freedom.' "

This particular chapter, as well as this entire book, was designed to stimulate a study of the nature and tactics of Communism and to translate that study into action. In this chapter we have sought to prove that: (one) Communism was and is essentially evil; (two)

Communism is not the foe of Fascism, but is actually Fascist; (three) Communism or Red Fascism, and Red Nazism in practice crush liberty of speech, of the press, and of political opposition; and (four) world Communism, despite the "good-conduct label" given them by the liberals of the United States, is still vital and more insidious than ever. This trio of evils — Communism, Nazism, and Fascism—are intrinsically wrong and not one who would save Christian civilization would collaborate with them in any undertaking whatsoever. Those who permit themselves to be deceived into lending their aid towards the triumph of Communism in any of these forms in their own particular countries will be the first to fall victims of their error.

CHAPTER V

THE IRRESPONSIBLE AND UN-AMERICAN LEFT WING AT THE TIME OF THE DEATH OF MR. KENNEDY

Harvard Professor H. Stuart Hughes in the "far left" publication *Nation*, December 14, 1963, expressed his disappointment that the assassin of Mr. Kennedy was not a "southern racist" by saying, "Indeed, if we look deeply into our souls, I think many of us will recognize that we were disappointed to learn that such was not the case."

A great American, M. Stanton Evans, editor of the *Indianapolis News*, said in the *National Review* bulletin December 10, 1963: "Professor Henry Steele Commager of Amherst concluded the ultimate blame for the President's murder rested with those who had, inter alia, stirred up antagonism toward Russia." His reason is — if a Communist murders our President, the fault belongs with those who tell us we should worry about Communism. Stubbornly, many of the liberals still refuse to consider the fact that Communism *internally* took the life of the President of the United States.

Max Lerner in the ultra-liberal *New York Post* said, in trying to blame the anti-Communists and conservatives for the death of the President: "When right-wing racist fanatics are told over and over again that the President is a traitor, a Red, a nigger-lover, that he had traduced the Constitution, is handing America over to a mongrelized world state, there are bound to be some fanatics, dull-witted enough to follow the logic of the indictment all the way and rid America of the man who is betraying it." It is amazing that Mr. Lerner, in his responsible position in one of America's best-known newspapers, refuses to recognize the threat of internal Communism which took the life of his President, John F. Kennedy.

A leading clergyman who tried to fix the blame on the anti-Communist community of the United States, was Bishop James A. Pike of the Episcopal Church, leading "light" of the National Council of Churches. Bishop Pike said: "In fixing the blame, we must include all those who, by their race hate and extreme radical-right propaganda, have constantly supplied the fuel which would fire up such an assassin."

It is apparent now that the liberals were disappointed that the assassin did not turn out to be a member of the John Birch Society, Christian Anti-Communist Crusade, Daughters of the American Revolution,

American Legion, or Christian Crusade. Within one hour after the death of Mr. Kennedy on the streets of Dallas, Friday, November 22, the television networks were blaming the anti-Communist community for the tragic event. Continually, they referred to the appearance of Adlai Stevenson in the same city a few weeks before, at which time he was picketed and allegedly spit on and hit on the head by a picket sign. There are some interesting "postscripts" to the treatment of Adlai Stevenson in Dallas when he appeared during the latter part of October, 1963 to address a Pro-United Nations Rally. In the first place, Dallas has over 400 Cuban exile families with a total population of 1200 Cubans. There are pro-Castro and anti-Castro groups among these Cubans. The assassin, Lee Oswald, himself was an organizer of the Fair Play for Cuba Committee and he lived and worked in the Dallas area. According to reports from people who observed the picket line in Dallas on the night that Stevenson spoke, the line was predominately Latin Americans, and probably Cubans, not "right-wing Americans".

Even until the day this book is being written, the press is still hashing over the Stevenson affair in Dallas, but I have yet to read a report concerning the later appearance of Governor George Wallace of Alabama on the campus of Harvard University in Boston. In the December 17, 1963, issue of the *National Review* publication, a Michael J. Cronin of Revere Beach, Massachusetts, reports: "Last evening Governor George Wallace of Alabama spoke at Harvard concerning his views on segregation and states' rights. Upon his arrival at Sanders Hall, he was met by a student demonstration of approximately 150 participants who spat at him, cursed him with hysterical fervor, and attempted to assault him. After his speech, he was prevented from returning to his automobile by a howling group of 300. His car's tires were slashed by members of the "non-violent" group and his auto was damaged. We are all familiar with the way our news media waxed indignant over the disgrace of the Stevenson incident. I am writing this letter twelve hours after Governor Wallace's speech, so I have not seen any comment in the news. But I am willing to bet my vote for Goldwater that there will be very little said about the Harvard demonstrators." Indeed, Mr. Cronin was right. In fact, this author has never seen any report in any newspaper in the United States on this disgraceful treatment which a governor of a sovereign state received on Harvard's campus. To our knowledge it was not carried by either the Associated Press or the United Press International, although certainly it was "news." Here is another example of managed news. Only those stories which will put the "anti-Communist" community in bad light will be featured by the wire services. Those stories that would expose the "Far Left" and the liberal community will be ignored and, in most instances, killed by the manipulators of the wire services.

Arthur Krock of the *New York Times* pointed out in his column that our U.S. tax-supported overseas broadcasting facilities, Voice of America, began immediately to blame the "extreme right-wing" for the assassination of the President within a few minutes after the death of Mr. Kennedy at 1:59 p.m., Friday, November 22. Other left-wingers and far-leftists blaming the anti-Communists for the death of the President included Ralph McGill of the *Atlanta Constitution*, James Restin, Jimmy Breslin, Walter Lippmann, Marquis Childs, Bob Considine, William B. Shannon, Harriet Van Horn, and Inez Robb. (Inez Robb said: "But the radical right . . . the superpatriots . . . prepared the climate for assassination.")

One of the Senators from the State of Oklahoma, Senator Howard Edmondson, devoted one-half of his monthly "Reports to the People" in December, 1963, to an article written by the leftist columnist, Walter Lippmann entitled "Murder Most Foul" which had previously appeared in the left-wing newspaper, the *Washington Post*. As you might expect, Walter Lippmann refused to consider the Communist threat internally and, in fact, suggested that the future of the American Republic is "at stake when extremists go unrestrained." He, of course, is not referring to extremists on the left; he is referring to what he believes to be extremists on the right. In fact, in his one reference to "the left", Mr. Lippmann makes an interesting comment: "In his alienation, Oswald turned to the left, but that was *incidental*." Mr. Lippmann feels that the Communist affiliation of Lee Harvey Oswald was unimportant. The important thing was that he lived in a city which was predominately right-wing or anti-Communist and this is the thing that caused him to take the life of the President.

This author wrote to Senator Edmondson and reminded him, "It is strange to me that neither you nor Mr. Lippmann have had anything to say about Fair Play for Cuba Committee and the American Civil Liberties Union, in both of which Lee Harvey Oswald, the President's assassin, had an interest. In fact, in our *Tulsa Daily World*, Thursday, December 12, there was an Associated Press article saying that the Communist who assassinated Mr. Kennedy, Oswald, had attended a meeting of the American Civil Liberties Union on the campus of the Southern Methodist University less than one month before the assassination. At that time, he was shown a real hate film called 'Suspect', put out by the ACLU. The film is designed to turn the liberals against the anti-Communists and conservatives of the United States.

"So if Lee Oswald assassinated the President because of a hate climate, may I assure you that, based on fact, Mr. Oswald's motivation was a hate film put out by an organization called the American Civil Liberties Union. He was not influenced by, let's say, 'Operation Abolition' put out by the House Committee on Un-American Activities or 'Communist Encirclement' put out by Harding College, both anti-Communist films. It was not an anti-Communist film that angered Mr. Oswald. If indeed he plotted the assassination of the President because of a 'hate climate' in Dallas, it was one which had been created by the liberal leaders of that community.

"It would be extremely difficult for either you, Senator Edmondson, or Mr. Lippmann to blame the assassination of the President of the United States on the anti-Communist community. Surely you know, as a lawyer, that the law of the land simply states that to falsely accuse innocent persons of being accessories to the crime of murder is criminal libel. Furthermore, it is a fact today that those who allege that *all of us* must share the blame for the murder of the President are either dupes who do so ignorantly or they are agents of the Kremlin who do so to detract attention from the Communist assassin."

When you take a look at Walter Lippmann's background, it is not surprising that he would completely overlook the internal threat of Communism and would, in fact, blame the anti-Communist elements in America for this tragic event. In September, 1958, when the Communists and their sympathizers were propagandizing for surender of Quemoy and Matsu to the Red Chinese, Lippmann proposed that Formosa, the island where Chaing Kai-shek and the anti-Communist Chinese are exiled, be "neutralized and de-militarized." He even advocated that the anti-Communist Chinese who had fled to Formosa for refuge should be "repatriated to the mainland of Communist China."

Lippmann is famous for his defeatist and "surrender to the Communist line" philosophy. It is little wonder then that the Communist *Worker* gives such enthusiastic support to the editorials written by Walter Lippmann. However, the best look at Walter Lippmann can be gained by reading his philosophies expressed in his column of September 16, 1963, in the *Newsweek* magazine, at which time he said: "No civilized society has long tolerated the despotic theory of private property. This conception of property is alien to the central truths of Christendom which have always held that property is not absolute but is a system of rights and duties that are determined by society." Here Mr. Lippmann shows his complete contempt for the American free-enterprise system and his loyalty to Socialism.

In my letter to Senator Edmondson, I also pointed out that the "current talk of hatred by these left-wing columnists and politicians is a concoction of the minds of people who would coldly seek to use recent tragic events for political purposes."

Raymond Moley pointed out in his editorial in the *New York Herald-Tribune*, December 8, 1963, that "Such collective indictments are in themselves a form of mob violence. They do not destroy hate. They are the very seeds of hate."

A man who has probably done more to discourage patriotism and evangelistic Christianity in the South than any single individual is Ralph Emerson McGill, publisher of the *Atlanta Constitution*. In column after column in his *Atlanta Constitution* which is, in turn, syndicated to other newspapers in the left-wing camp, McGill attacks the conservatives, anti-Communists, and orthodox clergymen.

In his much-publicized new book, *The South and the Southerner*, McGill equated sincere ministers of the gospel and with the Ku Klux Klan's speakers and lumped them together as the enemies of democracy and justice in the South. His contempt for "old-time religion" is expressed in one column in the *New York Herald-Tribune* on June 24, 1962: "The celebrated old-time religion was pretty bad. It was composed mostly of sulphuric hellfire and damnation. It was a religion of fear, coercion, and two-hour sermons."

In a column in 1963, he accused General Edwin A. Walker of becoming "warped in perspective and emotion by his obsession with unidentified things which even he can only describe, and not always coherently, as hidden." This, of course, is in keeping with the nonsense of the "mental health enthusiasts" of the "far left", that everyone who disagrees with them is a neurotic and in need of psychiatric help. This obsession that political opponents are mentally sick is shown in Ralph McGill's column on March 8, 1962 in which he says: "Perhaps the most pathetic and psychologically naked young men in America are the so-called conservative 'Young Americans for Freedom' in New York." Anyone with any degree of fairness knows of the excellent work that has been done by the YAF, Mr. McGill, to the contrary.

In the same column he minimized the threat of Communism internally, saying: "The Communist enemy constitutes a definite threat, but it is an external threat, not a domestic threat."

In one column on Thursday, February 8, 1962, he called upon the American government to "denounce the extremists" suggesting that immediate action should be taken against the anti-Communists of America.

In an editorial in the *Saturday Evening Post*, December 14, 1963, shortly after Mr. Kennedy's assassination, Ralph McGill again attempted to blame the anti-Communists and conservatives for the death of the President, calling these conservatives "Peddlers of hate, Anti-Negro, Anti-Semitic, Extreme Right." He lumps them all together in one big pot, marked in big, bold letters—"Un-American." Again, as with the rest of his "far-left" cohorts, Mr. McGill refuses to consider the threat of Communism internally and does not reveal any information concerning Fair Play for Cuba, of which Lee Oswald was an officer. One of the reasons that Mr.

McGill will probably say nothing about Fair Play for Cuba or other pro-Castro groups is that he himself was one of the most enthusiastic backers that Fidel Castro had, even after the overthrow of the Cuban government. In his *Atlanta Constitution* on Thursday, January 8, 1959, Ralph McGill told his readers that we should "aid the revolution of Castro." Then, refusing to accept the obvious — that Castro was a Communist — he said: "It should be obvious that Fidel has no intention of going Communist . . . It is apparent that if this revolution does not succeed, the next one will go far to the left . . . First, we should recall Ambassador Earl E. T. Smith. He several times referred to the revolutionists as 'bandits.' This stamps him as a most unobservant man, and an Ambassador who failed to give his country sound information."

Because Ambassador Smith tried to warn the American Government of the Communist inclinations of Fidel Castro, McGill branded him as a "most unobservant man". Now in light of later events, I wonder what decent men would say of Ralph McGill and his enthusiastic support of Castro?

That Ralph McGill has powerful friends in Washington, there is no doubt. On the night of the Mississippi crisis when James Meredith was being enrolled at Oxford, Mississippi, the Attorney General of the United States, Robert Kennedy, personally introduced Ralph McGill to a nationwide television audience to give his comments on the affair in Mississippi.

According to the *Atlanta Journal* on Wednesday, January 10, 1962, Ralph McGill was "named to a committee to advise the Pentagon on the best ways to *teach servicemen about Communism*." His appointment was made by Defense Secretary Robert McNamara.

In the *Atlanta Constitution* on Friday March 2, 1962, there was a notice that Ralph McGill, publisher of the *Atlanta Constitution*, "has been named by President John F. Kennedy to the new fifteen-man general advisory committee of the U.S. Arms Control and Disarmament Agency." Patriotic Americans can only shudder when they think of the influence that this extremely unjust and biased far-left liberal has on men in high places of government.

Probably the most outspoken pro-Communist daily newspaper in the United States is the *Gazette and Daily* published in York, Pennsylvania by one J. W. Gitt. An article during 1957 by Howard Norton, of the Moscow Bureau of the *Baltimore Sun* newspaper, provided an interesting comment on Moscow's opinion of the York, Pennsylvania *Gazette and Daily* published by Gitt. In regard to the *Gazette*, Mr. Norton wrote: "Among the better American newspapers in the opinion of the Soviet press is the York *Gazette* of York, Pennsylvania. The *Daily* was the only bona fide daily newspaper in the United States which came out for Henry Wallace for President in 1948."

In the Wednesday, December 4, 1963 issue of the *Gazette and Daily*, York, Pennsylvania, Publisher Gitt and Editor Higgins, in an editorial entitled "No Absolute Security," completely overlooked the Communist affiliations of the President's assassin, Lee Harvey Oswald. Of Oswald, they say: "He was a disturbed man who may have had no motive whatsoever than that of retorting in this way to the ills, real and imagined, he had suffered at the hands of society." It doesn't take a scholar now to figure out who is responsible for the "suffering" of Lee Harvey Oswald which drove him to the assassination of Mr. Kennedy. Of course, the right wing is to blame, according to Moscow-favored paper *Gazette and Daily* of York, Pennsylvania.

On the same page in an editorial entitled "Food for Thought," Mr. Gitt specifically blames the conservatives of Texas for the death of the President and further suggests that this spirit of conservatism "did not originate in Dallas, Texas, but it had a lot of support there and in other parts of Texas, and so did Billy Hargis and his outfit of character assassins, and so did a lot of other paranoiacs and gold diggers who plucked a lot of that precious metal or its equivalent from ignoramuses who had found liquid gold, oil, and lacked the mental balance to use it for good purposes." Wrapped up in one sentence is the entire philosophy of J. W. Gitt. Anyone who fights Communism is a "character assassin". Anyone who supports an anti-Communist cause is a "paranoiac". And in the first place, Texas didn't deserve all the wealth that they have because they are a bunch of "ignoramuses."

In the Thursday, December 5, 1963, issue of the *Gazette and Daily*, the Gitts again tried to blame the anti-Communists for the assassination of the President: "The point is that characters such as McIntire, Billy James Hargis, Fred Schwarz, and many more, no matter what their professed intentions, have been busy stirring up the emotions of upset Americans and focusing suspicion on political persons of one level or another with whom they disagree. They have been producing a climate of hate — of that there is no doubt whatsoever. They have been creating an explosive atmosphere." Then with a veiled threat, this York, Pennsylvania *Gazette and Daily* says: "We shall see, too, if many of us are going to continue in our indifference to the poison they . . . (McIntire, Hargis, Schwarz) . . . have been spreading, telling ourselves 'Well, after all, what real harm does it do?' Isn't the answer to that clear enough now?"

That a paper like the York, Pennsylvania *Gazette* would blame the anti-Communist movements and leaders as equally responsible for the assassination of the President should come as no surprise, especially in view of a report which had been put out by the Committee on the Judiciary of the United States Senate, April 25 through May 16, 1961, entitled "Fair Play for Cuba Committee. Here in this Government report there is a copy of an ad which appeared in a Communist publication on March 6, 1961, advertising a Fair Play for Cuba Committee Rally (Page 159). The speaker is announced as "James Higgins, Editor, York, Pennsylvania *Gazette and Daily*." It is no wonder that Mr. Gitt would like to shift the blame from the Fair Play for Cuba and the Communist Party to the anti-Communist movements, considering the fact that the editor of his newspaper has been a spokesman for the organization of which Lee Oswald was a member.

Newspaper editorial writers and television commentators were not the only ones who were clearly disappointed that a right winger could not be blamed for the death of the President. Before the apprehension of the Communist assassin, Lee Harvey Oswald, was made known. famed Americans such as Chief Justice Earl Warren were blaming the right wing. Even after the identity of Oswald became public information. Judge Warren, in his funeral oration at the bier of President Kennedy, said: "What moves some misguided wretch to do this horrible deed may never be known to us, but we do know that such acts are commonly stimulated by forces of hatred and malevolence, such as today are eating their way into the bloodstream of American life. What a price we pay for this fanaticism." Senator Mike Mansfield joined Judge Warren by blaming the "apostles of hate." As M. Stanton Evans pointed out: "Warren's stentorian utterance was particularly ironic. It is the Warren court which has turned the American Communists loose by the carload lots, struck down significant anti-Communist legislation and held that the Communist advocacy of violence is a mere abstraction not actionable under the U.S. Constitution. For Warren, under the circumstances, to speak as he did was an act of daring which leaves the mind limp with incredulity."

Senator Barry Goldwater, Republican of Arizona, tried to set the record straight in his syndicated column, Friday, December 6, 1963: "In the nation's initial shock at the assassination of President Kennedy, there was little time or opportunity for objective assessment of motivation. Immediately following the shooting, there were some misleading statements to the effect that the assassination had been engineered by the so-called 'radical right.' Even the U. S. Information Agency, in its broadcast to Russia, said the assassination had taken place in Dallas and described that city as a center of right-wing extremism. This broadcast was at the root of the Soviet contention that rightists were responsible for the killing and that the subsequent slaying of Oswald was part of a plot to cover up the conspiracy. Efforts to tie every group to the right of center, whether extreme or not, into the slaying have continued since, despite the long Communistic background of Lee Oswald himself. One columist even suggested that 'extremists' are bent upon such acts of violence and therefore we should do away with free speech. His reasoning was that our constitutional right of free expression leads to violent dissension and intemperate acts."

Former Major General Thomas A. Lane wrote an interesting editorial entitled " 'Right' is Blamed Wrongly" a few days after the assassination of Mr. Kennedy:

"The tragic death of President Kennedy should cause all Americans to pause and examine carefully the direction of our political institutions. Dangerous errors have invaded our thinking.

"Within a few hours of the President's death, Moscow radio was attributing the assassination to right extremists in the United States. When an American broadcasting representative was asked to explain the basis for this Soviet conclusion, he replied that he had heard this same attribution on the Voice of America program.

"Why did our Voice of America initiate so obvious a theme of Soviet propaganda when there was no evidence to support such an inference?

"In addressing the Senate soon after the news of the assassination was received, Senator Mansfield related this tragedy to sharp divisions within our society. Similarly, Chief Justice Warren said Mr. Kennedy was assassinated 'as a result of the hatred and bitterness that has been injected into the life of our nation by bigots.'

"These leaders expressed what was in the minds of most Americans. The consensus of our fears reveals how completely our minds have been conditioned by press, radio and television to believe that our radical right would be capable of so monstrous a crime.

"At the same time, we have been conditioned to believe that Communism is not a force in this country. As the Communist connections of the apparent assassin became known our news agencies and our leaders became stunned and silent. They tried to ascribe the crime to personal motivation of the assassin. They continued to deplore the political divisions which were not related to the crime but avoided mention of the Communist motivation which was the direct cause.

"The truth is that U.S. political forces holding power have created massive propaganda misrepresenting the purposes and methods of native political forces challenging the status quo. The distrust directed at bona fide American political movements provides cover for Communist underground political action. A list of the unsolved crimes and misdemeanors which have been attributed by U.S. public opinion to the radical right would be formidable.

"It is clear how greatly the Communist cause would have been served if the assassin had escaped. The crime would have been charged to those groups of the political right which have strongly opposed the Kennedy policies. Excoriation of the innocent would have been unrestrained. The fabric of our political institutions would have been seriously strained. Our public information agencies were poised for such an operation.

"Why is there no storm of righteous indignation against the Communist perpetrators of this dastardly crime? Why, against all we know about the Communist operating methods, do we pretend that Lee Harvey Oswald acted alone?

"The closest parallel in recent history to the assassination of President Kennedy was the murder of Leon Trotsky in Mexico City in 1940. The behavior of Oswald so closely paralleled that of the Trotsky assassin as to suggest that both had the same training.

"The murder of Oswald looks like the underground retribution for an agent who had failed to destroy himself.

"It is time for Americans to realize that we have no native political groups of the left which condone the use of crime as an instrument of politics. In the Western world, only Communism maintains a criminal underground for this purpose. We have obscured these realities with the verbiage of domestic politics and sacrificed our capacity for objective judgement."

In concluding this subject, let me add that the Communist influence in the United States is apparently so strong that every effort possible has been made to blame the anti-Communists for the death of the President, in spite of the fact that the assassin himself was a Communist. This is the only logical explanation.

William F. Buckley, Jr., in his column of November 27, 1963, stated: "The opinion makers of the country ... were getting ready to turn the President's tragedy into an excuse for a program against the American Right. Within a matter of minutes nationally known radio and television commentators had started in, suggest-

141

ing that the assassination had been the work of a right-wing extremist ... Goodness knows what would have happened if Lee Oswald had not been apprehended, or even if he had been apprehended a day or two later. Even as it was, the disappointment was more than some could bear, and the genocidal fury here and there broke its traces."

These opinions of Mr. Buckley of a possible blood-bath in the United States, had an anti-Communist been responsible for the assassination of Mr. Kennedy, are verified by a report written by the French correspondent, Hilaire du-Berrier, who was visiting in Dallas on the day of the assassination. His report is frightening but it deserves consideration:

"Out of the Dallas crucible came facts which realistic America must face: for meanness, viciousness, dishonesty, and absence of all sense of honor, the groups referred to as the American Right are no match for the organized, entrenched, and internationally-supported Left lined up against them. Radio, TV, the press, government agencies, and militant politicians took a position against America's interests and for the Left. Your correspondent was in Dallas when it happened. The first announcement of the killing was still coming over the air when the first threatening telephone call reached the home of General Edwin A. Walker who also lives in Dallas. A woman's voice said, 'We'll get you, you bastards.' For three days and nights the telephone threats and insults continued. Other known conservatives were likewise menaced. General Walker was out of Texas at the time of the death of the President. Had he been in Dallas, he would have been assassinated by the Left that is shouting 'Hate Mongers! Bigots!' today. A man ran up on the Walker lawn and threw the American flag to the ground. Day and night automobiles prowled the neighborhood 'casing' the Walker residence. Though out in force, Dallas police never stopped or questioned a driver circling the home of the General, who had been shot at on April 10, 1963, by the same Communist assassin who would later take the life of the President of the United States. These threats continued despite the fact that Oswald, the pro-Communist, had already been charged with the crime.

"No apology came over the phone lines of those marked for the harassment by the Left. Intimidation is the Left's weapon. Truth being no obstacle, Moscow immediately laid the crime on the Right. The Voice of America did likewise for like reasons. The Left was striking while the iron was hot. Only protagonists of the extreme left, hoping that a right winger had killed the President, would have made such statements without basis of fact. It was no accident. Chief Justice Earl Warren and Senator Maurine Neuberger (Democrat-Oregon) said the political right wing was responsible and abroad their statements supported Moscow. All the time in America cries against hate mongering and bigotry against a right that had never contemplated more than hand bills, signs, and paid announcements in the press, yet America said nothing.

"Within a matter of hours after the slaying, Boston's extreme left winger, Gordon Hall, was given the use of nationwide TV networks to 'pooh-pooh' Oswald's Communist connections and direct American fury against the Right.

143

"What points emerge from this marshalling of the facts? First, the American in the street showed himself to be unstable, incapable of thinking or acting in the crisis to save himself. Agencies and officials that should have shown themselves responsible, spontaneously became the tools of a revolutionary Left. What if an insane Rightist had commited the crime? There would have been no hog-wash about 'extremism on both sides' — only the Reuther program against the right.

"Suppose Oswald had made his getaway to Mexico that afternoon. The witch hunt (a favorite Leftist term) would have been in full swing against conservatives. Conditions were ideal for it: The Attorney General, with all the police and justice machinery of America within his grasp, was the slain man's brother. Vengefulness, veneered by a generation of wealth, would have been unleashed. Every man, group, and organization forming a counter-balance to the Left would have been destroyed. Patriotism, branded subversion. Opposition, dismantled. Only organized labor would have been allowed to exist as a force. Her citizens disarmed, America would be ripe for the takeover. The machine was in place. There was only one hitch: Oswald was caught and his Communist background revealed."

In an article published in many newspapers around the nation on December 14, 1963, Drew Pearson stated that the Earl Warren investigating commission was actually "investigating the FBI." This vicious left-wing propagandist went on to say: "What the public doesn't realize is that for the first time since the days of Warren Harding, the FBI itself is under investigation." Pearson further wrote as follows: "President Johnson knew the FBI would be in for investigation and also knew the sacrosanct position of the FBI when he went to great pains to pick a Presidential Commission of unimpeachable integrity to probe the Dallas tragedy"

What Pearson did not tell his readers, among other things, was that the U.S. Communist conspirators called for "an Extraordinary Commission" to be "headed by the Chief Justice of the Supreme Court" and "composed of citizens and experts who enjoy the confidence of the nation" at least three days prior to the announcement of the establishment of the Warren Commission. This Communist call for such a commission came in a feature front page editorial in *The Worker* of November 26 which undoubtedly went to press prior to that date. Since selection of the commission under Justice Warren, the Reds seem well satisfied with it, except for expressing doubts about two or three members of the commission.

Newspaper columnist Holmes Alexander and Senator John Tower of Texas brought up some much more fruitful prospects for an investigation than the investigation of the FBI which Pearson claims will take place. In an interview with Mr. Alexander, Senator Tower said:

"We have reports from Texas that the rightist figures were closely watched during the President's visit to Dallas on November 22. It appears that the leftist figures were not watched." In this interview Senator Tower also said: "The radical right is the symptom of the disease we call extremism. The radical left is the disease itself."

Let all thinking Americans ponder this analysis carefully. The radical left is the disease. Any excesses on the right are a result of this cancerous disease of the extreme left which is leading our nation into totalitarian tyranny. Americans might fight the roots of the disease itself and not the symptoms. Once the symptoms are destroyed, the disease itself is hidden and will not be discovered until it is too late.

In his syndicated column regarding the Tower interview, Holmes Alexander brought up some pertinent and extremely important questions. He wrote:

"Was there a failure in high places to take the Marxist menace as seriously as the Birchite menace? Did that failure contribute to the President's coming within gunfire of a leftist crackpot? It is a hideous thought to contemplate but it cannot be discarded for that reason. Why wasn't Oswald under surveillance? Was it because the Federal Government, and to some extent the general public, have really come to believe that foolish, ill-mannered hecklers who spit on Adlai Stevenson represent a graver danger than the Communist system whose members and fellow travelers are the terrorists in Venezuela, the guerillas in Viet Nam and the conquerors of Cuba? . . ."

In spite of the absolute, indisputable evidence that Lee Oswald's mind was molded by Communist conspiracy propaganda, that his hatred was of the American free enterprise system and all it embraces, and that no one with even the remotest connection with what is considered to be the extreme right has any remote connction with the entire hideous affair, the propaganda voices of the left continue to try to blame right wing conservatives for creating the atmosphere of "hate" which caused Oswald to commit the assassination of

146

President Kennedy. Do they really think the American people are that stupid?

Seventy-four hours after the assassination of Mr. Kennedy, on Monday Afternoon, November 25, at 3:00 p.m., this author wrote an article entitled "Reflections on the Death of the President" which was printed in our Weekly Crusader on December 6, 1963, which said at that time:

"It may be difficult for my readers to understand my fear upon hearing the right-wing accused of participation in President Kennedy's death. May I assure you, as one who has gone through a hate campaign directed at me by the liberals and left-wing element, and having seen the degree to which they will go to destroy anyone who stands in their way, my heart told me that their hatred knew no limitations and their vengeance knows no bounds.

"I know—and you know—that no true conservative in the United States would stoop to taking the law into his own hands. I know — and you know — that any man who would assassinate the President of the United States, in these days when we still have 'due process of law,' would not be a conservative or a patriot, but an anarchist. I hold them in the same contempt that I hold the Communists or any man who would go beyond the law to achieve an end. In my thinking, the end never justifies the means.

"Conservatives stand for law. We preach obedience to the law. For that reason, we opposed the racial demonstrators who took the law into their own hands and carried on racial agitations, defying state and local laws, without regard to 'due process of law.' My main criti-

147

cism of the racial agitators is the fact that they have no regard for the law — that they go beyond the law in an emotional period of American history to accomplish their end. No American — no minority group — no majority group — can ever justify breaking the law or circumventing the law to accomplish their self-justified goals.

"You would have to *lead* an Anti-Communist Movement to know what the liberals are capable of —the hatred, incriminations, intimidations and coercion they constantly throw at the leaders of the anti-Communist cause. I cannot describe adequately the heartache and persecution heaped upon any leader of an anti-Communist movement by the liberal left-wing. With unlimited finances, and being in control of the national media — television, radio and publications — they can destroy a man without any shrug of conscience or regard for 'due process of law.' It is this lawless spirit that is preached by the communists, and practiced by far too many liberals that we oppose."

CHAPTER VI:
"THE ENEMY WITHIN — FAR-LEFT PRESS"

"We have to influence non-Communists if we want to make them Communists or if we want to fool them, so we have to try to infiltrate the big press, to influence millions of people and not merely hundreds of thousands." These words were directed at the Communists of the world by Molotov in a memorandum in 1931. From that year on, Communist leaders, U.S.A., applied their satanic skills to this extremely important task of infiltrating and subverting the American press. There are

600 daily newspapers in the United States, with a circulation of over 59 million. In addition to these dailies, there are 8,000 weekly newspapers with additional millions in circulation.

The exposure of the Molotov memorandum was made by Igor Bogolepov, former Counselor of the Soviet Foreign Office, who defected from Communism at the end of World War II. In testimony before the Senate Internal Security Subcommittee on April 7, 1952, Bogolepov said that in the same memorandum Molotov admitted: "Only a few people who are already Communists read the Communist papers. We don't need to propagandize them." So they fixed their eyes on the "enemy press." Infiltration of the "enemy press" is always necessary before the Communists take over a country.

Revealing information regarding the techniques used by the Reds in infiltrating the "enemy press" was given in a report published by the Senate Internal Security Subcommittee during 1962, entitled "Communist Penetration and Exploitation of the Free Press." One section of the report deals with the Communist infiltration of the Bulgarian press prior to the Communist revolution in that country. The strategy used in Bulgaria was described for the Senate Committee by Dr. G. M. Dimitrov, President of the Bulgarian National Committee for Liberation:

"... Carrying out well-prepared, long-range plans, Soviet agents began planting Bulgarian Communists in all non-Communist publications, principally as journalists or printers. These Communist plants were instructed to go slow in their activities until the press was thoroughly infiltrated. They were to become friendly with all the personnel of the publication, from the editorial staff down to the printshop workers. They were to study the attitudes of the key members of the staff and to gauge how they can best be used by the Communists.

"After a Communist plant was well established in a non-Communist publication, his first task was to create favorable attitudes toward the Soviet Union ... Following the infiltration of the Bulgarian press, the Soviet Embassy in Sofia began to court openly the favor of Bulgarian newspapermen. Journalists of all convictions, even extreme anti-Communists, were invited to lavish vodka-and-caviar parties. As these parties became more frequent, the guests included political leaders as well ...

"The next Soviet step was to invite prominent journalists, writers, and political leaders to visit the Soviet Union and write about their impressions. The visitors, of course, saw only what the Soviets wanted them to see on closely-supervised guided tours. The Soviet officials did not expect glowing praises of the Communist system in Russia by the Bulgarian press at that time, but they sought to induce the Bulgarian visitors to write about the struggle of Russian workers and peasants to build up their backward economy after centuries of neglect under the Tsars ... Another familiar Soviet theme was their great desire for peace in the world. These tactics paid off and many Bulgarian newsmen and other prominent people, most of them anti-Communists by conviction, actually did write favorably of their impressions while visiting Russia.

"Partisan dinners for newsmen continued at the Soviet Embassy in Sofia. More and more editors and publishers softened their anti-Communist sentiments and were willing to accept leftists, and later even known Communists, on their staffs. At the same time the infiltration by concealed Red agents of the Bulgarian press and publishing houses continued ...

"At the time of the Hitler-Stalin Pact in 1939, the Fascist-oriented press of Bulgaria was thoroughly infiltrated by the Communists. The prominent pro-Nazi journalist, T. Kojoucharov, for example, wrote in the reactionary daily, *Slovo*, that 'nothing could be more natural than the unity of Nazi Socialism and Soviet Socialism' and that this unity would last forever. At the same time, the Bulgarian Communist theoretician, T. Pavlov, wrote a whole pamphlet in which he presented similar views.

"In 1944, the Soviet Union declared war on Bulgaria without any provocation or reason and the Red Army occupied the country without firing a shot because the allies assured the Bulgarian people that the Soviets were coming as 'liberators.' One of the first acts of the Communists upon gaining control of the country was to suspend all non-Communist publications and to place all newsprint under strict control. Soon the country was flooded with printed Communist propaganda with no opposition press to answer ...

"Most non-Communist publishers and journalists were declared Fascist or Nazi and sentenced to long prison terms by 'people's courts.' Some were even executed. Among them were publishers and editors who had harbored Communist journalists as insurance against just such an eventuality ..."

While their tactics may very somewhat from country to country, the Communist conspiracy's basic strategy in infiltrating the enemy press in any nation is the same. In the introduction to its report on "Communist Penetration and Exploitation of the Free Press," the Senate Internal Security Subcommittee warned Americans: "A free press can be lost. Let us know and understand what happened in nations which suffered this loss. Let us understand how and why it happened. And let us resolve that it shall not happen here."

Most newspapermen would protest vehemently if you accused their profession of being Communist infiltrated. Yet, in the years 1955 and 1956, the Senate Internal Security Subcommittee looked into Communist infiltration of the American press and concluded that there was "substantial evidence" of such infiltration. During January 1956, the Subcommittee questioned seventeen newsmen in New York City, fourteen of whom had been on the staff of the *New York Times*. Of the seventeen witnesses, fourteen invoked the Fifth Amendment on questions regarding their association with Communism. In its 1956 annual report, the Senate Internal Security Subcommittee summarized: "The subcommittee heard the testimony of more than a score of newspapermen during 1956. Except in a very few cases, it encountered a wall of resistance when it presented its evidence and information to them for reply. The resistance took the form of either a claim of privilege under the First or Fifth Amendments or outright defiance of the authority of the Sub-committee."

A majority of the so-called liberal newspapers refuse to recognize the peril of *internal* Communism. A typical example of this blindness was the June 10, 1961, editorial in the *Arkansas Gazette*, Little Rock. This editorial claimed that the Communist Party in the United States as a domestic political force was a "negligible factor." The *Gazette* claimed that the Communist influence on elections in our country was insignificant, its dogma abhorrent to the American people and repudiated by them.

The famed columnist, Art Buchwald, in his column of March 7, 1962, used the technique of ridicule to discredit anti-Communist activity in the United States when he said: "Unhappily, while there are more and more organizations being formed to fight Communists in the United States, there are fewer and fewer Communists around to fight, and the anti-Communist organizations are fighting among themselves over who has the right to fight Communists."

Some of the far-left publications, such as *Harpers* magazine, actually utilize their columns to attack the Federal Bureau of Investigation and the House Committee on Un-American Activities for insisting that there is a Communist threat internally. In the October 1949 issue of *Harpers*, there was an article by the late Bernard DeVoto entitled "Due Notice to the FBI," and here, in part, is what he said: "A single decade has come close to making us a nation of common informers. The Committee on Un-American Activities blasts several score reputations by releasing a new batch of gossip or we find out that the FBI has put at the disposal of this or that body a hash of gossip, rumors, slander, back-biting, malice, and drunken invention which, when it makes the headlines, shatters the reputation of innocent and harmless people and of people who our laws say are innocent until someone proves them guilty in court." Of course, this is simply vicious smear and nothing else.

One of the newspapers that jumped all over then-Congressman Richard Nixon and the House Committee on Un-American Activities for exposing Alger Hiss, was *the Washington Post*. Even after Alger Hiss' conviction, the *Washington Post*, in an editorial on January 23, 1950, gave the following strange explanation of Hiss' deception: "Alger Hiss had the misfortune of being tempted to betray his country in an era of widespread illusions about Communism and is being tried for perjury in connection with his offense in a period of cold war when the pendulum of public sentiment had swung far in the other direction."

In commenting on this editorial in the May 29, 1950 issue of the *Chicago Tribune*, an editorial stated: "The implication is that there was nothing shocking about a disposition to betray one's country, but that the traitor had to be careful about his timing."

As we mentioned in another chapter, from time to time editors and publishers of far-left newspapers appear on the platform of Communist-sponsored rallies. For instance, on June 7, 1962, a Communist-organized united-front rally against the McCarran Act was held at Manhattan Center, New York City. Top Communist leaders, Gus Hall and Benjamin Davis, were among the featured speakers. Another featured speaker was Murray Kempton, *New York Post* columnist. The Communists were so joyful over Mr. Kempton's speech that they printed lengthy excerpts from it in the June 19, 1962, issue of *The Worker*. Murray Kempton, in his speech, ridiculed the FBI and told the Communists at the rally that "This country has not been kind to you but this country has been fortunate in having you." He also advised the Communists that "I salute you and I hope for times to be better."

A very famous columnist, Walter Winchell, during the summer of 1962, resigned as columnist for the *New York Mirror* and King Features Syndicate. Winchell said that his editors on the *New York Mirror* had given him latitude but accused the *Los Angeles Herald-Examiner* of killing all items about Communism. King Features, he charged, killed five paragraphs about alleged Communists around the late President Kennedy, although according to Winchell his charges had been "cleared by the *Mirror's* legal department."

Probably the most prominent "far-left" American newspaper which constantly attacks anti-Communist investigations is the earlier-mentioned *Washington Post.* On May 22, 1950, the *Washington Post* published a lengthy editorial attacking anti-Communist investigations which stated as follows: "For weeks the Capital has been seized and convulsed by terror... akin to the evil atmosphere of the alien and sedition laws in John Adams' Administration." In this one editorial, the editors of the *Washington Post* referred to Congressional investigations of the internal Communist conspiracy as "witch-hunting" twelve times. Undoubtedly this smear of sincere Congressional investigations into Communism misled a large number of unsuspecting Americans.

One of the most famous examples of Communists infiltrating the newspapers is that of Carl Braden. Braden was on the editorial staff of the *Louisville Courier-*

Journal. His Communist activities first came to light when he bought a house in an all-white section of Louisville and transferred it to a Negro, Andrew Wade IV. When Wade's family moved in, trouble broke out. There was shooting and bombing, and racial tension became explosive. Braden organized a "Wade Defense Committee" which, by press, radio, and mass meeting, defended Wade's occupation of the house. The Commonwealth Attorney in Louisville, A. Scott Hamilton, investigated the whole affair and came to the conclusion that Communists had planned the whole thing, including the rioting and bombing, as a means of inciting racial hatred and trouble.

Carl Braden was indicted on a charge of advocating sedition. Braden denied that he had ever been a Communist. A great parade of witnesses testified in his defense, including his minister, the Rector of St. Stephen's Episcopal Church, writers, reporters, a professor at Indiana University, colleagues of Braden on the *Courier-Journal* staff, and local labor union leaders. But at the crucial moment in the Braden trial, the Louisville FBI released one of its undercover agents, Mrs. Alberta Ahern, who testified that Braden was an active secret Communist leader in Louisville. He had recruited her, in fact, into the Communist Party. He collected dues for the Red cell to which they both belonged. Braden was convicted and sentenced to fifteen years in prison. Braden not only worked for the *Louisville Courier-Journal* before his exposure, but he had done free-lance work for the *Toledo Blade, Newsweek* magazine, *Chicago Tribune, St. Louis Globe-Democrat, New York News,* and the Federated Press which serves the Communist *Worker*. He was an influential member of the American Newspaper Guild, Louisville's Chapter, and had written articles, speeches, and radio scripts for the AFL-CIO. When Braden's house was searched, they found almost a "truckload" of Communist educational and propaganda literature, some charging germ-warfare against the United States, some branding America as the agressor in the Korean War.

On February 8, 1962, in the *Chicago American*, columnist Irving Dilliard referred to Carl Braden as simply an "Episcopalian" and to the famous Communist, Frank Wilkinson, as a "Methodist." Mr. Dilliard contended: "All Americans who care what happens to liberties in our country should breathe a little easier now that these men, Braden and Wilkinson, are again free." Who knows how many innocent Americans may have been deceived by the mis-information in this one column by Irving Dilliard? This one column is typical of the many editorials appearing in far-left newspapers which deceive the American people concerning the threat of Communism internally.

While these left-wing newspapers and columnists befriend even known Communists, you will seldom, if ever, find left-wing writers and the press referring to anti-Communist conservatives in any type of complimentary language. The former pro-Castro enthusiast, Ralph McGill, of the *Atlanta Constitution* is a typical far-left editorial writer. When he refers to the conservatives or anti-Communists, he uses such terminology as "pathetic and psychologically naked young men" or "wild and wall-eyed radicals."

The influence which the Communist publications

themselves have on the far-left's daily newspapers is sobering to any patriot. For illustration, on April 5, 1950, soon after Senator Joseph McCarthy (Republican-Wisconsin) had begun his efforts to expose the Communist conspiracy internally, the Communist *Daily Worker* wrote: "Communists are keenly aware of the damage the McCarthy crowd is doing." On May 4, 1950, the term "McCarthyism" was printed for the first time in a *Daily Worker* article by Gus Hall, National Secretary of the Communist Party. He wrote, "I urge all Communist Party members and all anti-Fascists to yield second place to none in the fight to rid our country of the Fascist poison of McCarthyism." On November 27, 1950, the Communist Party in Maryland and the District of Columbia mailed out an article entitled "Unity Can Defeat McCarthyism." The author was Philip Frankfeld, Chairman of the Communist Party in Maryland, who was later convicted for his Communist activities. What kind of unity was Frankfeld speaking about? He was referring to unity of naive, uninformed non-Communists with the Communist conspirators to accomplish a very important objective of the conspiracy — destroy Joe McCarthy!

On June 18, 1953, an FBI undercover agent exposed the Communist plot to assassinate Senator Joseph McCarthy.

The December 1953 issue of the offical Communist Party organ, *Political Affairs*, carried an article by the National Committee of the Communist Party entitled "Unity Can Rout McCarthyism." Following are quotes from this article: "The name of this growing Fascist beast is McCarthyism ... Now is a time to deal a smashing blow at this monster. The sharp stand of the recent CIO Convention against McCarthyism sounds the right note. The issue must be taken to the great masses of the people...prepare them for a vast political movement that will defeat every candidate in the 1954 elections who does not specifically repudiate McCarthyism and all his filthy works . . . This situation is ripe for organized labor and its allies, by a united smash, to rout the McCarthyism pro-Fascists...This opportunity must not be missed."

The April 1954 issue of *Political Affairs* continued the draft program of the Communist Party written by the National Committee of the Party. This directive to the conspirators was divided into seven sections, and five of the seven attacked McCarthy or McCarthyism. Section IV was devoted entirely to Senator McCarthy and was entitled, "The Menace of McCarthyism — The Growing Danger of Fascism." In this program the conspirators again rated McCarthyism as their number one enemy as they exhorted their members and dupes: "To defeat this menace is the first task of the hour." In the same issue William Z. Foster urged the Communists to "give everything we have to the development of this great struggle."

This Communist-inspired operation against a sincere American patriot ended in a disgraceful and unjustified censure. The Communist conspirators were in the thick of this phase of the battle against "the Fascist poison of McCarthyism." *The Daily Worker* entitled an editorial of September 28, 1954, "Throw the Bum Out." In it they called Senator McCarthy the "arch-conspirator against the American Constitution." In this editorial and throughout the entire period of this-time-wasting episode in our Senate, the Communist conspirators urged their members, fellow travelers and sympathizers to insist that the Senate vote for censure. It was a major issue in the Communist conspiracy publications. Why? The answer is obvious. The Communist conspirators and their sympathizers knew what they were fighting for, but millions of innocent American victims of the Communist Party line did not know what they were doing. Unfortunately, millions of these Americans still do not have the vaguest notion of what all the furor was about, even though they think they know. They think just as the Communists still wish them to think.

In the May 1956 issue of *Political Affairs* the Communists said, "The democratic masses finally cracked down on McCarthy," and that "The recent curbing of the McCarthy pro-Fascist menace by the American people augurs well for the future." Whose future? The author, William Z. Foster, was certainly not speaking of the future of the American republic which was established by our Christian founding fathers. He is looking forward to a Soviet America and is confident of this end result in the great struggle going on today. Upon the death of this persecuted and hounded American patriot, the Soviet News Agency Tass said he was a "double reactionary" who "baited and persecuted by terroristic methods anyone who came out against the domination of a handful of billionaires."

The word "McCarthyism", a Communist-coined smear word, became something horrible beyond imagination in the minds of many Americans. Communists and their sympathizers kept up a steady fire of smear attacks against Senator McCarthy resulting in a united effort by the far-left to destroy "the enemy" — not Communism, but Joe McCarthy.

Among the popular magazines with large circulations, therefore exerting enormous influence upon public opinion in the United States, which joined in the smear attacks against Senator McCarthy, was *Time* magazine. In his newspaper column of November 20, 1951, Fulton Lewis Jr. summarized some of the choicest terminology used by *Time* magazine in reporting on Senator McCarthy's fight against Communism: "Rash-talking Joseph R. McCarthy; pugnacious Senator Joe McCarthy; loud-mouthed; wretched burlesque; scare-head publicity; desperate gambler; a fool or a knave; weasel-worded statements; vituperative smear; half truths; wild charges"

In his newspaper column of November 16, 1951, Fulton Lewis Jr. revealed a tremendous error *Time* magazine made in smearing Senator McCarthy in the Gustavo Duran case. Lewis wrote: "In an effort to smear McCarthy, *Time* magazine said: 'Duran, never a Red, was definitely and clearly anti-Communist — he worked for the United States Government in Cuba during World War II tracking Axis and Communist agents.'

"What the editors of *Time* did not know when they tried to peddle this is that McCarthy had in his files a private memorandum from *Time* magazine's Washington office that labeled Duran exactly what McCarthy called him. And then, just to impale themselves solidly on the hook, *Time*'s editors added: 'Every word in *Time*'s story, incidentally, was thoroughly checked for accuracy of fact and interpretation. It is a policy the Senator would do well to follow.' " Mr. Lewis went on further in his column to quote from the *Time* magazine memorandum which coincided with Senator McCarthy's charges.

In a letter to Henry Luce, publisher of the magazine, Senator McCarthy described the *Time* article on the Duran case as a "vicious and malicious lie being broadcast to millions of American people in clearly deliberate, dishonest attempt to discredit my fight against Communism." He went on to tell Mr. Luce, who owns the *Time* and *Life* magazines: "If freedom of the press is to be maintained, then the editors of a national magazine such as yours, regardless of how much they want to discredit my fight against Communists, do owe some honesty and decency to the public."

Perhaps the leading newspaper to parrot the Communist Party line against Senator McCarthy was the *Washington Post*. In its May 22, 1950, editorial (which was run as a paid advertisement in other newspapers), the *Post* referred to "McCarthy-Goebbels-Vishinsky technique of the lie." In the same editorial, readers were told: "The mad-dog quality of McCarthyism has become so apparent that its power for sowing confusion and suspicion has probably spent its force ..." This was less than three weeks after the Communist publiction coined this smear word, "McCarthyism."

In 1954, a series of articles smearing Senator McCarthy in the *New York World-Telegram*, a Scripps-Howard newspaper, was too much for one member of the Scripps family — Mrs. William Loeb Jr., grand-daughter of E. W. Scripps, founder of the chain. In a sizzling wire to her brother, Charles E. Scripps, Chairman of the chain, and Jack Howard, President of the newspapers, Mrs. Loeb said that the articles on McCarthy were "rotten, biased journalism which would make my grandfather, E. W. Scripps, who above all stood for integrity and fair play in the handling of news, turn in his grave in disgust and shame."

In his book, *McCarthyism — The Fight for America*, Senator McCarthy referred to the policies of "managed news" practiced by the rewrite desks of the large wire services — Associated Press, United Press International, etc. The Senator wrote: "After several experiences, there was impressed upon me the painful truth that the stories written by the competent, honest Associated Press, United Press, or International News Service men assigned to cover the Senate or the House might not even be recognized by them when those stories went on the news ticker to the thousands of newspapers throughout the country. Before being sent out to America's newspapers, the stories pass across what is known as a rewrite desk. There, certain facts can be played up, others eliminated. For example, so often we found in the stories about me a word like 'evidence' was changed to 'unfounded charges.' 'McCarthy stated' would become 'McCarthy shouted.' 'Digging up evidence' became 'Dredging up evidence.' In one case, I recall the story as written on Capitol Hill was 'McCarthy picked up his briefcase full of documents and left.' When the story left the rewrite desk, it was 'McCarthy grabbed his briefcase and stormed from the room.'

One young reporter for the *New York Herald-Tribune*, Dave McConnell, reporting on the un-American treatment given to Senator McCarthy, wrote in his paper May 16, 1960, that the unfair treatment of Senator McCarthy "has come as a surprise to many newspaper veterans who cling to the old mandate that personal bias or personal opinions belong on the editorial page and not in the news columns ... The uproar in the press section during Senator McCarthy's testimony at one point made it difficult even to hear what the Wisconsin Republican was telling the subcommittee."

Of course, not all the newspapers in the United States smeared McCarthy. From the very beginning, the *New York Daily Mirror* supported Senator McCarthy. In an editorial March 16, 1950, they referred to the investigations of Senator McCarthy as "one of the most important events of our time ... McCarthy has courage. He has facts. He knows what he's talking about ... That opposition-Senators and protectors of the State Department would like to smear McCarthy, throw up all manner of smoke-screens to divert attention, and achieve an eventual whitewash is not the issue — and the people will not permit it to be made the issue ... They want the mess cleaned up in Washington. Go to it, Joe McCarthy."

In an interview during 1950, J. Edgar Hoover, Director of the Federal Bureau of Investigation, commended the anti-Communist activities of Senator McCarthy, which was ignored by most of the large left-wing daily newspapers. Mr. Hoover said: "He is earnest. He is honest. He is sincere. Whenever you attack subversives of any kind you are going to be the victim of the most extremely vicious criticism that can be made."

American newspapers and publications have enormous power. They have the power to make or break men and organizations. Favorable or unfavorable images of certain movements and their leaders can be planted in the American minds without recourse to the subject.

William Randolph Hearst boasted that with one telephone call he made the name of Billy Graham a household word and in later years, Billy Graham admitted this. Upon hearing Billy Graham on the radio during a little-publicized revival in Los Angeles, Hearst called his Los Angeles newspaper and told them to "build him up." Build him up the Hearst papers did indeed, making Billy Graham the number one evangelist, as far as fame is concerned, in the world today.

While it is possible for the press to build an unknown minister into an internationally-famous personality, it is also possible for them to picture a staunch and dedicated patriot as a dangerous, irresponsible "hate monger," and ruin his influence.

In the McCarthy days, some of the far-left press actually stooped to printing outright lies about Senator McCarthy in their determination to destroy his effectiveness as an anti-Communist crusader. On October 19, 1951, the *Post-Standard* newspaper of Syracuse, New York, published an editorial in which Senator McCarthy was accused of paying money, through an intermediary, to a man named Charles E. Davis for forging the name of a Communist to a telegram sent to John Carter Vincent, then United States Ambassador to Switzerland. This editorial also accused Senator McCarthy of framing Senator Tydings of Maryland with a fake photograph showing Tydings in alleged conversation with Earl Browder, and made other accusations which were vile and contemptible against the Senator from Wisconsin.

Almost one and one-half years later, on March 5, 1953 the *Syracuse Post-Standard* published another editorial on "The McCarthy Record." This editorial stated:

"An editorial published in this space, October 19, 1951, has been the subject of a suit for libel by Senator Joseph R. McCarthy of Wisconsin. Since publication of this editorial the statements therein have been subjected to careful study in the light of all the facts now available.

"The *Post-Standard* in the light of all the pertinent facts wishes in fairness to its readers to correct certain statements that were written in good faith and in a sincere belief in their truthfulness, but which have nevertheless proved to be untrue and unfair to Senator McCarthy."

The editorial went on to inform readers that the newspaper's investigation had shown that Senator McCarthy "had not committed any act deserving of criticism" in connection with the so-called Charles E. Davis forgery. It stated that the newspaper was satisfied that Senator McCarthy was not responsible for the photographic "framing" of Senator Tydings, and that "responsibility has been clearly fixed on another individual who had no connection with Senator McCarthy."

Once while visiting in Senator McCarthy's office, I said to my friend whom I loved dearly and who proved to be such a great inspiration to me as a young minister fighting Communism in the early days of Christian Crusade, "Why don't you sue some of these people who tell these lies on you?" As I recall, we were alone in his office. It was at the close of the day. I was to accompany him to his home for dinner. He smiled and pointed to a quotation which he had framed and which hung over his desk. It was a quotation by Abraham Lincoln which simply stated: "If I were to read, much less answer, all the attacks made on me, this shop might as well be closed for any other business."

There should be no question in the mind of any patriotic American about the enormous damage done to the cause of freedom and Americanism by those far-left newspapers and magazines which joined in the Communist-inspired attacks against Senator Joseph McCarthy. The only way this damage can ever be rectified is by these periodicals launching a courageous and vigorous campaign on behalf of the Constitutional concepts and historic Americanism. However, it is extremely unlikely that a far-left newspaper will be converted to Americanism in our time. The attacks, smears, lies, innuendoes, half-truths, character assassination, guilt by association originally directed against Senator McCarthy are now being used against anti-Communist men and movements in 1964 who dare resist the Communist threat internally.

In December 1960 the Communists of the world were told in Moscow by the Communist dictators to step up their activities against anti-Communists in the United States. Edward Hunter, psychological warfare expert (and one of the ten most effective anti-Communist voices in America today), testified before the Senate Internal Security Subcommittee July 11, 1961, concerning this Moscow directive against United States anti-Communists. Mr. Hunter said that it was planned in Moscow that the America news media be used by the Communist International to discredit the anti-Communist movements in the United States. Indeed, immediately following the Moscow 1960 meeting, American far-left newspapers and publications began their vicious attacks against the so-called "radical right" or the anti-Communist movements of America.

Guilt by association? Sure, the far left will use guilt by association to discredit the anti-Communist cause. In the February 9, 1962, issue of *Life* magazine, Keith Wheeler, author of a smear article against the anti-Communist movements of America, pulled a shabby trick of including anti-Communists and Nazis together in the far-right classification. He wrote: "The far-right ranges all the way from the respectable conservatism of a Barry Goldwater to the vicious lunacy of the American Nazi Party." This is a typical example of the satanic deception perpetrated under the false theory of Communism and Nazism as opposite extremes, when all the time Communism and Nazism share the Socialist foundation.

Newsweek, Look, Time, New York Times, Washington Post, Atlanta Constitution, every star of the far left, parrot the Communist Party line against the ani-Communist or conservative movements in the United States with amazing continuity. As Ed Hunter said before the Senate Committee on July 11, 1961: "The players know only the conductor in front of them and he may be totally ignorant of who selected the music, arranged the program and why. The extraordinry orchestration (against the anti-Communist movements) that preceded and appeared in leading American newspapers and magazines. . . is in full accord with the new 'unity line' of the Red Manifesto..." Edward

Hunter also pointed out during his testimony that during these smear drives against anti-Communists, "Few in the wolf pack know why they are barking." This is true in the case of non-Communist Americans following any phase of the Communist Party line. As Jesus said when facing the ordeal of Calvary, "Father, forgive them, for they know not what they do."

By April 1962 the smears against the anti-Communist organizations were so successful that Gus Hall wrote in the Communist publication *Political Affairs* that there was a "mass upsurge against the ultra-right which started with our statement ten months ago that warned of this danger and outlined tactical approach for the mobilization of the democratic forces to oppose this menace." He assured fellow Red conspirators that "this fanatical Fascist-like fringe of the ultra-right will be pushed back into its lair."

In the June 23, 1962, issue of the *Portland Reporter*, Philip Hager wrote that Americans are standing in line "waiting their turn to lash out at the extremists of the right." Non-Communist Americans are practically lined up to attack not the Communist conspirators but opponents of the Communists. The attack on the anti-Communist movements are so vicious and unfair that Edward Hunter commented in our *Weekly Crusader*, June 15, 1962. "In my thirty-five years in journalism I have never read or seen so much sheer dishonesty and outright faking outside of the Communist press as I have been witnessing in the newspaper and air coverage of the anti-Communist movement."

The attacks against me personally and against Christian Crusade started on January 1, 1962 when that much-publicized "champion of all liars." Drew Pearson, triggered the smear attack against me by accusing me of "flamboyant hate preaching." The words of Senator Richard Russell of Georgia on the floor of the Senate May 19, 1950, explains the Pearson phenomenon: "Drew Pearson uses the freedom of the press for political blackmail ... It would be impossible for any Senator to attempt to add to Mr. Pearson's stature as the Prince of Liars ..."

If any American wants to know the effectiveness of any minister, writer, broadcaster, or politician against the Communist conspiracy, all he has to do is read faithfully the Communist publications. If you are an effective anti-Communist, you will be smeared mercilessly by the Communist press. If your statements aid and abet the cause of Communism, you will be applauded continuously by the Communist press. The Communists hold Walter Lippmann in high regard. In a column in *The Daily Worker*, November 24, 1957, A. B. Magil praised Mr. Lippmann as "one of the wisest of contemporary capitalist political philosophers." An article in the November 10, 1962, issue of the West Coast Communist newspaper *Peoples World* referred to James B. Reston of the *New York Times* as being "as knowledgeable and informed a correspondent as there is in the nation's Capitol" and as "a responsible journalist." When the Communists speak in such complimentary terms of a writer, we can be sure that the writer so praised is not putting out much in the way of facts which would be harmful to the Communist cause.

On August 20, 1961, *The Worker* reported favorably on the *Portland Daily Reporter* as follows: "Born as a weekly strikers' publication in February 1960, it grew in one year to a daily paper with an avowed ambition to be a liberal independent daily. In the face of incredible handicaps it survived...the first daily newspaper that has been started in the United States in fifteen years." *The Worker* article pointed out that stock of this paper was owned by some 6,000 shareholders in forty-six states, including Oregon's United States Senators, Wayne Morse and Maurine Neuberger, the State Attorney General, the Mayor of Portland, and White House advisor, Arthur Schlesinger, Jr. The Communist writer states that Senator Morse was instrumental in obtaining Associated Press service for the newspaper. If this is the first newspaper to be started in our nation in fifteen years, it is a tragic commentary on the state of the public mind in the United States that it has to be a paper which rates so highly with the Communist conspirators.

In the December 23, 1962, issue of *The Worker,* the *Detroit Free Press* was applauded by the Communists because the Detroit paper had attacked the House Committee on Un-American Activities. During October 1961. *The Worker* rated a news account in the *Cleveland Plain Dealer* newspaper as a "straight-forward news story." From time to time the *Christian Science Monitor* has been praised by *The Worker,* including a complimentary editorial on the front page of *The Worker,* May, 22, 1962.

One of the publications that the Communists attack most frequently is *Barron's Business and Financial Weekly.* In one editorial, November 4, 1962, *Barron's* was attacked by the Communists because the publication had called "for a purge of all those in the government who advocated a lessening of world tensions. and hinted at a nation-wide witch hunt against peace advocates." Of *Barron's*, *The Worker* said that this menacing, Hitler-like demand is not being made by a Birchite, but by a leading spokesman for big business.

The *Chicago Tribune* is high on the list of Red enemies among United States newspapers. An article in *The Worker* of October 15, 1961, attacked the *Chicago Tribune* for printing anti-Communist editorials, as follows: "No right-wing inspired story emanating from the offices of Dixiecrat Strom Thurmond or from the prolific press-agentry of the House Un-American Activities Commitee or from the weekly Manion Forum of the air ... escapes the *Chicago Tribune*'s news hawks. They all get printed and in great length ..." In an article in *The Worker*, January 14, 1962, the Communists attacked the *Chicago Tribune* as follows: "The *Chicago Tribune* has a long and odious record. For a century it has poisoned America's atmosphere."

There is little or no criticism in the Communist press for such publications as *Look* and *Newsweek*.

Within one hour after the assassination of John F. Kennedy in Dallas on Friday, November 22, 1963, the Communist press in Moscow was blaming the anti-Communist and conservative forces of the United States for the death of the President. This, therefore, became the Communist Party line. The Communist press itself denied any Communist connections with Lee Harvey Oswald, the President's assassin. The pro-Communist press in America shifted the blame to the anti-Communists in another way — the premise of some of the far-left critics is that certain anti-Communists in Dallas had created such an atmosphere of hate for President Kennedy by maintaining that consciously or unconsciously he and certain of his decisions were soft on Communism, that a Communist on whom the government had been very soft had killed the President. In other words, a hardened Communist killed the President because the President was criticized by some anti-Communists. The mind to which this logic makes sense, especially in view of the fact that there is absolutely no evidence to prove their position and all the evidence is against it, is a mind which is in the grip of powerful illusions or a mind which is just passing on,, without evaluating, the gossip which it has heard. Some liberals went so far as to suggest that since the President had to be killed, it was a shame that some anti-Communist didn't take his life. The twisted logic of these illusionists is further illustrated in the fact that their great outcry is against the right and not against the Communists. The official Party line is that the anti-Communist elements of America are to blame. By the "right," they have reference to all active anti-Communists who call for a firmer stand against internal and external Communism. It is quite obvious why the Communists blame the anti-Communists. Anything in their non-moral outlook is truth if it can in some way advance the Communist Party and discredit their opposition.

Here are some examples of non-Communists parroting the Communist Party line by blaming the right-wing elements of the United States. On November 23, the *New York Herald-Tribune* carried an article on page eight on "Dallas, Long a Radical's Heaven." Of course,

Oswald was born in New Orleans, had lived some in New York, and had been in the USSR for several years. He had been a Communist in his thinking from about fifteen years of age. Thus, whether Dallas had been a haven of so-called radical right-wingers or not had nothing to do with making Oswald a Communist. He was not a product of Dallas or America, but of Karl Marx. (However, in all fairness, we should point out that on the same day this article was carried in the *Herald-Tribune,* another columnist, Stuart H. Loory, wrote in the same paper that the politicians in the nation's capital "were only too eager to believe" at first that it had been done by someone on the far-right wing.)

Newsweek magazine, who, with *Look* magazine, is constantly in a battle for first place in the far-left publication race, in its issue of December 9, 1963, was still blaming the right-wing for "creating an atmosphere of violence." In the same publication, *Newsweek* reported on Castro's reaction to the death of Mr. Kennedy and headed the report: "The Grief Of A Foe." Castro is a Communist. He deceived Cubans and many others into thinking that his revolution was not communistic. He has executed many people. He hates the United States. He had more than once called for the death of Kennedy. Really, isn't it a bit too much to believe that Castro was filled with grief as *Newsweek* magazine suggests?

Drew Pearson wrote a column shortly after the death of Mr. Kennedy claiming that President Kennedy was a victim of a hate drive by people on the right, such as the editor of the *Dallas Morning News*, Robert Dealey. He called the assassination "Dallas' answer" to the President's plea for good will and reason. He quoted an Arizona editor that "the hatred preachers got their man. They did not shoot him: they inspired the man or men who did it."

A Communist shot the President: therefore, anti-Communists in Dallas are to blame. A man who learned his hate, not in Dallas, but elsewhere, and mainly from Marxism, murdered the President; so Dallas is guilty. However, even James Reston of the *New York Times* had to admit: "All the evidence to date indicates that the right-wing had nothing to do with the death of Kennedy and that the deed could have been done in New York just as well as in Dallas." It is indeed frightening then to contemplate the editorial in the *Wall Street Journal* which was reported in the Congressional Record December 3, 1963: "In their obsession with the far-right, some people seemingly refuse to believe that the deranged killer was a man of the far-left."

Of course, the AFL-CIO Executive Council had to join in with these attacks on the anti-Communist movements as always. On November 26, the AFL-CIO Executive Council said: "Hatred — blind, bitter, savage hatred — is on the rise in America. There is the hatred of which Birmingham has become the symbol. There is the hatred exemplified by the John Birch Society and the followers of General Walker. There is the hatred of the fanatical Communist. There is no choice among them, for hatred in any form is evil." To classify members of the John Birch Society or friends of General Walker with the Communist Party is an evil and vicious thing. There may be some members of the John Birch Society who hate and there may be members of the AFL-CIO who hate. Perhaps the Executive Council of the AFL-CIO is guilty of hatred — hating the John Birch Society and General Walker. However, hate is an official doctrine of the Communist conspiracy, but hate is not an official doctrine of the conservative right-wing organizations. Why didn't the AFL-CIO say something about the black racist, Malcolm X, who indicated after the death of Kennedy that he was glad that the President had been shot?

Ralph McGill of the *Atlanta Constitution* immediately wrote an article on the "Harvest of Psycopathic Hate" in which he did not make one little reference to the extreme left, but most of it dealt with racial violence and those whom he viewed as extremists on the right. He made no specific reference to the fact that the man who killed the President was a Communist.

As we read these irresponsible charges against the anti-Communist elements of America by the left-wingers, the following question is raised in our minds: "Can this outpouring of accusations against those whom the far-left label the ultra-right be an indication of hate on the part of some of these accusers?"

In a speech before a convention of broadcasters, former Florida Governor Leroy Collins indicted the so-called Southern right-wing extremists for the death of the President. Senator Mansfield in his funeral eulogy called for "the strength to do what must be done to bridle the bigotry, the hatred, the arrogance and the iniquities and inequities which marched in the boots of a gathering tyranny to that moment of horror." Not a word about the bigotry, hatred, arrogance, iniquities, and inequities of Communism. Are we afraid to pinpoint on Communism the responsibility for the murder of the

President, lest we offend the feelings of some Communists? Must we talk about sinners in general, or haters on the far-right specifically, lest the real criminal, Communism, be exposed in its brutal nakedness?

In attack after attack, leaders of the far-left single out the right-wing for criticism, but there was not a word about Communism, which was responsible for the murder of the President, from the lips of these liberal political, religious, and educational leaders. What lamentable, warped logic: Communism killed the President; therefore it is the fault of someone else. One on the left murdered the President; therefore, the right is responsible. We wonder if some of those who talk so much about hate being the cause of the President's death without implying that it was Communist hate, but rather insist it was rightist hate, may not, by their irresponsible statements, be stirring up the hate and violence of some people. Almost immediately after the death of the President, Senator John Tower, a conservative opponent of the administration, began to receive threatening phone calls. His wife had to go into hiding.

The *Chicago Tribune* reported that Senator Barry Goldwater "has been stunned and shocked by the number of abusive letters and telegrams which he has received since the death of President Kennedy." There has been an outpouring of satanic abuse such as he has never seen in his life.

Hate did kill the President, but it was not the hate of which some in their illusions, some in their blind and bitter sorrow, and some in their shallowness, have spoken. It was the hate which is an inherent part of Communism which killed the President.

Thank God there are here and there patriotic newspapers that are faithfully presenting the pro-American and anti-Communist positions Such newspapers as the *Chicago Tribune, Dallas Morning News, Chattanooga News-Free Press, Omaha World-Herald, Tulsa World, Tulsa Tribune, St. Louis Globe-Democrat, Jackson Clarion-Leader, Shreveport Journal, Amarillo Daily News, Borger News-Herald, San Diego Tribune*, and many, many others are worthy of the support and respect of the American people. Only by reading responsible dailies such as those mentioned above and truth magazines such as *Christian Crusade, Weekly Crusader, Christian Beacon, Human Events, National Review, American Opinion, Dan Smoot Report*, etc., can the floodtides of Communism be dammed in the United States.

One of America's best authorities on the Communist conspiracy is Dr. J. B. Matthews, former chief investigator for the House Committee on Un-American Activities and for the McCarthy Committee. In his excellent book (which I recommend to every student of Americanism), called *Odyssey of a Fellow Traveler*, Dr. Matthews stated:

"Hate is at floodtide in the world today, a hate born of the doctrine that man is arrayed against man in an irreconcilable conflict of classes. It is a hate more deep rooted and terrible than that of international war ..

"However much Communists might prefer to be the only political group immune to all criticism and however much they may attempt to enforce this immunity with vituperation, it is important that the critics of Communism employ the restraint of civilized emotions, a fine sense of balance, and perhaps above all, their sense of humor while proceeding fearlessly to the work of criticism."

CHAPTER VII
RUTHLESS REUTHER
STAR OF THE "FAR LEFT"

On January 28, 1958, a great pro-American news paper columnist, George Todt, reported on the "Reuther-Goldwater Verbal Tilt." Mr. Todt explained this verbal exchange as follows:

"Last Wednesday in Detroit, the vice-president of the United World Federalists in the United States and an ardent champion of so-called mental health legislation found himself ideologically bankrupt of ideas, so what did he do? In his desperation, he lashed out in the most churlish and despicable manner at his chief opponent — a great United States Senator who is his intellectual superior — and told a captive audience that he was a lunatic.

"Unable and fearful to meet Senator Barry Goldwater in honest face-to-face debate, here is the rude and ungentlemanly quote from Walter Reuther, confided to 3,000 delegates at his UAW Convention and these are his exact words: 'Goldwater is mentally unbalanced — he needs a psychiatrist, he needs help. Ford, Chrysler and General Motors provided a platform in Detroit for the country's number one political fanatic, the number one peddler of class hatred, Senator Goldwater.'

"Here is the Senator's calm reply to the hate mongering of Reuther: 'This man cannot meet the charges that I, as well as others, have made about him in his drive for political power ... so he now resorts to the age-old practice of name calling. He cannot stand to have the truth told about him. The only defense he can muster is to cry foul or that his opposition are liars.'"

As recently as Thursday, December 26, 1963, Senator Barry Goldwater reported on the "hate mongering" activities of Walter Reuther in his syndicated newspaper column:

"Two of the greatest champions of the 'hate-by-association' theory of the assassination of President Kennedy undoubtedly are the AFL-CIO and the Americans for Democratic Action.

"They insist we must open a campaign against 'hate mongers' and imply that this includes everyone who has been critical of the New Frontier.

"The AFL-CIO and ADA obviously should not have anything to do with engendering hate themselves. However, this is not the case.

"The mighty labor complex and the radical ADA are principal supporters of something called Group Research Institute, although the sponsorship is as sub-rosa as it can be kept. GRI publishes a monthly newsletter which costs $25 and a $100-membership is prerequisite to subscribing. GRI is the left-wing bible on who, what and how to hate.

"It lists individuals and groups upon which all good radicals, liberals and others of the left should vent their hatred, because, in the opinion of this 'research' organization, they are right-wing extremists.

"Among the persons so classified are former Presidents Herbert Hoover and Dwight Eisenhower, Gens. James Van Fleet and Omar Bradley, FBI Director J.

Edgar Hoover and Ozzie and Harriet Nelson.

"Even Mrs. Eisenhower is included in this company, because she dedicated a new building to house the Freedoms Foundation of Valley Forge, Pennsylvania.

"GRI tells its subscribers to watch their newspapers for announcements of visits of such 'extremists' as these and outlines a program of action to counter what the hated 'rightists' may have to say. Subscribers are told to hound local newspaper offices and radio and television stations with information about the 'dangerous positions' held by the listed persons, to attend and interrupt public meetings where they speak and generally carry on in a childish and demonstrative fashion.

"GRI was incorporated early in 1962 by two lawyers, Daniel Singer and N. W. Heller. The papers of incorporation were notarized by Mary C. Asay.

"Singer is a former board member of the Council for Abolishing War. Heller was Washington secretary for the American Civil Liberties Union and was counsel for Kendrick Cole, central figure in one of the better-known security cases in recent years. Miss Asay was the office secretary of Joseph Rauh, Jr., long-time ADA official and lawyer for left-wing causes and individuals.

"GRI's service is subscribed to by the AFL-CIO's Committee on Political Education (COPE) and is given wide circulation throughout the federation by its industrial union department. Other funds come from ADA, of which Walter Reuther is a board member and a former co-chairman.

"It is not difficult to understand that, with such a lineup, GRI is exceptionally well equipped for its task."

That Walter Reuther is first and foremost an in-

ternationalist-minded politician there can be little doubt.
Twenty-five years ago, Walter Reuther took off his union
mask and allowed the politician to show through. Said
Mr. Reuther: "Political action ...shall have first call
upon my time and energy as president of the International Union." In other words, political action would
be Reuther's first priority, not collective bargaining. On
January 20, 1958, Senator Barry Goldwater said: "Walter Reuther, by his own statement, sees himself primarily
as a politician. The union appears to be merely a con-
venient stepping stone."

Congressman Clare E. Hoffman, (Republican-Michi-
gan) on Tuesday, February 18, 1958, accused Walter
Reuther of having "long politically controlled Michigan." Congressman Hoffman said that "vicious, lawless
violence has been his weapon, misuse of union funds
their practice." Walter Reuther has long channeled his
political activities through an AFL-CIO-sponsored committee called COPE—Committee on Political Education. However, in 1963, he had his fingers in another
"hate group" described by Senator Barry Goldwater
above — this organization being called Group Research.
So, armed with COPE and Group Research, Walter
Reuther is determined to control the political set-up of
the United States of America. It should be said that at
no time in the political history of this country has there
been such a well-organized, heavily-financed or better-
disciplined organization than that formed by the political activities of Walter Philip Reuther. It is alleged that
Walter Reuther spends a half-million dollars of union
funds annually for personal public relations. But
stripped of all his press-agentry, the fact is that Walter

Reuther is one part labor boss and nine parts political adventurer. America's far-left crowd finds it difficult to wax eloquent enough to describe this demagogic character whom they consider some sort of Twentieth Century "messiah." The *New York Times* said of Walter Reuther that he possessed a combination of "the most engaging qualities of Albert Einstein and Van Johnson," while the *Saturday Evening Post* referred to him as "an undissipated Prince of Wales." One of the far-left crowd who considers himself an advisor to Presidents is Arthur M. Schlesinger, Jr., of Harvard and Americans for Democratic Action (ADA) fame. Schlesinger, writing about Reuther, has stated: "Walter Reuther, the extraordinarily able and intelligent leader of the United Auto Workers, may well become in another decade the most powerful man in American politics." Many concerned patriots are convinced that Reuther has attained his goal.

Let's take a careful look at Reuther's background.

Walter Philip Reuther was born in Wheeling, West Virginia, September 1, 1907 the son of Valentine Reuther.

Walter's grandfather, Jacob Reuther, was a dairy farmer in Mannheim, Germany. Jacob Reuther was well-known as a dissenter in the old country. He was a Socialist, a militant pacifist, and a labor agitator. His enmity toward "Prussianism" led Jacob Reuther to migrate to the United States in 1892 with his two small sons. He was determined that they should not grow up to be inducted into the German Army. Jacob's son, Valentine, Walter's father, was eleven years old when they arrived in New York. They settled on a small farm near Effingham, Illinois. In the Illinois farm home, Jacob gave his sons a thorough indoctrination course in Socialism, pacifism, and trade unionism. In religion, Jacob was a rebel, eventually withdrawing from the Lutheran Church as a result of doctrinal disputes with the local pastor.

As a young man at the turn of the century, Walter's father, Valentine Reuther, moved to Wheeling where he became a steel worker. In 1904, at the age of 23, Valentine was elected president of thee Ohio Valley Trades and Labor Assembly. He was only 26 years old when his son, Walter, was born. Valentine left the steel mills to take a job as a teamster for a Wheeling brewery. He became active in the teamster's union local. Valentine Reuther, like his father, was steeped in pacifism and the socialist dogmas. These, he in turn, passed on to his children. He boasted a personal friendship with Eugene V. Debs, the outstanding Socialist leader at the beginning of the century. Walter says he once went with his father to visit Debs in the penitentiary at Moundsville, West Virginia.

Throughout Walter's childhood and youth, Socialism was a lively topic of discussion in the Reuther house.

Reputedly because of the smallness of the elder Reuther's wages as a teamster, Walter quit high school in 1924 at the age of 16. He went to work immediately for the Wheeling Steel Corporation as an apprentice tool and die maker, and at once, according to his own account, plunged into unionism. In 1927, he was fired, and set out for Detroit to seek a job in the automotive industry. Despite his youth, he is reported to have arrived in Detroit as a skilled tool and die maker.

Walter's first job in Detroit was at the Briggs body

plant. In a few weeks, he switched to Ford where higher wages were being paid.

Walter had night work at Ford's, and so he took up his high school studies once more. In 1929, he received his high school diploma, and entered the College of the City of Detroit (now Wayne University).

In 1930, his brothers, Victor and Roy, came to Detroit and enrolled at Wayne University. All three became known as campus agitators. Continuing what was by then a Reuther tradition, the brothers set out to harnangue the Wayne students into an acceptance of Socialism.

In 1932, during the presidential campaign, Walter brought a chapter of Norman Thomas' League for Industrial Democracy into being on the Wayne campus. It was altogether natural for Walter himself to be chairman of this little Socialist organization. He also organized and became chairman of the Wayne University Social Problems Group.

When an effort was made to establish an ROTC on the Wayne campus, Walter and his brothers put their radical agitation into high gear. A Wayne professor who joined them was suspended from the faculty and brought up on charges before the Detroit Board of Education. The Reuthers promptly organized a demonstration in behalf of the suspended faculty member. Victor started the proceedings off and Walter closed them. Their campaign was successful. The Wayne University authorities dropped the plans for ROTC.

The Reuther brothers were openly members of the Socialist Party in this Wayne University period. They campaigned around the city in behalf of the presidential candidacy of Norman Thomas.

A few weeks after the 1932 election, Walter and Victor decided to abandon the formal education of Wayne University in favor of a less academic preparation for their messianic careers, namely, experience in the workers' paradise of the Soviet Union.

Despite the wholesale distortions and false impressions, the simple fact is that the Reuther brothers — Walter and Victor — embarked on an enthusiastic pilgrimage to the Soviet Union. That was their goal when they boarded ship in New York Harbor in February 1933. That was the goal they had achieved when they walked down the gangplank in San Francisco, in October 1935.

By the beginning of 1934, Walter and Victor were in the Soviet Union at work in the large automobile plant at Gorky. They were writing letters to their friends in the United States, giving vent to unqualified enthusiasm over what they had found in the Soviet Union.

In February 1934, Roy Reuther reported that Walter and Victor had "gone completely Stalinist." He had received letters from them saying that they were done with the Socialist Party. Allegedly, Walter's and Victor's political adventuring had taken them wholeheartedly into the camp of the Stalinists. At that particular time, Roy Reuther was something of a Trotskyite, having spent a period of study at A. J. Muste's Brookwood Labor College. Roy expressed some disappointment that his brothers had become so enamored of Stalinist Communism.

One letter written by Walter and Victor Reuther from Russia to Melvin and Gladys Bishop has been widely quoted, particularly the final paragraph which says, "Carry on the fight for a Soviet America." This letter, written from the Soviet Union, January 21, 1934, is so indicative of Reuther's feelings at that time that it should be widely circulated.

On October 21, 1938, the entire letter was incorporated in sworn testimony before the Committee on Un-American Activities, and Chairman Martin Dies invited the Reuther brothers to refute the charges under oath, but the invitation was ignored.

The authenticity of the letter is beyond question. Melvin Bishop, to whom the letter was sent, has publicly acknowledged having received it and verified the accuracy of its contents at a UAW Convention at Buffalo, New York, in August 1949. Also in a letter to the *Saturday Evening Post* in August 1948, Walter Reuther tactitly admitted co-authorship. A partial text of the "Mel & Glad" letter follows:

"Dear Mel and Glad:

"What you have written concerning the strikes and the general labor unrest in Detroit, plus what we have learned from other sources of the rising discontent of the American workers, makes us long for the moment to be back with you in the front lines of the struggle; however, the daily inspiration that is ours as we work side by side with our Russian comrades in our factory, the thought that we are actually helping to build a society that will forever end the exploitation of man by man, the thought that what we are building will be for the benefit and enjoyment of the working class, not only of Russia, but the entire world, is the compensation we receive for our temporary absence from the struggle in the United States...

"Now that we have already experienced the thrill, the satisfaction of participating in genuine proletarian democracy, we are more than just sympathetic to our country (Russia), we are ready to fight for it and its ideals.

"And why not? Here the workers, through their militant leadership, the proletarian dictatorship, have not sold out to the owning class...Here are no bosses to drive fear into the workers...Here the workers are in control ...

"In our factory...there are no pictures of Fords and Rockefellers, or Roosevelts and Mellon. No such parasites, but rather huge pictures of Lenin . . . etc., greet the workers' eyes on every side. Red banners with slogans 'Workers of the World Unite' are draped across the craneways. Little Red flags fly from the top of presses, drill presses, lathes, . . . etc. Such a sight you have never seen before...

"Mel, once a fellow has seen what is possible where workers gain power, he no longer fights just for an ideal, he fights for something which is real, something tangible . . . We are witnessing and experiencing great things in the U.S.S.R....We are daily watching Socialism being taken down from the books on the shelves and put into actual application. Who would not be inspired by such events? ..

"Carry on the fight for a Soviet America.

(Signed) 'Vic and Wal' "

Based on this letter, it is no wonder that the *New York Herald-Tribune* editorially described Walter Reuther after his election to the UAW presidency in 1946 as a "dangerous and disingenuous opportunist, a reckless politician" and commented upon his "aggressive demagoguery."

Many examples could be cited of Walter Reuther's collaboration with known Communists. From the Detroit police department files a story has become known in recent years of a Communist rally held on May 3, 1937, in Detroit which was attended by a highly-skilled investigator of the police department, Sgt. Harry Mikuliak. According to Sgt. Mikuliak's account, this meeting was held in the auditorium of the Central Methodist Church in Detroit. The meeting was originally scheduled to be held in the Cass Technical High School, but permission had been denied by a representative of the Board of Education, a Mr. DeGalen. Anna Louise Strong, well-known Soviet propagandist of that period, was the speaker at this meeting in the Central Methodist Church. The meeting was held to raise money for the Communist side of the Spanish Civil War. The money-raiser was none other than Walter Reuther. The amount collected in cash that night was $522.67. Reuther was then president of UAW Local 174. Walter Reuther knew Anna Louise Strong from his Soviet days. He knew her, as did everyone else who had ever heard her name, as a Soviet apologist. To my knowledge, Reuther has not denied this collaboration with the Communists. Obviously, he cannot.

Walter Reuther deserves a place in American history as the "generalissimo of the sit-down strikes." His present position as the head of one of America's largest labor unions rests entirely upon those acts of violence in which he collaborated to the fullest with the Communist Party of the United States. Reuther became president of the UAW in March 1946. Walter's victory over R. J. Thomas was tenuous indeed. The vote was 4,444 for Reuther and 4,320 for Thomas. This smallest of majorities catapulted Walter toward his ultimate goal. It is further interesting to note that Reuther gained the presidency of the UAW with a subtle witch hunt of his own in which his opponent, R. J. Thomas, was accused of being allied with Communism. Reuther had ranted up and down the ranks of the UAW with patriotic-sounding attacks upon the Communists in the union. The acknowledged leader of the so-called Communist faction in the UAW was George Addes, the union's secretary-treasurer. It was assumed on all sides, because of the sudden anti-Communist crusade of Walter Reuther when he was campaigning for the presidency, that Addes would be the first ousted from his strategic position in the union. It is difficult to imagine the shock the convention delegates received when, after the poll of the votes was completed, Reuther stood up and faced the convention and said, "I want now to extend my hand to George Addes ... and tell him that together we can unite this organization." Although Addes was an acknowledged leader of the UAW Communist faction, he and his Communist followers refused Reuther's "extended hand."

One doesn't need to go back to Reuther's enthusiasm about the Soviet Union in 1934, or to his hand-in-glove collaboration with the Communist Party in the sit down strikes of 1936-37, in order to assess correctly the sincerity of Reuther's professed opposition to Communism. It is clear beyond any doubt in the minds of American conservatives that Reuther's present-day mild anti-Communism is just a maneuver of a confirmed political adventurer. He is not one whit less the Socialist that he was in former days.

Based on the career of Walter Reuther, his aims and ojectives are clearly understood. One, he is a firm believer in world government. At a convention of World Federalists, he said, "I do believe that the work you people have been doing is the beginning of something that has tremendous importance in the world. I hope that the day is not too far off when I can officially join with you." The odd political character of the World Federalists is underlined by the assortment of Communist fellow travelers, ex-Communists, liberals and internationalists who compose it.

Two, most of the Reuther ideas, his numerous "memorandums and plans," are plagiarized from British Socialism. While fundamentally a Socialist, he is also an unscrupulous opportunist. He has demonstrated consistently that he is not in the slightest averse to the use of any method to achieve his ends. There have been many so-called "Reuther plans" dished out to the American people in the last twenty years. Some of them have commanded considerable attention from the press. All of these "Reuther plans" have one thing in common: They call for greater and greater government control over all the aspects of our economic life. (His most famous plan, the Reuther Memorandum, will be discussed at the conclusion of this chapter).

Three, having been a national board member of the Americans for Democratic Action (ADA), in my opinion the ADA was unquestionably the vehicle in which Reuther and his crowd expected to take over the entire

Democratic Party, U.S.A. Over thirty key officials of the ADA were able to infiltrate the Kennedy Administration. What future the ADA will have with President Johnson is not yet clear. (More will be said of the ADA in subsequent chapters).

Four, Walter Reuther was not yet forty years old when he defeated R. J. Thomas for the UAW presidency. His next step is to become president of the entire AFL-CIO. Some day we may learn of the retirement of George Meany from the arduous tasks of that position. Reuther is eager to succeed him (in spite of the "friction" between Meany and Reuther) and has built up a personal political machine within the AFL-CIO which makes it certain that he will do so.

Five, somewhere along the line is the step which involves the complete control of the Democratic Party. Failing this, the master plan calls for the disintegration of the Democratic Party as it now exists and the formation of a brand new Farmer-Labor Party. If he succeeds in capturing President Lyndon B. Johnson and the entire Democrat hierarchy, his dictated program will be one of national Socialism leading to the destruction of most of our free American institutions.

A look at the newspapers over the last few years shows the far-left philosophy of this ruthless man, Walter Reuther. On July 19, 1963, Walter Reuther urged Congress to strengthen civil rights legislation by making "direct payment of damages to persons discriminated against in public facilities." He said that anyone who has been "wrongfully excluded from a public facility should be entitled to recover a flat sum in damages." On May 4, 1962, Walter Reuther announced that he would "seek legislation to compel employers to pay double time for overtime after 40 hours a week." At this time, he warned that the "labor movement may get fat, soft, and flabby if it does not keep its militancy and social idealism."

Prior to becoming Attorney General of the United States, Robert Kennedy worked as counsel for a Senate committee investigating labor unions. All the major unions were investigated with the exception of Reuther's. In fact, Robert Kennedy became famous for his anti-Jimmy Hoffa crusade. Tom Anderson of Nashville, Tennessee, stated in his syndicated column, "Straight Talk," in March 1958: "Hoffa... unlike Reuther, is a brass-knuckle hoodlum whose dreams are more down to earth: Money and power are his gods, not making America over . . . Reuther's blueprint for creeping Sovietization would eventually break the automobile industry, would force the government to take it over and run it 'producing for use and not for profit' in the 'public interest'... The average union leader's goal is: 'more.' But Reuther's goal is not average, his goal is Socialism."

In the January 12, 1958, *Arizona Republic*, there was an editorial which stated: "Walter Reuther is fighting viciously to prevent the Senate Rackets Committee (Robert Kennedy's committee) from investigating the United Auto Workers. Reuther's objective is to make it seem that the committee's investigation of the Teamsters Union was a public service, but any probe of the UAW would be just low-down politics. Just last week, John L. Lewis, one of the great leaders of labor in America, referred to Reuther as 'an earnest

Marxist inebriated by the impetuosity of his own verbosity.' No fair person wants an investigation solely for the purpose of discrediting any branch of organized labor. No investigation should be undertaken for partisan political reasons, but neither should any investigation be avoided for such reasons. If Reuther is clean, an investigation won't hurt him. If the methods he uses are fair, he need not fear the result. But in any event, the public should know what goes on and the Senate Rackets Committee is the only means it has of finding out. The Committee cannot succumb to Reuther's present violent attack if it wants to retain the respect it has won from the American people."

As a historical postscript, we should add that Robert Kennedy resigned from the Senate Committee the day the Committee started its probe into the Reuther Union. Thus, the probe was ended before it ever started.

Reuther's attitude toward free enterprise is shown in an Associated Press release dated January 22, 1958, in which he is quoted as telling a special convention of the UAW that big corporations are putting the nation's economy in peril because "they take so much in profits." Senator John Marshall Butler (Republican-Maryland) pointed out: "The well-worn legend that businessmen have been reaping 'excessive profits,' is once more abroad in the land. As usual, the charge is advanced by some leaders of the labor union movement — particularly by Walter Reuther. Reuther's accusation and the facts concerning the wage-price spiral of the American economy need to be examined carefully. Consider these significant facts: An examination of distribution of the increase in the national income through this decade shows that for every additional dollar of corporate profits after taxes, employees receive an additional $40. Furthermore, labor's share of the total national income rose from 65.3% in 1947 to 70.3% in 1956. On the other hand, corporate profits after taxes dropped from 9.3% of the national income in 1947 to only 6.1% in 1956."

No long look into the personality of Walter Reuther would be complete without referring to a famous speech by Walter Reuther delivered at the Masonic Temple in Flint, Michigan, on March 18, 1936, at which time he gave a glowing account of his pilgrimage to Moscow, lauding the Soviet Union with fervent enthusiasm. In response to a question about religion in Russia, he said: "We (including himself as a Soviet proletarian) do not believe in God, but that Man is God." A friendly biographer of Walter Reuther, Paul F. Douglass, writes: "Although Reuther takes no active part in organized religion, he is widely recognized, by the Protestant Churches in particular, as a Christian liberal." How an athiest can be a "Christian liberal" is hard for me to understand.

Reuther's long-time romance with the National Council of Churches began shortly after he became head of the union. He converted the "Christian clergy" by extending an invitation to the far-left National Council of Churches to send a delegation of ministers to CIO conventions "to hear its speakers and get acquainted with its leaders." This Reuther idea of comradeship with the National Council of Churches paid off handsomely, for in February 1950, both Walter and Victor Reuther were invited to the Federal Council's second National Study Conference on the Church and Economic Life attended by 450 ministers and laymen from 37 states. Reuther's collaboration became so close that on November 10, 1952, he wrote a letter on the stationery of the National Council of Churches to all CIO unions commending the far-left National Council for its Labor Sunday message which opposed universal military training and denounced "the attempt to enforce conformity or to silence people by character assassination, guilt by association, or the use of unfounded charges," which, of course, was the typical Communist Party line of the moment. He then asked that each International Local Union send in contributions up to $500 payable to the National Council of Churches.

Two years later in 1954, Reuther prevailed upon the CIO's Philip Murray Memorial Foundation to contribute $200,000 to the National Council of Churches, the check for which he presented in person.

One officer of the National Council of Churches, Bishop Grant D. Batorf of the United Brethren Church in Christ, made a public statement in which he declared:

"The Political Action Committee has the affrontery to insult the church by telling it what should be its program, even to suggesting a creed which leaves God out and makes no mention of Christ, but instead is in substance nothing but the bitter pill of Communism with a little sugar coating.

"We cannot work with a group claiming to represent labor when it is contrary to our Christian faith, our American form of Government, and in the last analysis harmful to the working man himself."

It is difficult to explain how a Protestant university, Wilberforce University (a Methodist Church institution), was prevailed upon to confer a degree on Walter Reuther as a Doctor of Humanities. Another "Christian university," Boston University, conferred upon Reuther an "honorary degree of Doctor of Laws." Why these Christian institutions select an extreme radical like Reuther for this honor is somewhat of a mystery, especially since he has made it known that he doesn't believe in God.

Not only did Protestant churches defile the name "Christian" in presenting these honorary degrees to Walter Reuther, but Reuther was honored with the appointment as Gaston Lecturer at Georgetown University, a leading Catholic institution outside of Washington, D. C. Furthermore, he was presented a Doctor of Laws by the Catholic St. Mary's College in California. In conferring these honors, both institutions apparently ignored the papal Encyclicals of Pope Leo XIII, who warned against Marxism, Communism, and Socialism in whatever forms and Pope Pius XI, who declared: "The doctrine of modern Communism . . . is in substance based on the principles of dialectical and historical materialism previously advocated by Marx . . . Communism is intrinsically wrong, and *no one who would save Christian civilization may collaborate with it in any undertaking whatsoever*."

A letter written on the official letterhead of *Life* magazine January 24, 1961, signed by Beverly Bennett "for the Editors" is quite amusing, especially this comment: "It is true that in his youth Walter Reuther was a radical. Since then, he has settled down into a more sober, responsible maturity. He is now identified with the 'right-wing' union leaders." I should imagine after publication of this book that Mr. Reuther will sue *Life* magazine for damages for calling him a right-winger.

As I suggested earlier, Walter Reuther is well-known for his "memorandums and plans." His hatred of the pro-American conservatives and the anti-Communist movements of our time is shown by his "Political Memo from COPE" published bi-monthly by his AFL-CIO Committee on Political Education, 815 16th Street Northwest, Washington 6, D.C. Almost every issue of "Political Memo from COPE" has an attack against some spokesman of the anti-Communist cause. In the April 22, 1963, issue, COPE attacks Billy James Hargis and Senator Barry Goldwater. In the July 1, 1963, issue, he levels a two-page attack against Robert Welch, whom he accuses by headlines as the "messiah" of the anti-Communist cause. In the July 15, 1963, issue, he attacks Billy James Hargis, General Edwin Walker, the John Birch Society, former Congressman John Rousselot and the Republican Party in general. He claimed in this issue that the young GOP's had been taken over by the "extreme right-wing." His headline for the article is entitled "Old Fuddy-Duddies Take Over Young GOP." In the headline article in which he attacked me personally, it is identified "When Rightists Pick A Target, They Saturate It."

In the July 29, 1963, issue, he attacks *Human Events*, Senators Strom Thurmond and Barry Goldwater, Admiral Ben Moreell, and the John Birch Society. In this particular issue, he says that Senator Barry Goldwater boosts the John Birch Society. In the August 26, 1963, issue, he comes out in favor of the nuclear test ban treaty with the Soviet Union in a headline article entitled "Test Ban: AFL-CIO Boosts It, Right Wing Bombs It." In this article, he attacks Dean Clarence Manion, Young Americans for Freedom, "ultra-right" Harding College, and the Business-Industry Political Action Committee. The August 12, 1963, issue of "Political Memo from COPE" is given over entirely to an attack on Senator Barry Goldwater, and in the September 9, 1963, publication of COPE, he tried to prove that the leaders of the right-wing organizations have some sort of mysterious and secret alliance with a "conspiracy" directed by the John Birch Society.

In issue after issue, he pours out his hate on the anti-Communist and pro-American groups of America, never criticizing nor mentioning the left-wing organizations, such as Fair Play for Cuba, of which Lee Harvey Oswald, the assassin of John F. Kennedy, was a member.

It is apparent that Walter Reuther considers the organized anti-Communist community in the United States his number one enemy. Since the conservative movement is critical of both Communism and those members of the far left who knowingly or unknowingly further the cause of internal or international Communism, Walter Reuther and his far-left crowd have joined the Communists to repudiate and destroy this pro-American influence on American life.

As we have stated earlier, the Communists were so fearful of the powerful Christian conservative emphasis that they called an international meeting of Communists in Moscow in December 1960 to devise ways and means to repudiate anti-Communism around the world, but especially in the United States.

(Every reader of this book should send fifteen

cents to the U.S. Government Printing Office, Washington, D.C., and ask for the vital government publication exposing this Communist program, "The New Drive Against the Anti-Communist Program," based on testimony before a U.S. Senate Committee by the famed anti-Communist authority, Edward Hunter.)

In a recent smear book by two far-left authors, Donald Janson of the *New York Times* (stationed in the *Times'* Kansas City, Missouri, office) and Bernard Eisman of CBS Television (CBS News, New York City), reference was made to a "secret memorandum" by Walter and Victor Reuther, written at the request of President John F. Kennedy and Attorney General Robert Kennedy. The "Reuther Memorandum" was prepared at the behest of the Attorney General, according to this book. The story is as follows: In the fall of 1961, Walter Reuther, president of the United Auto Workers Union and vice-president of the AFL-CIO, was asked by Attorney General Robert Kennedy to write a memorandum on what should be done with the conservatives and anti-Communists in the United States. The memorandum was written by Victor Reuther primarily, but submitted in the name of both Reuther boys to Bobby Kennedy. (Janson and Eisman referred to the memorandum as "a 24 page blueprint for action against extremists.") The memo was submitted on December 19, 1961. Subsequently, the office of the Attorney General, Washington, D.C., printed extra copies of the Reuther memorandum and submitted them to leading "liberal" and far-left Senators and Congressmen in Washington, D.C. (A copy of the full Reuther memorandum can be obtained for fifty cents by writing Christian Crusade,

Tulsa 2, Oklahoma.) As you read this "secret document" you will see liberalism in action with the facade removed. The far left intends to stop the grass-root conservative movements of America with regard to their civil liberties or their civil rights, Suppression of freedom of speech, government coercion and intimidation, all the earmarks of Nazism and Communism, are suggested in this Reuther report as appropriate action against the enemies of the "liberal establishment."

Congressman James B. Utt (Republican-California) has prepared an excellent summary of the Reuther memorandum:

"Now let us examine the recommendations of the Reuther brothers to be used for your own destruction. The first recommendation was that 'the radical right inside the armed forces poses an immediate and special problem requiring immediate and special measures.' Under this heading, he recommended that Secretary McNamara investigate the extent of the radical right in the military. The memorandum claimed that it was widespread pressure from right-wing generals and admirals in the Pentagon which brought about the recall of General James Van Fleet to active duty. What was wrong with General Van Fleet? Simply this, he was a member of the board of 'For America,' he endorsed the Florida Coalition of Patriotic Societies, and he was on the board of advisors of H. L. Hunt's 'Life Lines.' The memorandum complained that all that Van Fleet accomplished was to embarrass Adlai Stevenson by saying that Stevenson was to blame for the U. S. failure to provide air support in the Bay of Pigs invasion, and that General Van Fleet would have fired Stevenson. Had I been President, I would not have fired Adlai Stevenson for the simple reason that I would never have hired him in the first place.

"The number two complaint in the Reuther memorandum was that the Attorney General's list of subversive organizations is lending aid and comfort to the radical right. The memo goes on to state, 'although the radical right poses a far greater danger to the success of this country in its battle against international Communism than does the domestic Communist movement, the latter has been branded subversive by the government and the former (radical right) has not.' The memo goes on to state, 'the list today is almost like a Good Housekeeping seal for the radical right and as long as it exists' (indicating it should be abolished) 'it should not remain one-sided and permitted to work in favor of the radical right.' It is interesting to note that the adjective 'radical' precedes any mention of 'right.' You see, radicalism has always been an offensive word to the American people; and, if the brothers Reuther can implant the word radical in connection with conservatism or right-wing movements, it would prove destructive.

"The memo continued that 'it might be advisable for the Attorney General to announce at this time that he is going to investigate one or more of these organizations with a view of determining whether charges will be filed and hearings held on the question of listing one or more of these organizations. The mere act of indicating that an investigation will be made will certainly bring home to many people something they have never considered — the subversive character of these organizations and the similarity to listed groups on the left.'

Now that is really something. Many of these organizations to which Reuther refers have requested an investigation and I can assure you that if one is held there will be no witness who will take the Fifth Amendment.

"One specific proposal in the memo was that FBI agents infiltrate ultra-conservative organizations to determine whether they should be classified as subversive or not. My dear friends, the FBI does not have to infiltrate these organizations. They have an open invitation to join with any of them.

"The third suggestion was 'The flow of big money to the radical right should be dammed to the extent possible.' You should note that the word 'dammed' is spelled with two m's although their direct intent was to spell it the other way. The proposal further states, 'As funds are a source of power to the radical right, action to dam up these funds may be the quickest way to turn the tide now running in their favor.' At least that is an admission never before heard, that the tide is running in our favor. The memo suggested that tax exemptions be carefully checked and that the list of major donors to the far right be made public and that the Federal Communications Commission check radio and television stations carrying far-right propaganda, but listing the program, 'Know Your Enemy,' emanating from Tucson, would be a good place to start.

"Incidentally, immediately after the memo was circulated, the income tax reports of Walter Knott of Knott's Berry Farm, one of the greatest exponents of free enterprise, and a true patriot, were examined and he was found liable for deductions which he had taken on contributions to support the California Free Enterprise Association. It is amazing how easy it is to deduct money for contributions to the Fund for the Republic and other left-wing organizations which support the socialistic Communist ideology, but when you attempt to educate people on the free enterprise capitalistic system, you are then dispensing political propaganda. When you consider the massive political propaganda spewed forth by the National Education Association, the Rural Electrification outfit, and even the National Council of Churches, the double standard becomes so apparent that a school child would recognize it.

"Skipping one recommendation, I go to the fifth, which was that 'The domestic Communist problems should be put into proper perspective for the American people, thus exposing the basic fallacy of the radical right.'

"Now we come to the real 'meat and potatoes" of what seems to be bothering the liberals, and that is that the director of the FBI, J. Edgar Hoover, 'exaggerates the domestic Communist menace at every turn and contributes to the public's frame of mind upon which the radical right feeds.' The memo further charges that assistant Attorney General J. Walter Yeagley, who continued in charge of internal security matters, has always maximized the domestic Communist menace. 'There is no need,' the memo continued, 'of a further effort to dramatize the Communist issue, the need now is to rein in those who have created the unreasoned fear of the domestic Communist movement in the minds of American people and to slowly develop a more rational attitude toward the strength of this movement.' In other words, the rational attitude which the pseudo-Liberals want is that we should appease and even embrace the international Communist menace. The memo suggests that it would not be well to forbid dissenting officials from expressing a contrary view for fear of the charge that the administration was attempting to muzzle J. Edgar Hoover, but that 'any effort to take a more realistic view of the leaders of this administration would probably cause most of the administration officials to fall in line, and even some legislators might be affected thereby.'

"This, then is the key to the recent attacks upon our patriotic conservatism by some members of the U. S. Senate and some members of the House, and, if you will read these attacks appearing in the Congressional Record, you will be amazed to see how closely they have followed the substance and the language used in the 24-page memo of Victor Reuther."

Proof that the far-left in some places of responsibility is carrying out the Reuther memorandum is the July 26, 1963, release of the Federal Communications Commission, Washington, D. C., entitled "Broadcast Licensees Advised Concerning Stations' Responsibilities under the Fairness Doctrine as to Controversial Issue Programming." The Reuther memorandum suggested that certain anti-Communist organizations be eliminated altogether by Federal force and that radio stations that carry anti-Communist broadcasts, either on a paid or free basis, be the subject of an investigation by the Federal Communications Commission, implying that such stations will have their licenses removed unless their programming meets the approval of the Liberal Establishment.

Since the Reuther memorandum specifically suggests that my movement called Christian Crusade be subject to government action, I feel that we are acting clearly within our right to inform the American people of this "secret action."

It is clear to me that the Reuther memorandum of December 1961 has been implemented in the communique from the Federal Communications Commission dated July 26, 1963. In fact, the very thing that Walter and Victor Reuther called for in 1961 is fulfilled in this July 26 action — that is, the threat of repressive action against radio and television stations that carry "anti-Communist" or "religious" broadcasts. The July 26 communique has been referred to by one station owner as the beginning of the new FCC reign of terror."

Among the "impossible" requests of the July 26 memorandum from the FCC is this: "When a controversial program involves a personal attack upon an individual or organization, the licensee must transmit the text of the broadcast to the person or group attacked, wherever located, either prior to or at the time of the broadcast, with a specific offer of his station's facilities for an adequate response." How on earth is a radio station going to contact every individual and organization mentioned on a "news commentary program" or "news editorial program" prior to the broadcast to offer them equal time? I don't know.

The July 26 "Public Notice" further spells out those to whom the orders are directed — those stations that carry programs designated by the terms "Americanism," "anti-Communism," "states' rights" and *religious*."

Nowhere does the notice mention any possibility that this July 26 memo applies to leftist or socialist-slanted broadcasts. The only program specifically mentioned as being "controversial" are pro-American and/or Christian broadcasts.

Liberals piously maintain that they are not attempting to control freedom of speech, and yet this July 26 memo makes such freedom so difficult and threatening that many radio stations will drop their conservative and anti-Communist programs rather than struggle through the red tape or jeopardize their licenses.

Already the July 26 memo is being enforced. In the *Broadcasting* magazine (the trade publication of the radio and television industry) dated September , 1963, there is an article entitled "Closed Circuit" which reports that at President Kennedy's luncheon with nineteen prominent broadcast station owners August 22 in the White House, he made plain his "deep concern" over use of radio and some television by "right-wing groups." Somehow, all government leaders must understand that radio and television stations are for the use of *all* Americans, whether they are liberal or conservative, and when we deny freedom of spech to one group, it will ultimately mean the abolition of freedom of speech for all independent thinkers and independent Americans, and will be tantamount to an absolute dictatorship.

Furthermore, this issue of *Broadcasting* suggested that the late President Kennedy believed that these groups using the "media," even on a paid time basis, are doing it for political reasons. I would like to take this opportunity to assure the new President of the

United States, the Federal Communications Commission, and every radio station and television station in America which carries my Christian Crusade programs, that my messages are not for political purposes, but are my religious convictions, and to those who have not read it lately, a re-examination of the First Amendment of the Constitution of the United States might be enlightening at this time. The Amendment says: "Congress shall make no law respecting an establishment of religion or prohibiting the free exercise thereof; or abridging the freedom of speech or of the press."

The FCC, the President of the United States, Congress, or anyone else cannot determine what constitutes the Gospel of Jesus Christ or religious dogma. I have the same right to speak out against the admission of Red China to the United Nations or the nuclear test ban treaty or foreign aid to Communist countries, as the National Council of Churches (also a tax-exempt organization) has to speak out in favor of the admission of Red China to the United Nations, the civil rights march in Washington, D. C., to influence legislation, federal aid to education, or any of other dozens of legislative-related subjects on which they have expressed themselves in the name of religion.

Furthermore, it is of great concern to me as a clergyman, to read that the National Council of Churches, according to the June 17, 1963, issue of *Broadcasting*, page 62, has made a proposal to the United States Government, to the FCC Chairman, specifically, for "tighter government control of broadcasting." The June 17 issue of *Broadcasting* editorialized on this by saying: "The general board of the National

Council of Churches, which represents some thirty Protestant and Eastern Orthodox denominations, has thrown its powerful support behind the campaign to impose tighter government controls on television and radio. In these recommendations (by the NCC) are contained all the elements that are needed for complete government control over radio and television programming. Let the government adopt the whole package and it will have deprived broadcasting of the right guaranteed by the First Amendment."

To show you how ridiculous this July 26 release from the FCC is, in the September 2, 1963, issue of *Broadcasting*, page 61, there is an article entitled "Equal Time Request Follows Manion Show." Dean Clarence Manion, former dean of the Law School of Notre Dame University of Indiana, has a news commentary heard on 300 radio stations each Sunday. On one of his broadcasts in August 1963, he discussed the nuclear test ban treaty, which he opposed. An organization calling itself Citizens Committee for a Nuclear Test Ban Treaty, an organization no one has ever heard of before, and which was probably organized for just this project, sent a request to the FCC and the 300 stations that carry Dean Manion's program demanding equal time free of charge, although Dean Manion had *paid* for his time, to deliver a commentary favoring the treaty. Heretofore, this would have been laughed at. However, under the July 26 ruling, this unheard-of organization, demanding equal time to defend a point which Dean Manion opposed, was given free time on most of the 300 stations. Dean Manion did not criticize this organization. He had never heard of this organization. He was talking about the nuclear test ban treaty.

America will become a jungle of confusion and vigilante acts unless this unfair, discriminatory practice and suppression of the freedom of speech is immediately halted by the FCC. There is no end to such a ridiculous policy.

The National Association of Broadcasters again according to *Broadcasting* magazine, dated September 2, has asked the FCC to rescind its July 26 policy statement.

Since Lyndon B. Johnson has assumed the Presidency of the United States, Mr. E. William Henry, Chairman of the Federal Communications Commission, has announced that he will continue to pursue the same policies that he inaugurated under the Kennedy Administration.

Besides Walter Reuther's COPE, as we stated earlier in this chapter, he and his cohorts introduced in 1963 a new "American Gestapo" called Group Research, Inc. The following editorial by the syndicated columnist, Edith Kermit Roosevelt, explains the purpose of Reuther's Group Research. Walter Reuther's program might well be called "blueprint for total federal regimentation and the sovietization of the United States in the 1960's." An informed citizenry can prevent it from becoming a reality. Wrote Miss Roosevelt:

"The name 'Group Research, Inc.' sounded intriguing. I decided to look into it. I have been a reporter for more than a decade but this gave me a new experience.

"Wesley McCune, head of the three-room office, was out. While awaiting his return, I noticed a wall chart. When I began taking notes, the staff of three girls leaped up suspiciously and a young man came from an outer office. The scene ended with me being ordered to leave.

"Next day, I tried again, and met McCune. He gave me a velvety welcome which turned to harsh negatives when I began to ask questions.

"Group Research, Inc. has been quietly operated for more than a year. Only last month, a syndicated newspaper dispatch said the orignization was investigating where and how 'right-wing' groups got their financial backing. An informant told me it specialized in accumulating dossiers on anti-Communists and so-called 'rightists.' When anti-Communists do this, it is called a blacklist.

"My decision to do some researching into Group Research, Inc., was hastened when I was told that its headquarters at room 422, 1404 New York Ave., N. W., (Washington, .D. C.) was crammed with filing cabinets — one of which contained a card about Edith Kermit Roosevelt.

"I wondered why the dossier on me including such details as that I had 'discussed the folly of shipping foreign aid to India.'

"Why should this go into a record in an office listing itself as 'non-profit' and 'educational?"

"I was in eminent company. Also listed are writers, educators and scholars of world renown. Dr. Wilhelm Roepke, who helped guide West Germany's miraculous post-war economic recovery is one. Why? Also anyone who was a sponsor of groups like Young Americans for Freedom, or is listed on the masthead of publications such as *Modern Age*. This academic-type quarterly features contributions by such 'extremists' as Philip E. Mosely, director of studies, Council on Foreign Relations, New York, Msgr. J. M. Lally, editor of *The Pilot*, and Louis L. Gerson, professor of political science at the University of Connecticut.

"Who compiles this 'educational' information? McCune was assistant to Charles F. Brannan when he was Secretary of Agriculture, and later was public information officer of the National Farmers Union.

"Group Research's certificate of incorporation is signed by two Washington attorneys: Daniel M. Singer of 5410 39th St., N. W., and James H. Heller of 3916 Ingomar St., N. W. Heller is secretary of the Washington chapter of the American Civil Liberties Union which vigorously opposes dossiers on pinkos and pro-Reds.

"The chart in this office listed a dozen organizations opposed to Communism, such as the Farm Bureau Federation, the Association of American Physicians and Surgeons, Freedoms Foundation of Valley Forge, American Security Council, American Committee for Aid to Katanga Freedom Fighters, American Enterprise Association, Young Americans for Freedom, Committee Against Summit Entaglement, Harding College, and the Foundation for Economic Freedom.

"Above these names were colored balloons bearing the labels, 'racism,' 'book-burners,' 'bogey of inflation — the balanced budget,' 'pro-military,' anti-Cuban extremists,' 'anti-UNICEF,' 'anti-semitic,' 'anti-medicare,' 'states' rights primitives,' 'censorship,' and 'anti-federal aid to education.'

"As I copied this, the young man came forward. He bluntly asked me to leave. 'We don't want publicity,' he explained. The receptionist, a blonde with an upsweep hairdo, declared, 'This is a private organization. You aren't supposed to take inventory. We told you to leave.'

"I saw fear in her eyes, mingled with hate. Of what? What was there to hide?

"One of the questions I naturally asked McCune was: 'For whom are you compiling these names and data?' I pointed to the 100 filing cabinets and drawers lining the offices. 'That's my business,' he said.

"'Who are the people behind your group?' That's my business,' he said.

"This secretiveness and the smear labels on the chart raised many questions. I thought of the curiously synchronized campaign alleging the wealth of anti-Communist groups, broadly implying that anti-red leaders were raking in huge profits. These smears are false but they dried up many contributions, forcing serious cutbacks in the work of these anti-Communist groups.

"A final question: 'Who pays for "Group Research?' I asked McCune. He said: 'that's my business.'"

"I think it is *my* business — and that of the public!"

So the "smear-bund" of the far-left, with its unlimited funds, pushes its "hate campaign" full speed ahead

CHAPTER VIII

MEN AND MOVEMENTS OF THE FAR LEFT

That America is being led today, for the most part, by a strange breed of individuals who have formed an intellectual, sophisticated cult bent on the destruction of Constitutional Government and orthodox Christianity, there can be little doubt. Often these socialist-minded idealists are referred to as "left-wing liberals," "the liberal establishment," and again as "anti-anti- Communists." Perhaps the best "classic" identification of by these individuals to whom he refers as pseudo-liberals. Mr. Hoover wrote:

In the August 1956 issue of *The Elks Magazine*, J. Edgar Hoover warns of the danger to America posed by these maladjusted individuals to whom he refers as pseudo-liberals. Mr. Hoover wrote:

"The individuals who belong to this cult are not members of the Communist Party. They even deny any sympathy with Communism. But they live in a never-never land. Seemingly ignorant of the existing conspiracy, duped by Communist contacts which they are apparently incapable of recognizing, the pseudo-liberals constantly take off on intellectual flights that inevitably end on an enticing airstrip planned for them by the Communists. Even when the concealed pitfalls on that strip bring each subsequent flight to a disastrous conclusion, the experience apparently holds no lesson. The pseudo-liberals flit off eagerly again to a rarefied stratosphere, and inevitably as before, return to the Communist hangar.

"These misinformed dupes are among the persons who offer blanket opposition to all security programs now in effect and to all that are suggested. They are among the ones who demand removal of all measures designed to eliminate security risks from government. They add their voices to those that rant endlessly at patriotic committees of the Congress whose efforts are dedicated to exposing the conspiracy and to alerting citizens to the danger. These persons indulge in sabotage by semantics — they stigmatize patriotic Americans with the obnoxious term 'informer' when such citizens fulfill their obligations of citizenship by reporting known facts of the evil conspiracy to properly constituted authorities ... Communism is ... they say, simply a political party like the Republican and Democratic Parties. These incredible people profess to find the tyranny of Communism compatible with Christianity and synonymous with academic freedom! Our difficulties today, they proclaim, stem from a myth created out of fear and hysteria. These simple-minded souls would have you believe that this foreign-directed conspiracy, which already has enslaved approximately one-third of the people of the earth, and is resolutely working night and day to bring us to our knees, is a myth! The antics of these vociferous individuals create a smoke-screen which helps to conceal the deadly menace of Communism ..."

This inimical group is also strangly dominant among those voices crying for more and more government spending and more government control over our one within their ranks. Senator Joseph S. Clark, Jr., (Democrat-Pennsylvania), writing in the *Atlantic* lives and property. In fact, this admission comes from *Monthly* said, ". . . a Liberal is here defined as one who believes in utilizing the full force of government for the advancement of social, political and economic justice at the municipal, state, national and international levels." It is these socialist-minded characters who have changed, by usurpation of power, our Constitutional form of government.

In his *Techniques of Communism*, Louis Budenz, former member of the (U.S.) National Committee of the Communist Party, called such dupes by their official Red terminology when he said:

"All groups which the Communist Party is seeking to penetrate are termed 'mass organizations' in Communist parlance, and by Red penetration and eventual control they are to be made into 'transmission belts' for broadening the influence of the Party. In *Foundations of Leninism*, Stalin lays down this use of 'transmission belts' by a centralized, disciplined party as an essential feature of Communist efforts (V. 113).

"The Communists are always aware that they must make all 'mass organizations,' religious, labor, educational, and scientific groups, 'transmission belts' for the Communist line . . . they made great gains in this respect, inducing many organizations, newspapers and other agencies of opinion to forward the Communist line . . ."

Just to quote from Louis Budenz, Benjamin Gitlow, Bella Dodd or other ex-Communists who are now fighting Communism is sufficient to awaken the ire of the left-wing liberals. They found no fault in these people when they were serving America's deadly enemy, but now that they expose their former comrades and the workings of the Communist conspiracy, the left-wing liberals, these anti-anti-Communists, viciously attack them from all sides. Their ridiculous attitudes cannot be explained outside of a satanic influence over their thinking processes.

It is extremely difficult to distinguish between a naive left-winger and a dedicated Communist conspirator. Since ordinarily they stand for the same thing, it is indeed a problem to ascertain their true intention.

In this book we are not accusing the pseudo-liberals and anti-anti-Communists of being *intentionally* pro-Communist or *outright* Communists. But, we are saying that their activities aid and abet the Communist cause. Certainly their fight against Constitutional concepts, orthodox Christianity and dedicated pro-American patriots does not hamper the Communist cause, but instead, helps the Communist cause.

Senator William Fulbright of Arkansas has been one of the most outspoken pseudo-liberal spokesmen against the conservative movement in the United States. In a speech in Fayetteville, Arkansas, on July 23, 1962, Senator Fulbright classed Billy James Hargis, along with Dan Smoot, as "either maladjusted fanatics or cynical exploiters." Again there is the hint that anybody who disagrees with the "Liberal Establishment" is in need of psychiatric care. This is a fundamental belief of the entire Far Left.

For years, the Communist conspirators and the Far Left have seemed to be well aware of the opportunities offered to their cause through the new and enlarged concepts of mental health. In the November 1949 issue of *Masses and Mainstream*, a Communist monthly, Francis H. Bartlett, a psychiatrist, explained "how Capitalism causes neurosis." In the same issue, Joseph Wortis, another psychiatrist who has since invoked the Fifth Amendment, described how "progressive" psychoanalysts deliver public lectures on the "psychological consequences of Capitalism." Dr. Joseph Wortis is the man who introduced shock therapy in America.

During hearings of the House Committee on Un-American Activities in San Francisco, May 13, 1960, an identified Communist by the name of Vernon Brown shouted to the staff director of the federal committee, Richard Arens: "I am of the opinion that you are beginning to sound a little bit like you ought to see a psychiatrist."

On April 9, 1962, Communist leader Benjamin Davis told the students of Upsala College at East Orange, New Jersey, that "the poison of the ultra-right . . . obviously creates a mental insanity that has been demonstrated by the performance of General Walker, Senator John Tower and Senator Strom Thurmond." The Communist *Worker* of April 15, 1962, claimed that this remark that conservatives and anti-Communists were in need of psychiatric help received much applause from the students.

During a speech at Swarthmore College in Pennsylvania, reported in the Communist *Worker* of May 6, 1962, Gus Hall said: "Anti-Communism is a political poison which brings shame to our country in all nations . . . the fact is that anti-Communism creates political and personal insanity."

One famous Protestant clergyman, Dr. George A. Buttrick (former president of the Federal-National Council of Churches) said in his book *Christian Fact and Modern Doubt*: "Probably few people who claim to believe every word of the Bible really mean it. That avowal, held to its last logic, would risk a trip to the insane asylum."

The current "mental health legislation" emphasis of the far left should be carefully investigated. As Dr. Lewis A. Alesen, in his book *Mental Robots*, says: "The mental health program, so called, is particularly disingenuous and disarming because it professes the goal of solving a health problem recognized to a greater or less degree by all, but it cleverly conceals beneath a barrage of beautiful verbiage, a group of most sinister objectives ..."

Undoubtedly, the vast majority of those working in the mental health program at local levels are sincerely working to help the insane and those who really need mental help. We feel that promotion of the new concept and misuse of "mental health" for political purposes is being done by a small minority working behind the scenes, just as is the case in many other areas of the determined assault on freedom by forces of the far left.

Members of the far left cannot tolerate opposing views. This is indicated in a speech by Senator Fulbright at Stanford University on July 28, 1961, when he said:

"The President is hobbled in his task of leading the American people to concerted action by the restrictions of power imposed on him by a constitutional system designed for an Eighteenth Century agrarian society, far removed from the centers of world power. It is imperative that we break out of the intellectual confines of cherished and traditional beliefs, and open our mind to the possibility that basic changes in our system may be essential to meet the requirement of the Twentieth Century ... The North Atlantic nations ...

219

must surrender far more of their jealously guarded sovereignty than they have already done, and press forward with the development of supernational institutions."

In this speech, Senator Fulbright contended that public opinion should be educated in order that the American people would follow the line of thinking he promotes.

In these remarks one can see immediately the vast ideological differences between Senator Fulbright and anti-Communist conservatives. We conservatives know that the Constitution of the United States is not outmoded and that our problem is not a need for more power in the hands of a President. We believe the very opposite. As a nation grows larger and larger there is more and more reason to limit the power in the hands of fallible men, not to increase that power. We contend, in opposition to Senator Fulbright's principles, that the principles of freedom expressed in our Constitution left us by our founding fathers are even more sorely needed today than they were at that time.

From this disagreement with Senator Fulbright on the present-day value of our Constitution and of national sovereignty stems other disagreement which we feel prompted the Senator's harsh attacks on anti-Communists. Senator Fulbright's dim view of the value of our national sovereignty came to life in his maiden speech on the floor of the United States Senate, according to an article by Willard Edwards, Capitol Hill correspondent of the *Chicago Tribune*. This article appeared in the February 3, 1962, issue of *Human Events*. Here, in part, in which Mr. Edwards said about the first Senate speech by the Junior Senator from Arkansas:

"As a freshman Senator, he scorned to obey the rule recommending respectful silence for a period. In his maiden speech March 28, 1945, he lectured his colleagues on internationalism and sovereignty. Americans were confused about sovereignty, he said, and must be ready to sacrifice some of their 'most cherished prejudices' to attain world order."

Mr. Edwards also pointed out that in the same speech Senator Fulbright deplored "unbridled and intemperate attacks" on Russia and Communism. According to Mr. Edwards, Senator Fulbright further said: "The Russian experiment in socialism is scarcely more radical for modern times than was the American Declaration of Independence in the days of George II."

In this *Human Events* article, Mr. Edwards also pointed out that Senator Fulbright "first aroused the attention of the liberal establishment by joining the small minority which voted against continuance of the House Committee on Un-American Activities, then headed by Representative Martin Dies."

Of course, Senator Fulbright's foreign policy views are also at complete odds with those of anti-Communists whom he labels with such attractive names as "irresponsible radicals" or "maladjusted fanatics." The basic reasoning behind his foreign policy views was revealed clearly in a Senate speech on March 6, 1959, in which the Senator contended that "the public opinion of the world will cause the Russian people to relinquish their control of the once-free peoples of Poland, East Germany, Hungary, Czechoslovakia, Latvia, Estonia, Lithuania, Rumania, and Bulgaria."

Can you imagine a statement based on a more total ignorance of the Communist conspiracy than this statement? In the first place, it is not the *Russian people* who have control of these enslaved nations; it is the Communist dictatorship, Nikita Khrushchev and his associates. In the next place, public opinion of the world means nothing to these satanic conspirators and anyone who contends otherwise is void of knowledge about the Communist conspiracy. The only thing which the Communists respect is determined opposition; that is all that will cause them to back down in any given situation.

Another statement which vividly demonstrated Senator Fulbright's complete ignorance of the Communist conspiracy was contained in an article he wrote in 1946 that was included in a book entitled *Assignment in Exposition*. This book was written by Louise E. Roabacher, and was published by Harper and Brothers especially for college students. In the chapter called "The Price of Peace is the Loss of Prejudices," Senator Fulbright stated:

"Another powerful prejudice which has affected our policy is our fear of Russia and Communism ... Until the revolution in Russia we had always been on friendly terms with that nation. We had never fought her. Yet, after the revolution was established by Lenin, we refused to recognize Russia until 1933 . . . I do not believe that the Soviets desire to dominate the world as the Germans did. They have given no evidence that they believe they are supermen ... I can see no reason why we cannot get along peaceably . . . "

In view of this evidence, it is no wonder that Senator Fulbright insisted in his famous "Memorandum" that military officers be gagged from making public statements on the evils of the Communist conspiracy. It would appear that he sees little evil in this satanic conspiracy.

In an article in the January 1962 issue of the *American Legion Magazine,* Irene Corbally Kuhn contended, "The harm that Fulbright has done with his memo denigrating the military is incalculable..."

Of course, the Communist conspiracy took a brighter view of the Senator's memorandum, advocating muzzling of the military. The Communist *Worker* of August 27, 1961, devoted a headline article on page five to the Senator's memo. This article was entitled, "Senator Fulbright's Memo Exposing Ties of Military Chiefs to the Ultra-Right." In this article they gave lengthy quotes from the Senate speech by Senator Fulbright, defending his memo and attacking anti-Communists.

A *highly respected* leader of the far left who has been identified many times before federal committees as an outright Communist is Dr. Harry F. Ward, who for twenty years was professor of "Christian Ethics" at the Union Theological Seminary and is the "father" of the National Council of the Churches of Christ and the Methodist Federation for Social Service.

The National Council of Churches came into existence through a series of events that began in 1907. It was the outgrowth of an organization of socialist clergymen called "The Methodist Federation for Social Service," which had been organized in 1907. In a Congressional document entitled "Investigation of Communist Activities in the New York City Area," dated July 7,

1953, we read concerning this organization of Dr. Ward: "The Methodist Federation for Social Service was organized by a group of socialist, Marxist clergymen of the Methodist Church headed by Dr. Harry F. Ward, twelve years before the organization of the Communist Party of the United States in 1919."

This was the first "united-front" effort of the Communists to organize the clergy of the United States in a socialistic revolution. Dr. Ward was the champion of this "social gospel" cause. On May 21, 1946, on a broadcast, Dr. Ward stated: "The Soviet Union is progressing and growing up economically and politically since the time of the Czars, while capitalist society is starving and going down."

Out of the Methodist Federation for Social Service came the National Council of Churches, then called the Federal Council of the Churches of Christ in America, in 1908. (In a constituting convention held in Cleveland, Ohio, November 28 - December 1, 1950, the name Federal Council of Churches was changed to "National Council of Churches of Christ in the United States"; in 1948 in Amsterdam, The Netherlands, the Federal Council of Churches further broadened its activities on a world scale by establishing the World Council of Churches.)

In recent years there have been several well-documented books and articles, including the now-famous "Air Reserve Center Training Manual" issued by the Air Force in 1959 which contained a section partially based on my writings entitled "Communism and Religion." I have written a book detailing Communist infiltration of churches called *The Facts About Commu-*

nism and our Churches.)

Because of this public attention focused on many pronouncements of the National Council of Churches which strangely parallel the Communist Party line, in true "Reuther style", the religious hierarchy that leads the group began defending its organization by defaming the character of its opponents. Even the Communist Party itself has rushed to the defense of the National Council of Churches time and again when exposures of the socialistic-minded ecumenical group were printed. After the release of the now-famous Air Reserve Center Training Manual, which contained many documented criticisms of the National Council of Churches, the Communist *Worker* on February 28, 1960, carried a page-four headline article entitled "Army Attack on Clergy Traced to Pro-Fascists." Of course, as we have pointed out before, anyone or any organization opposing Communism is Fascist or pro-Fascist to them, so when Communists say pro-Fascist, they actually mean anti-Communist.

This February 28, 1960, *Worker* article told the Communist conspirators that these pro-Fascists were "parties to a plot to destroy the National Council of Churches" and that the House Committee on Un-American Activities, which the Communists called a "House Un-American Committee," was active in the plot. In this article defending the National Council of Churches, the Communists viciously attacked Air Force officials. Here is what the *Worker* article said: "These arrogant characters ... were happy to have the clergy smeared with a phony Communist label. Like the rest of the Pentagon, they are afraid of what many pastors are saying about the need of H-Bomb bans, disarmament, peace ..." This same Communist article branded me as "a pro-Fascist evangelist who heads an outfit called Christian Crusade." Two weeks later in the March 13, 1960 issue, the Communists devoted an entire article to smearing me. In this article, they called Billy James Hargis a "Red baiter from way back." Since that time, Christian Crusade and Hargis have been attacked from time to time by the Communist *Worker*.We were attacked in feature articles during January and February of 1962. However, it is interesting to note that we were never attacked in the pages of the Communist *Worker* until we criticized the National Council of Churches of Christ.

Many of the far-left publications, in their attempt to defend the National Council of Churches from these truth charges, went way out on a limb. For instance, in an article which appeared in the "slightly biased" *Look* magazine of April 24, 1962, written by Louis Cassels of the Associated Press staff, entitled "The Rightist Crisis in our Churches," Cassels attacks the anti-Communists whom he characterizes as "radicals of the right." Then he attempted to use Mr. J. Edgar Hoover and the FBI as a smoke-screen to cover the provable facts regarding the pro-Communist activities of clergymen in the National Council of Churches hierarchy. Mr. Cassels certainly implied in his article that Mr. Hoover had given a clean bill of health to the National Council of Churches. However, this is not true.

During the summer of 1961, a Tulsa, Oklahoma, patriot, Mrs. Margaret West, wrote Mr. Hoover in regard to an inference made on a local television program by a local spokesman for the National Council of

Churches, Rev. David O. Reece. According to Mrs. West and others who saw this television program, the Rev. Mr. Reece inferred that the FBI had cleared the National Council of Churches of charges made in the Air Force Manual. Mr. Hoover answered Mrs. West's letter on July 8, 1961, as follows:

"I would like to point out that the FBI does not issue clearances of any kind. There was no specific investigation made in connection with the subject of your inquiry. Any remarks by a representative of this Bureau should not be interpreted as a defense or endorsement of any group, since this is not a proper function of the FBI."

Mr. Hoover is on record concerning Communist infiltration of religious groups. For example, in the *Redbook* magazine of February 1949, there was an article by Mr. J. Edgar Hoover entitled "God Or Chaos?" This article deals with Communist efforts to use American religious groups. In this article, Mr. Hoover said:

"Many Communist fronts have operated under the guise of some church commission or religious body. It is ghastly to see the monster, atheism, being nourished in the churches which it seeks to destroy. Church leaders can stop this nefarious infiltration by taking vigorous action in the boards and commissions under church supervision. Individual ministers and church members can avoid being hoodwinked if they will stay close to the fundamentals of their faith."

One of the most ridiculous lines of argument used by those apologizing for the National Council of Churches is a contention that those exposing the dangerous left-wing activities of high-ranking clergymen are the ones who are helping the Communists. Mr. Cassels makes this oft-repeated claim at the end of his article, and he uses as evidence a generalized statement which he attributes to an anonymous FBI official.

The clearest expression of this unfounded claim was made by Dr. Roy G. Ross, General Secretary of the National Council of Churches. This remark was published in a pamphlet put out in 1960 entitled "What About the National Council of Churches?" Dr. Ross had this to say about those who have exposed harmful left-wing activities and influence in the National Council:

"Among the loudest, if unconscious, supporters of Communism in America today are a handful of hate-mongering, dissident persons who are devoting their lives to the undermining of the churches and their regularly constituted agencies... Those who would destroy our churches and weaken our democratic society, to the delight of Communists everywhere, persist in spreading their poison..."

The Communist conspirators themselves explode this type of asinine claim through their vigorous support of left-wing clergymen and their left-wing activities. Obviously, such activities are of much aid and comfort to the Communists. For example, large headlines at the top of the front page of the Communist *Worker* of April 8, 1962, read "500 Church Leaders Bid Gov't Halt Arms Race."

One quote from this statement should provide ample reason for the Communist conspirators seeing fit to grant it favorable front-page billing. Among other things, these left-wing clergymen said, "We plead with the leader of our government not to persist in piling up nuclear arms even if other nations are not prepared to agree on the same course, but to formulate and call on our people to support programs of unilateral withdrawal from the nuclear arms race ..." This is simply a call for the government leaders in our nation to render our nation helpless before a surrender ultimatum by Khrushchev or his successor.

Among the signers of the dangerous, surrender-type statement are well-known names in the modernistic theological field such as George A. Buttrick of Harvard University, Herbert Gezork, president of Andover-Newton Theological Seminary, and Rev. Martin Luther King (*Time* magazine's "Man of the Year" — 1963). *The Worker* only listed a few of the names. Undoubtedly, a thorough check of the 500 signers would reveal many from National Council affiliated denominations.

The March 13, 1962, Communist *Worker* granted one of its front-page headlines to a letter issued by the General Council of the United Presbyterian Church. This letter was a vicious attack on anti-Communists and obviously it was highly pleasing to the Communist conspirator. The article in the March 13 *Worker* was headlined "PRESBYTERIAN COUNCIL WARNS AGAINST BIRCHITES." The article stated:

"The General Council of the United Presbyterian Church warned its 3.2 million members last Thursday that the ultra-reactionaries, such as the John Birchites, were boring from within the church to disrupt and divide its congregation in the name of anti-Communism.

"The 52-members of the Presbyterian church's highest national administrative body charged that its ministers, officers and the members were being threatened by these virulent reactionaries. The Presbyterian leaders . . . called on their co-religionists not to be duped by 'a campaign of anti-Communism based on a distrust of our free American institutions.' "

The Worker of March 11, 1962, contained a favorable article on page two in regard to the booklet attacking anti-Communists which was written by Rev. John F. Cronin of the National Catholic Welfare Conference. Communist conspirators seemed especially pleased with the ridiculous remark in this booklet that "extremists of the right" are fomenting a "violent form of disunity that is weakening the nation." (Louis Cassels' article in the April 24, 1962, *Look* magazine used the Presbyterian letter and the Cronin booklet to back up his attempt to discredit patriots who are fighting for the survival of this nation. It is quite strange that the Communist conspirators also take such a favorable interest in both of these documents, instead of avoiding them or attacking them as something harmful to the Communist cause.)

In the May 28, 1961 *Worker*, the Communist conspirators complained about those who engage in "vilification of the National Council of Churches as 'Communist led.' " Further down in this same article, the Communists again defended appeasement policies of the National Council of Churches. They said:

" . . . the National Council of Churches has endeavored to further peaceful co-existence and peace on earth . . ."

This completely unfounded claim that those opposing left-wing activities of Protestant clergymen are really the ones who are helping the Communists was used widely by National Council apologists in defending the Council against facts in the Air Force Manual.

In 1963, in fact, immediately prior to the assassination of John F. Kennedy on November 22, 1963, a false statement was issued by the "Joint Commission on Ecumenical Relations of the Episcopal Church" which said: "After consulting with the House Un-American Activities Committee and the FBI, the Committee could find no substantiation to the charges of 'Communism among leadership of the National Council of Churches' and charged the purveyors of such unfounded rumors are irresponsible." (You will notice that this Episcopal Committee used the Communist terminology "House Un-American Activities Committee" instead of referring to this Congressional group by its proper name, House Committee on Un-American Activities.)

On October 23, 1963, the Director of the House Committee on Un-American Activities, Mr. Francis J. MacNamara, whote an inquirer: "The Committee staff members did not 'clear the National Council of Churches and its leaders of all Communist line support activity.' They did not have the authority to do so. Committee findings pro or con, on any individual or group, are made only in its officially published reports." This letter from Mr. MacNamara states that representatives of the Episcopal Joint Committee had completely misrepresented the House Committee on Un-American Activities. In fact, the House Committee on Un-American Activities is on record opposing certain leaders of the National Council of Churches:

"Thus far of the leadership of the National Council

of Churches of Christ in America, we have found over 100 persons in leadership capacity with either Communist front records or records of service to Communist causes. The aggregate affiliations of the leadership is now, according to our latest count, into the thousands and we have yet to complete our check which would certainly suggest on the basis of the authoritative sources of this Committee that the statement that there is infiltration of fellow travelers in churches ... is a complete understatement." (Government document: "Issues Presented by Air Reserve Center Training Manual," February 25, 1960, page 1303.)

The *Tulsa Sunday World*, December 18, 1960, exposed the "world government" dream of the National Council of Churches in an editorial entitled "Are Churchmen Burying Us?":

"The National Council of Churches is the nation's largest Christian organization. Its membership is made up of representatives from 33 Protestant and Orthodox denominations.

"The Council met last week in San Francisco, and we are impelled to the conclusion that a more weak-kneed, ill-advised and faithless conclave it would be impossible to imagine.

"As a result of actions taken by the Council we believe every American church member who hasn't the time or the inclination to read his daily newspaper, or assimilate the meaning of the things that are going on around him, ought *at this very moment* to commune with his preacher and the leadership of his church — not to seek guidance but to *offer* guidance!

"Why do we feel so strongly on this?

"Well, first we'll quote from an Associated Press report on the Council meeting:

" 'The United States may soon have to subordinate its will to that of the United Nations. Citizens must be prepared to take it.'

"Now, let's quote from a resolution on the subject of U.S. subordination which was *adopted* by the Council membership:

" 'We believe citizens should prepare themselves for such eventuality. It would not then be an undue shock to public opinion, since people would have a more mature view, better able to interpret democracy at work on a world scale, with the benefit as well as the risk that the extension of democracy always entails.'

"There it is, in a nutshell — the United States in the process of being sold down the river by some of its highest, most respected churchmen.

"We can scarcely believe it. We cannot understand by what process some of the finest brains in all of Christianity have become so confused, so soft, that they would subvert this nation to the will of the polyglot that makes up the United Nations. We are asked to surrender ourselves, our freedoms, our dreams, to the will of non-believers, to ignoramuses barely emerging from the Dark Ages, and to despots who speak loudly before the assemblage of nations we call the UN.

"Surely the religious leaders of this nation cannot believe that to submit to United Nations omnipotence is the 'mature' thing to do, or that the majority of the UN represents 'democracy' at work.

"Are 200 years of faith and work and hope to be sacrificed before the altar of nations who have been unable to duplicate the masterworks that are the possession of the people of the United States? What have we been fighting for? The things we have achieved through our work and prayers — are they no longer considered important enough to preserve? Is it no longer fashionable to be free and American? Is it no longer Christian to hold fast to the sovereignity of one home, one nation, one God?

"To the National Council of Churches, we direct a sincere question:

"Is the 'Brotherhood of Man,' in 'One World,' within the capacity of human beings to achieve?

"Let us, for God's sake, be realists!"

St. Mark's Episcopal Church in Shreveport, Louisiana, appointed a Committee to study the National Council of Churches at a June 1960 meeting. After about a ten-month study this committee released a lengthy, fully documented report. Among the conclusions of this report was the following: " . . .we conclude with firm conviction and only after long study and prayer, that the National Council of Churches, as it is presently constituted and operated, is a harmful and highly dangerous institution." As a result of this report the Vestry of the Church adopted a resolution at their April 2, 1961, meeting calling for the Protestant Episcopal Church to withdraw from the National Council. The *Shreveport Times* reported fully on this important opposition from within the National Council, but it was given little attention by national left-slanted papers.

There are ten "major Communist Party objectives" which are promoted by the National Council of Churches:

MEN AND MOVEMENTS OF THE FAR LEFT

1. That the United States recognize Red China and that Red China be admitted to the United Nations.

2. That the United States suspend atomic tests, unilaterally if necessary, indefinitely.

3. That the United States throw itself at the mercy of the World Court of the United Nations.

4. That a purely national concept of security is wrong from every point of view.

5. That the concept of nuclear retaliation or preventive war is contrary to Christian principles.

6. That the United States abolish universal military training.

7. That the United States subordinate its will to the majority decisions of the United Nations.

8. That the United States abandon our military alliances with our allies such as SEATO.

9. That the House Committee on Un-American Activities should be curbed and even dissolved.

10. That the Congress of the United States repeal the McCarran Immigration Act, which restricts flow of immigrants and constitutes our first line of defense.

In 1949 the late Reuben H. Markham tried to awaken the Protestant churches concerning the way Communism is trying to destroy our American churches, in a book entitled *Let Us Protestants Awake!*. He said:

"Communism debases some churches by using them as its political instruments, in the manner of many tyrants during the last 2,000 years. Whenever a church allows itself to be used by imperialistic, atheistic materialists who scorn all religion and ridicule every sort of belief in God, such a church is worse than useless. There are a number of such cases in Russia and Eastern Europe.

"Secondly, Communists, by a carefully worked out strategy, try to infiltrate into churches and turn one against another, as Protestants against Catholics or Orthodox against Uniats or Hussites against Lutherans.

"Thirdly, Communists, after debasing some churches and weakening others through fear and dissension, crush all that dare show resistance. Communists have persecuted more Christians, destroyed more churches, arrested more priests and preachers and terrorized more laymen than any type of government anywhere in modern times — not excluding Nazis, Fascists or non-Christian Oriental rulers. And this persecution of Christians is increasing now in many lands."

Earlier in this book on the "Far Left," we mentioned that the Communists featured the apostate Methodist clergyman who has been identified as a Communist, Dr. Henry F. Ward, as their speaker at a Communist rally in New iork City on Saturday, September 28, 1961, at St. Nicholas Arena. In six appearances before federal investigating committees, ex-Communists identified Dr. Harry F. Ward as a "card-carrying Communist." In spite of this, many of the leaders of the National Council of Churches refused to "turn their backs" on Dr. Ward. In fact, on October 15, 1963, a birthday party was held at Carnegie Hall, New York City, to honor Dr. Harry F. Ward. Such famous clergymen, leaders of the National Council of Churches, as Dr. John Bennett (the new president of Union Theological Seminary, New York City, where Dr. Ward taught for twenty-five years), Bishop James Baker, Bishop John Wesley Lord, Dr. John A. MacKay

(Presbyterian leader who has long urged diplomatic recognition of Red China by the United States and the entrance of Red China into the United Nations), Bishop Walter Mitchell, Bishop Edgar A. Love, Rev. Henry Hitt Crane, Rev. Edward L. Peet, Dr. Ralph Sockman (Methodist clergyman of New York City who has broadcast over NBC Radio free for over twenty years each Sunday), and many, many others were among the sponsors.

The Worker, Communist publication of October 15, 1963, stated, concerning Dr. Ward: "Dr. Ward is a link between the Christian Socialist preachers of the late Nineteenth Century, who sought to end the church's neutrality in the class struggle (or subservients to the Capitalists) and the pastors of the Twentieth Century, who have joined in humanity's struggle for peace and a decent life of brotherhood. Many Christian ministers who cast their lot with mankind were inspired and taught by Dr. Ward. He mobilized the churches in support of the Unionists. He helped set up the American Civil Liberties Union in 1920, becoming its first chairman. He became a firm advocate of friendship with the Soviet Union. We're going to be at Carnegie Hall this Tuesday evening, October 15, to wish this grand man many more birthdays. We (the Communists) are sure we will see you there."

When you see our Protestant leaders honoring a known Communist in such a way, it is extremely discouraging then to read in the October 20, 1963, issue of *The Worker* that the "International Convention of the Christian Churches (Disciples of Christ) is deserving of the highest praise by all democratic Americans for warning its two million members against the ultra-rightists who use anti-Communism to carry out their reactionary aims. But, the church leaders did more than warn the members of their congregation. They issued a document telling them how to identify these enemies of the people." It is difficult to imagine a Protestant denomination with some two million members not even mentioning the danger of Communism externally or internally at their national convention, but instead, con-concentrating on upholding and carrying out the main objective of the Communist Party, U.S.A., at this time—that is the destruction of the anti-Communist movements.

A question for the National Council of Churches of Christ and their followers to consider at this time is: "How long do you think you can continue to condemn the ultra-right as hate-mongers before the American public finally recognizes it for what it is, namely the Communist Party line?"

Edward Hunter, the expert on psychological warfare, wrote in December 1963, "A nationwide squeeze-play has been organized against those who believe in traditional American principles and who are anti-Communists. A blacklisting enterprise has been set up in Washington, D.C., for this purpose (Group Research Institute) with tentacles extending nationally and with the co-operation of the Administration in power in Washington. The 'black and gray' clandestine tactics that I helped develop in World War II for use against the enemies of the United States, are being used nowadays against the American people and the Congress."

One of the leaders of this "squeeze-play" in the

238

United States is one Gordon Hall. Earlier in this book we quoted from Hilaire du Berrier, who said that one of the major television networks interviewed Gordon Hall within minutes after the apprehension of Lee Harvey Oswald. Hall tried to "pooh-pooh" Oswald's Communist connections and shift the blame to the anti-Communist conservatives. In recent weeks, the *Saturday Evening Post* has done a complimentary feature on the activities of this "character."

Mr. Hall uses many aliases as he goes around the country fighting the anti-Communist leaders and movements. The original smear artist of the far left was John Roy Carlson, author of the libelous book, *Undercover*, which viciously smeared many good American patriots. In fact, Gordon Hall worked for a few months for the same outfit that financed John Roy Carlson in his full-time defamation activities. This Gestapo-like "smear-bund" was called Friends of Democracy, run by Rex Stout, former editor of the Communist publication, *New Masses*, and by the so-called "Rev." Leon M. Birkhead. Gordon Hall was employed as an "underground agent" for this smear-bund. At times he would pose as a violent anti-semitic distributing anti-semitic literature to outspoken patriots with the hope that he could trap the patriot into some "anti-semitic" remark which he could use against him. Of course, the Communists have long tried to stir up race hatred and "civil war" among the Jews, Protestants and Catholics. No character is more slimy than the "agent provocateur" who stirs up this hatred specifically for the purpose of being able to accuse others of having yielded to it.

In recent years, Gordon Hall has gone around the

country speaking before church groups, P.T.A. groups, civic clubs, etc., where he spews his subtle but deadly poison. Often he begins by announcing that he is vigorously opposed to Communism, but insisting that we must not allow our fear of Communism, which is of little consequence internally anyhow, to cause us to listen to people who, in fighting Communism, will do more damage to our ideals and our democracy than would the Communists themselves.

According to the records, this professional "hate-monger" was born in Queens County, New York City, on December 9, 1921. His education consisted of grammar school and uncompleted high school. He served in the Air Force during World War II and in 1946 went to work for "Friends of Democracy." However, he was actually discharged from the U.S. Air Force in November of 1945 and was employed by Grumman Aircraft Company between his discharge and his employment in December of 1946 by Rev. Birkhead. The records of Grumman Aircraft Company show Hall as "discharged because of anti-minority agitation."

Some of the aliases that Hall uses are G. D. Hill and Gordon Walker. According to the records, Hall was associated with the Anamist Party (National Renaissance Party). Among his associates in this party were James H. Madole, Charles R. Allen, Jr., and Vladimar Stepankowsky. Stepankowsky, formerly editor of a Communist paper in London, was expelled from several European countries for Communist activities and was identified as a Soviet agent by Elizabeth Bentley, who further advised that Stepankowsky was on the payroll of the notorious spy chief, Jacob Golas. Charles R. Allen,

Jr., has a long history of Communist front affiliations. (See *Strategy and Tactics of World Communism*, U. S. Senate Internal Security Subcommittee, pages 1173, 1180, 1184.)

Allen and Hall at one time published a pamphlet called *Countertide* out of Boston (it lasted seven issues) which attacked Senator Karl Mundt, former President Herbert Hoover, and Fulton Lewis, Jr., known anti-Communist leaders.

The Anamist Party, led by Gordon Hall, Charles R. Allen, Jr., and Stepankowsky, held meetings in a hotel on West 46th Street, New York City. This group distributed violently anti-semitic literature. Among the patriots this group attacked were Congressman Cox, Senator W. Lee O'Daniel, and ex-Chairman Wood of the House Committee on Un-American Activities.

According to the *Boston City Reporter* of June 1950, Hall was appointed executive director of the Francis Sweeny committee. In this capacity he would gather information on anti-Communist leaders and movements and deliver them to such men as Gordon Allport, who has a record of over a dozen affiliations with Communist fronts, and Max Lerner, who has a record of over three dozen affiliations with Communist fronts, and these "educators" helped Gordon Hall gather more facts.

In a feature article in the *Christian Science Monitor*, written by Robert P. Hey during 1961, the author quotes Hall as stating that he has collected information on 1,000 organizations, generally classified as members of the "ultra-right." His attacks on the anti-Communists and the right-wing movements have been consistent. But, occasionally, he attacks "fundamentalist church groups," I suppose for the fun of it. The *Boston University News* of October 9, 1962, reported: "Gordon Hall, famed hate expert, spoke on hate groups and the U.N. First, he mentioned the American fundamentalists who have called the U. N. an atheist and pagan organization because it does not mention the name of Jesus in prayers." In this attack, Hall indicted millions of dedicated Christians who do not care for the United Nations. However, the fallacy of his statement is apparent since the United Nations does not have prayers at all.

Mr. Hall's attacks against anti-Communist movements are numerous. He was quoted in the *Boston University News*, October 9, 1962, as having accused Robert Welch of the John Birch Society of inspiring white women in New Orleans to spit in the faces of Negroes. According to the *Christian Science Monitor*, December 6, 1961, he said the John Birch Society "is not really conservative or anti-Communist," but shares the techniques of the Communist, Fascist, and Nazi tyrannies. According to the *Manchester Union Leader*, September 8, 1961, he told the *Harvard Crimson* in 1952 that Bill Buckley, publisher of the *National Review*, "is even more Fascist than he is cracked up to be." In a lecture before a group at the Y.W.C.A., Detroit, Michigan, on March 18, 1954, Hall stated that the Daughters of the American Revolution (DAR) have been wrong on every issue since the beginning of time and he said that the American Legion are "dupes" and further stated that Senator Joe McCarthy helped Communism, as do those who support him. According to public records, Gordon Hall has attacked the following: American Legion,

Daughters of the American Revolution, Dean Clarence Manion, American Council of Christian Churches, United States Day Committee, House Committee on Un-American Activities, Fulton Lewis, Jr., Senator Barry Goldwater, General Edwin A. Walker, former President Herbert Hoover, Dr. Carl McIntire, Young Americans for Freedom, the film "Operation Abolition," Billy James Hargis, etc., etc.

Frank A. Capell, editor, *The Herald of Freedom*, New York City, says of Gordon Hall, he is a "self-confessed espionage agent for 'one of the most vicious Communist organizations ever set up in this country,' associate of Communist fronters; pupil of Communist fronter educators . . . a rabble-rouser, a hate monger, an irresponsible opportunist who attacks patriots, anti-Communists, veterans, Christian religions, Congressional Committees, Senators, Congressmen, even the American Legion, DAR and YAF, all dedicated to the preservation of our country and it's freedom. By attempting to stir up hatred, to set group against group, by smearing anti-Communists, by creating fear, by character assassination, by failure to concentrate on the true enemy of our country, Gordon B. Hall is serving the internal Communist conspiracy."

When speaking of smear artists in the United States, we have to give attention to Drew Pearson, the trigger man for the far left. Whenever Drew Pearson begins attacking a man or movement in his column, look out. The sky is about to fall in. The first evidence that Christian Crusade had of impending smear by the Communists was a series of attacks on us in the columns of Drew Pearson. Immediately following the Pearson series, every Communist publication in the world began its attacks on Christian Crusade.

Senator Joseph McCarthy exposed Pearson's pro-Communist associates in a speech on December 15, 1950, which appears in the Congressional Record. He said: "Only a man as diabolically clever as Pearson could continue to maintain his huge reading and listening audience after being so completely and thoroughly labeled an unprincipled liar and a fake... The heads of any of our intelligence agencies will testify that one of the principal aims of the Communist Party is to gain control of our lines of communication; that is newspapers, radio, television, motion pictures, and so forth. It, of course, would be a miracle if they had not recognized in Pearson the ideal man for them... an unprincipled, greedy, degenerate liar — but with a tremendous audience both in newspapers and on the air waves — a man who has been able to sugar-coat his wares so well that he has been able to fool vast numbers of people with his fake piety and his false loyalty.

"Pearson has long had working for him — part of the time officially on his payroll, and part of the time in a slightly different status — one David Karr. The relationship is such that it is difficult to know who is the master and who is the servant. I may say that just what his status is, is difficult to know, except that they are still working together today. (This speech was delivered in 1950. We have no way of knowing if Karr is still associated with Pearson.) I will give you a picture of this man David Karr. Let me quote Martin Dies, head of the Un-American Activities Committee, on page 512 of the Congressional Record for February 1, 1943.

This link between Pearson and Karr is the important link: 'Here is the case of David Karr who is Assistant Chief of the Foreign Language Division of the Office on War Information at a salary of $4,600 (that was Lattimore's Division). For two years, Karr was on the staff of the Communist Party's official newspaper, *The Daily Worker*. There is not the slightest doubt that all members of *The Daily Worker* staff were required to be members of the Communist Party. Karr was a writer for the Communist-front publication, *Equality*, whose editorial council was composed largely of well-known Communists and Communist fellow travelers. David Karr was also public-relations director of the American League for Peace and Democracy, one of the Communist fronts which Attorney General Biddle branded as subversive. Karr was a frequent writer for the league's magazine, *Fight*.'

"I also quote from a statement made by Congressman Dondero on the floor of the House, page 9702 of the Congressional Record of October 10, 1945: 'The ink was hardly dry on the Japanese surrender when a barrage of vilification and slander was launched against General MacArthur, led by the Communist *Daily Worker*, *PM*, and Drew Pearson, who is the voice of David Karr formerly with *The Daily Worker*. For more information on this subject, I refer you to the story in the *Washington Daily News* of October 8, 1945. Even Dean Acheson, our own Acting-Secretary of State, participated in this hue and cry, and it was echoed in London by Soviet Commissar Molotov. It has reached a climax in the Russian proposal to hamstring MacArthur with a four-power control board, the fruition of a well-synchronized and thought-out plan to sacrifice American interests to those of the Soviet Union.'"

Now, comes the summary of Senator McCarthy's lengthy report on Drew Pearson: "I have discussed this man Pearson with practically every former member of the Communist Party whom I have met during my recent and present investigation of Communists in Government. Almost to a man, they were agreed on a number of things — No. 1: That Pearson's all-important job, which he did for the party without fail, under the directions of David Karr, was to lead the character assassination of any man who was a threat to international Communism. No. 2: That he did that job so well that he was the most valuable of all radio commentators and writers from the standpoint of the Communist Party. No. 3: In order to maintain his value, it was necessary that he occassionally throw pebbles at Communism and Communists generally, so as to have a false reputation of being anti-Communist.

"It appears that Pearson never actually signed up as a member of the Communist Party and never paid dues. However, that has not in any way affected his value to the party; nor has it affected his willingness to follow the orders of David Karr, who, of course, is a most active member of the Party, and who carries instructions and orders to Pearson.

"I ask those who are skeptical as to whether Pearson actually has been doing a job for the Communist Party to stop and review Pearson's record over the past ten years. You will find that he has always gone all-out to attack anyone who is attempting to expose individual and dangerous Communists, while at the same time he goes through the fakery of criticizing Communism and Communists generally. The heads of the House Committee on Un-American Activities have always been targets. You will find also that he has always consistently and without fail launched a campaign of personal smear and vilification against any man in public life who has stood against any plan of socialism in this country . . ."

Among the men that Drew Pearson helped smear and destroy in American minds were Senator Joseph McCarthy, General Douglas MacArthur, Chiang Kai-shek, and James Forrestal. Since Pearson has now turned his guns on me and my movement, I am encouraged at the success Christian Crusade must be having in the fight against Communism, and I am honored to be singled out with the others whose names I have mentioned for attack by this slimy character assassin.

Propaganda and psychological warfare operations of the Communist conspiracy are done by experts. Only know-how by dedicated, conservative patriots can counteract this and save our free society. Present events underline the great need.

CHAPTER IX

MANIPULATION OF PUBLIC OPINION
BY THE FAR LEFT

Men and movements of the far left are engaged in an indisputable psychological warfare effort, directed against the anti-Communist and conservative patriots of the United States. The Liberal Establishment has used the hideous assassination of John F. Kennedy as a weapon for the destruction of old-fashioned American-ism and the grass-roots anti-Communist movements in this country, but the American people and their Congress have become their real target. Actually this effort is aimed at all who believe in our Constitutional check-and-balance system of government and who do not want to be ruled by dictatorship of the self-proclaimed "elite." If we, as a people, come to believe that Communism is not a deadly peril right here or anywhere else it exists in the world, the United States of America will have to pay the same price that John F. Kennedy did. Prior to the assassination of Mr. Kennedy, we already were being successfully conditioned into acceptance of this delusion — that Communism is no menace here in America. The consequences of our stubborn refusal to combat this evil internally could be more tragic than what happened at Dallas.

Since this is a battle for men's minds, the far left is determined to manipulate public opinion in order to socialize the American economy and throw this government into a world government state.

Perhaps the most influential of the far-left organizations is the Americans for Democratic Action (ADA). Senator Barry Goldwater called upon President Kennedy, prior to his death, to "purge his own Administration" of the members of the ADA. He referred to the ADA members who had infiltrated the Administration: "The extremist groups of the left are far more dangerous than those of the right."

The Americans for Democratic Action was born in the Willard Hotel during April 1947 in Washington, D.C. Among those involved in the founding of the ADA was Senator Hubert H. Humphrey, who was Mayor of Minneapolis, Minnesota, at that time. Humphrey described the ADA's aim as "militant political action from the grass roots right through to the national level without turning into a third party movement."

On June 2, 1954, the late Congressman Kit Clardy of Michigan made a speech on the floor of the House of Representatives regarding the Americans for Democratic Action, which he called a "Trojan Horse." Mr. Clardy said that in his opinion the ADA had probably done more than any other group in the nation to "foster and promote many of the aims of the Communist Party" while "loudly protesting that it was anti-Communist."

In an analytical examination of the ADA, Mr. Clardy revealed that:

"... They fought against the adoption of the Subversive Control Act, calling it a dangerous and futile attempt to repress the Communists, as though repressing Communists was a bad thing. I regard it as an act of self defense. They urged withdrawal of our recognition of the Chiang Kai-shek government. They opposed adoption of the Smith Act, under which many Communists now have been convicted ... They pilloried the FBI for daring to bring Judith Coplon to trial, saying: 'It has given the public a chance to see how silly an FBI report can really be.'

"They have urged a continuation of diplomatic relations with all the Communist nations. They have opposed the rearmament of Germany ...

"If they have ever openly attacked the Communist Party position on any subject, it has not been called to my attention. They have contented themselves with relatively mild generalizations, and in the very next breath, have urged the program I have thus far detailed. They deny the existence of an internal threat and speak softly about the problem in far-off lands. I challenge anyone to name a single Communist tracked down and exposed by the ADA. While I can cite many instances where ADA members have defended Communists exposed by others, I have never found them on the firing line where Communists were being uncovered. I have never found them exposing Communist fronts or denouncing Communist propaganda ... If embracing a large segment of the Communist Party line makes one an anti-Communist, then they qualify. But the real point I want to make is that ADA is a Trojan horse infiltrating our lines for the purpose of selling us socialism ...

"ADA's tolerance of Communists and Communism in our midst . . . may stem from their lack of understanding of Communist philosophy. They seem totally unaware of the fact that Communism demands the destruction of all other societies ... They continually speak of the threat of Communism in America as a phantom . . . They have never admittted the guilt of Alger Hiss. If we followed their advice the Communist conspiracy would soon take over."

Over thirty influential "ADAers" are prominent in the Administration in Washington, D.C. At the turn of this new year, 1964, they include: Theodore C. Sorensen, Arthur S. Schlesinger, Jr., Chester Bowles, G. Mennen Williams, James Loeb Jr., Adlai Stevenson, George L. P. Weaver, Orville Freeman, Frederic C. Belen, Archibald Cox, and Robert C. Weaver.

During October 1958, the ADA invited Roy

Cohn, former Counsel to the McCarthy Senate Subcommittee investigating Communism, to speak at a meeting in New York. Apparently this invitation was a move to show that they "tolerate" opposing views. Roy Cohn bluntly told them what he thought of the organization. He said:

"I am unalterably opposed to just about everything for which you stand. It is the fuzzy irresponsible thinking of you and those associated with you which has contributed to the gains made by the atheistic communistic conspiracy in the world . . . Your activities have aided Communism, not fought it . . . There is no useful purpose to be served by your continued existence."

One of the most powerful organizations which consistently attempts to "brain-wash" Americans, young and old, with the gospel of the far left is the National Education Association. The NEA has now departed from its historic role as a "counselor to education" to become a sort of gestapo operation that blackballs members of the "far right."

Rosalie M. Gordon, author of that great book, *Nine Men Against America*, wrote in the publication, *America's Future*: "One of the most active practitioners of this guilt-by-association is a big educational lobby in Washington known as the National Education Association — NEA for short. NEA is supported by the dues of hundreds of thousands of teachers all over the country. It uses the money which these teachers pay into NEA's treasury . . . But NEA is not, as many believe, merely a *nonpartisan* educational organization. It is a *lobby* — one of the largest in the Capitol . . . Looking at NEA's activities over many years, it is hard to escape the conclusion that its ruling hierarchy is part and parcel of the liberal establishment."

A few years back, the liberal officials of the NEA announced a new project . . . they would spend some of the teacher-members' dues in a four-year program which would collect "extensive files on the critics of education" and/or NEA. In plain English, that means the collection of dossiers by a private organization whose influence reaches high in Washington, D. C. circles, on individuals or organizations who dare criticize "liberal" education or the promoters of unorthodox educational standards, the National Education Association.

The Tulsa World (Tuesday, March 27, 1962,) ran an excellent editorial entitled "The NEA Blacklist' Could Include You!" which we reprint below:

"If you are opposed to Federal aid to education have you ever said so, out loud? Have you ever expressed doubt or question of the adequacy or competence of the public school system? Have you ever asked searching questions about school finance or administration?

"If so, you might be a non-conformist member of a very exclusive new club — the National Education Association *blacklist*.

"It takes only a reasonably thorough perusal of the addresses and proceedings of the 1961 national convention report of the NEA to learn that critics of public education in the U.S. are not only classified by the educationists as 'enemies' of education but are the subject of prepared 'dossiers.'

"We're not going to accept this thing so seriously as to fail to recognize how really ludicrous it is. Yet, what amazes us is that the National Education Association so obviously takes the attitude that critics of educational policies are trying to 'destroy' our system of education.

"The truth is that many people have sincere doubts about the efficiency and adequacy of our educational system; but the doubts they voice and the activities in which they engage are not designed to 'destroy' education but to *improve* it.

"Like other bureaucracies, the NEA assumes the attitude that those who question its motives or doubt its efficiency are sworn enemies and intent upon destroying it. Nonsense!

"*The Tulsa World* has frequently criticized educational policy; it has expressed sincere doubt of the basic 'need' for Federal aid to education and has on occasion openly attack the waste and misuse of public funds in Oklahoma's educational program.

"These activities, the NEA obviously believes, makes *The Tulsa World* an enemy of public education. The truth is, what we want and what most parents want is a dollar's worth of education for every dollar spent; in short, the best for our children at all times.

"What is the NEA attitude on all this? Let's quote directly from a report by the 'National Commission for the Defense of Democracy,' an agency of the NEA!

" 'About 1,000 requests for information concerning individuals or groups thought to be causing trouble for the schools or the profession were received during the year. Several new fact sheets and information bulletins concerning critics of education were prepared. The Commission has, probably, the most complete files of their kind on critics of education.'

"With an annual budget of more then $8 million, the NEA assuredly has the funds to run down and investigate the 'enemies' of education.

"But, that is not all that worries the National Education Association. It wants to keep alert to the situaion, and does so this way:

" 'Local and state associations appoint contacts for the NEA Commission in order to keep the Commission alerted to controversies and destructive criticism damaging to schools in their areas.'

"A pretty stern warning, we should say, for an American people that has long stood firmly for the right and privilege to speak out against those things they believe detrimental to their best interests. Now we find that if we oppose Federal aid to education we are 'enemies' of education and want to destroy public schools."

After reading Communist publications, studying the Communist conspiracy for many years, observing transcripts of Communist conclaves, and listening to Communist speakers, the author can draw no other conclusion than that the Communists intend to rule the world. When members of the Communist hierarchy in the United States make their speeches, and they make many of them, their sole purpose is to promote the cause of Communism's war to conquer the United States. The *truth*, according to Communist definition, is anything which aids the Communist cause. The speeches of Communist speakers are designed to deceive, not inform, their audiences. In spite of the satanic nature of Communism and the deception in Communist speeches, these conspirators are being welcomed with open arms on many American college campuses. The realities of this tragic situation are covered under a phony smoke-screen called *academic freedom.*

According to the Communist *Worker* of December 3, 1961, Herbert Aptheker, editor of the Communist conspiracy's official monthly, *Political Affairs,* spoke to a standing-room-only crowd on the Wayne University campus in Detroit. According to *The Worker,* "... the students gave Aptheker warm rounds of applause." Neglect of parents to teach our youth Christianity and Americanism has made the Communist talk of deceiving American youth much easier. Let us remember the key directive to Communist conspirators in the July 1959 *Political Affairs,* which warned them that success for Communism was not possible unless they could "win a solid base among the youth."

This ridiculous and foolhardy state of affairs has gone so far that the president of the University of Oregon was given an award by *The American Association of University Professors* for allowing Communist Gus Hall to speak on his university campus. This victory for the conspiracy rated a front-page article in the Communist *Worker* of May 1, 1962. This article said:

"The victorious struggle of the students and faculty of the University of Oregon to hear Gus Hall speak early in February, became a nation-wide symbol last week for freedom of speech throughout America's colleges and universities. On Friday, the American Association of University Professors annual meeting in Chicago gave its annual Alexander Meiklojohn Award to Arthur S. Flemming, President of the University of Oregon and Secretary of Health, Education, and Welfare under President Eisenhower. The award honored Flemming's decision to let Hall speak. The association has 50,000 members at 1,400 institutions covering the entire range of education in the United States."

Just how idiotic can things become in this tragically brainwashed nation of ours? While concerned Americans, often referred to as *extremists, super patriots,* or *anti-Communists*, are either restrained from speaking or are smeared, maligned or lied about in an effort to discredit them, a noted educator is rewarded for providing an audience for an enemy of our nation. Here again is an evidence of the vicious *double standard* fostered by the "soft on Communism" attitude promoted by the liberals.

Just who is this man, Gus Hall, whose appearance on the Universtiy of Oregon campus occasioned an award to that university's president by the Association of University Professors?

In a report on the Seventeenth National Convention of the Communist Party, which was held in New York City during December 1959, FBI Director, J. Edgar Hoover, described Hall as "an ex-convict, propagandist, unabashed emissary of evil, and rabid advocate of a Soviet United States."

Mr. Hoover went on later in his report to describe Hall as a "Moscow trained, utterly ruthless, Communist leader."

It is no wonder that we are losing the struggle against the Communist drive to enslave our nation when the American Association of University Professors honors a university president for letting this vicious conspirator speak on a college campus.

What is the attitude of the American Association of University Professors when a college moves to protect our nation and its students from Communist subversion? Does the AAUP bestow similar honors on that college president? Does the AAUP even remain neutral in such cases? No, they definitely take sides. The following are a few examples:

In 1956 the American Association of University Professors condemned Washington University for firing two Communist professors and censured the following educational institutions for firing Communists and those who refused to deny Communist affiliations under oath; the University of California, Ohio State, Temple, Jefferson Medical School, Rutgers, and Oklahoma University.

According to an article in *Human Events*, January 7, 1960, by Professor Anthony Bouscaren of Le Moyne College, each of the censured schools had only ten minutes to defend itself, and the whole procedure of the 1956 convention was of the nature of a star chamber proceeding.

In 1958, the American Association of University Professors blackballed the University of Michigan for firing two professors who refused to testify concerning their Communist affiliations, and Dickinson College was censured for dismissing a faculty member who refused to deny Communist affiliations under oath. In 1959, this professors' organization censured New York University for firing two professors with Communist affiliations.

The AAUP is willing to reward a college president if he allows a Communist to speak on a college campus, under the guise of *academic freedom*. They would be expected to be just as concerned about *academic freedom* if an anti-Communist professor is fired because of his belief. However, this is not the case. In 1956, American University in Washington, D. C., fired Professor Herbert Fuchs, a former Communist who broke with the Communist conspiracy. There was no complaint from the American Association of University Professors concerning the firing of anti-Communist Professor Fuchs by the American University.

It would seem that the Association of University Professors remains constantly on guard against those who interfere with the Communist conspiracy. In a speech at Philadelphia, Pennsylvania, on September 29, 1959, the late Representative Francis E. Walter, Chairman of the House Committee on Un-American Activities, said:

"The American Association of University Professors has, over the course of the last few years, followed the trail of the Committee on Un-American Activities like a ● dog after a meat wagon. Contrary to the propaganda of the Communists and their sympathizers, the Committee on Un-American Activities has never investigated education, labor, professional groups, or any segment of our society as such. We follow the trail of Communists wherever they lead. On several occasions in the course of the last few years we have found members of the Communist Party who were engaged as professors in schools or colleges. On most of these occasions the school or college in which the Communists were employed has fired them, but consistently and promptly the American Association of University Professors has issued a censorship of those schools or colleges for firing the

Communist on the grounds that it was an interference with *academic freedom* ...the American Association of University Professors still thinks that a Communist professor is something less than a Communist and that it is wrong to remove him from the arena in which he can do his most deadly work."

The mere suggestion that there is substantial Communist influence in America's racial strife will draw ridicule from uninformed citizens who consider themselves active promotors or sympathizers of all-out racial integration in America. In examining this question we do not contend that the Communists are the only ones behind America's racial strife. Readers can decide for themselves to what extent the Reds are involved after reading the factual evidence in this chapter.

Some integrationists contend that the Communists merely point out America's racial shortcomings and in so doing, do us a favor. We have even heard the contention that it is all right for Americans to co-operate with Communist fronts in racial integration activities because it is such a good cause.

In examining the evidence in America's racial problems, we need to consider the question as to whether the Communists are merely taking advantage of a situation or whether they have also been an important influence in creating and expanding racial strife in America.

In *The Worker* of May 26, 1963, Communist conspirators were informed that the current Negro uprising in America was "central to our entire national present and future." A feature editorial in the June 30 *Worker* told the Communists, "Nothing in the affairs of our nation is more important than this great struggle (racial strife) that is rolling over our country like a mighty wave." This editorial spoke of our nation's race strife as "this great revolutionary democratic struggle which is making radical changes in our nation in our days."

In short, America's determined enemies consider the current racial strife which is sweeping our nation as the key to their take-over of the United States. The lead article in the July 1963 issue of *Political Affairs*, official Communist monthly, referred to racial strife in the U. S. as "the key to all other struggles." Furthermore, the Communists claim that years ago they were the instigators of this shameful mess in America. An article in *The Worker* of June 30, 1963, made the following claim:

". . . It was the Communists, who for the first time in the 20th century projected the Negro question on to the national political scene for solution.

"Before the Communist Party came into being in 1919, the question of equality for the nation's Negro citizenry had been pigeonholed since 1876 . . ."

The article went on to explain that the Communists understood that our country could not move forward to its destiny, meaning Communism, unless "the commitment of the Civil War was honored." Since we cannot take the word of Communists, we must dig into the factual background for ourselves.

According to Joseph Zack Kornfeder, former Communist leader, Communist activities among American Negroes started around 1921 and "were prompted by a letter sent to the American Party by Nikolai Lenin . . ."

The Communist International, meeting in Moscow

during 1922, declared: "The Negro problem has become a vital question of the world revolution."

During the 1920's, a Communist leader by the name of Joseph Pogany came to the U. S. to advance the conspiracy's cause. Pogany was a leader of the Red terrorists in the first Red Hungarian revolution under Bela Kuhn. In the United States he went under the name of John Pepper and was attached by the Comintern to the leadership of the U. S. Communist Party. He was also a member of the Communist Negro Commission.

During 1928, a booklet by John Pepper entitled "American Negro Problems" was published by the Communists. In this booklet Pepper told the U.S. Communists that "The Negroes of the South are disfranchised politically" and he called their attention to "the tremendous revolutionary possibilities" available to the Communists through exploiting this situation. This Kremlin agent informed Communists in the U. S. that one of their biggest tasks was to extend their activities to the "solid South."

Communist leaders further developed their satanic scheme to use American Negroes at the Sixth World Congress of the Communist International in 1928. The May 3, 1929, issue of the official Communist International publication, *The International Press Correspondence*, told Communists that "The struggles" of "the black toiling masses . . . in Africa, America, the world over, are links in the chain of the world revolutionary struggle. The role of the Communist Party is to draw these oppressed masses into the world revolutionary movement . . ."

Also during 1928, the Communist Party in the

United States published a list of demands on the Negro question in the May 26, 1928 issue of the *Daily Worker*. The Communist racial strife plot in the United States included exploiting all racial inequities and injustices, real or imagined, to create a picture of "national oppression" which would serve as the basis of the Red theory that American Negroes are an "oppressed nation within a nation" and therefore entitled to the "right of self determination."

This plan for a Negro Soviet Republic in the South was rejected by Negro leaders in America and in turn, these leaders were attacked by the Communists with names such as "enemies of the Negro masses." As a result of the rejection by Negro leaders of the Negro Soviet Republic in the South idea, Communists modified their demand, and adopted a strategy of working for a "people's front among Negroes."

Since the basic goal of the Communist plot is to destroy free enterprise, Communists expressed opposition to Negro businesses from the start. In his 1928 booklet, "American Negro Problems," John Pepper gave the Reds some 1924 statistics on Negro businesses and advised them, "This Negro bourgeoisie is closely tied up with the white bourgeoisie; is often the agent of the white capitalists..." In his book *Color, Communism and Common Sense*, Manning Johnson said that Negro business was a bulwark against Communism and that "Consequently, the Reds seek to discredit, discourage and liquidate Negro business."

Manning Johnson, who did much great work in exposing the Communist plot after leaving the Party up until the time of his death, explained in *Color, Commu-*

nism and Common Sense the Red technique of creating hate among Negroes. He wrote:

"The Red propagandists distort the facts concerning racial differences for ulterior motives. All the right is not on the Negro side. Neither is all wrong. The same holds true with regard to the white man's side. The repository of good or evil is not to be found in any particular race ...

"White men sold white men as slaves. Black men sold black men as slaves. Black rulers are no more humane than yellow, red or white rulers. Neither are they less brutal.

"The placing of ... everything, right and just, among the darker races is a dastardly Communist trick to use race as a means of grabbing and enslaving the whole of humanity.

"Moscow's Negro tools in the incitement of racial warfare place all the ills of the Negro at the door of the white leaders of America. Capitalism and imperialism are made symbols of oppressive white rule in keeping with instructions from the Kremlin." Manning Johnson went on to explain that this Red trickery gave the Negro a persecution complex and a warped belief that the white man's prejudices, the white man's government were responsible for all of his problems and troubles.

In this extremely important book, Manning Johnson referred to Communists, pro-Communists, and left-wing race troublemakers who invade the South as "missionaries." He clearly explained their evil work as follows: "Like a witch stirring her brew the 'missionaries' stir up all the sectional and racial bitterness that arose in the wake of the Civil War and Reconstruction. They open old wounds. They thumb the pages of closed chapters. They rake over the dying embers of old grudges, old grievances, old fears and old hates, that time has been gradually consigning to history ..."

No Federal investigating committee has ever labeled the National Association for the Advancement of Colored People as a Communist front. In fact, J. Edgar Hoover, Director of the FBI, emphatically states that the NAACP is not a Communist front. There have been, however, known Communists associated with the NAACP from its beginning. The NAACP was originated in New York City in 1909, primarily by white people. The only Negro among its founders was the late W. E. B. DuBois who served as one of the organization's leaders for years. DuBois had a record of over 75 affiliations with Communist fronts and pro-Communist causes. He served on the faculty of the Communist Party's Jefferson School of Social Science. His articles were featured in Communist publications and his books were promoted by the Communists for many years. Louis Budenz, former editor for the Communist *Worker*, testified that "Dr. Du Bois became a member of the Communist Party approximately in 1944, when this was called to my attention officially by Jack Stachel." During November 1961, Dr. Du Bois dropped his "secret" affiliation with the Communist Party and openly joined the Party. This event was featured in front-page headlines in the November 26, 1961, issue of *The Worker*.

During its early days, the NAACP was attacked by the Communist Party. Communist strategy then was to attack socialists and their political fronts. This included the NAACP which was a socialist front. This policy of direct attack against socialist organizations was changed by Stalin in 1933. After that, the Communists concentrated on infiltrating Socialist organizations and working within them. By February 1950, the Communists were able to brag in their official monthly magazine, *Political Affairs*, that the success of their racial plans was "unmistakable and clearly discernible in the NAACP." By January 1956, *Political Affairs* was saluting the "heroic" leadership of the NAACP and urged Communists to "support the NAACP in the struggle with every ounce of energy at our disposal." Needless to say, *The Worker* currently publicizes favorably the activities of the NAACP including their drive for so-called "racial balance." Proof that the NAACP has been troubled over the years with the problem of Communist penetration is to be found in a resolution adopted at the NAACP convention in 1956 which reads as follows: "As in the past, the association will employ every reasonable measure in keeping with democratic organizational principles to prevent the endorsers, the supporters and defenders of the Communist conspiracy from joining or participating in any way in the work of the NAACP."

On November 11, 1957, the *New York Times* reported that the NAACP had rejected the membership application of Benjamin J. Davis, New York State Chairman of the Communist Party, and had declined a gift of $50 offered by Davis. The statements and actions of the leaders of the NAACP in opposition to Communism appear to be clear and decisive but they tell only half of the story.

At this point, we call upon the expert testimony of Dr. J. B. Matthews, formerly head of the Socialist Party and later Chief Investigator for the Martin Dies and Senator McCarthy Committees The following information was presented under oath by Dr Matthews at a public hearing of the Florida Legislation Investigation Committee on Monday, February 10, 1958, at the State Capital in Tallahassee, Florida:

"The other half of the story is that many of the leaders of the NAACP have been unusually susceptible to joining, supporting, and defending the front organizations of the Communist conspiracy.

"The indisputable truth of the matter is that the leaders of the NAACP, taken as a whole, have been extraordinarily soft toward the Communist conspiracy.

"In the so-called anti-Communist resolution adopted at the San Francisco convention in 1956, there would appear to be a big loophole in the phrase, 'every reasonable measure in keeping the democratic organizational principals.' Obviously, 'democratic organizational principles' do not prevent a person from holding high position in the NAACP and high position in a Communist organization at one and the same time.

"Two examples of NAACP officials who are currently prominent in the affairs of Communist organizations will illustrate the interlocking of the NAACP and the Communist apparatus.

"Andrew D. Weinberger, a national vice-president of the NAACP, is listed as treasurer on the 1957 letterhead of the Emergency Civil Liberties Committee, one of the most active Communist organizations in the United States at the present time.

"John Wesley Dobbs, a national vice-president of the NAACP, is a member of the board of directors of the Southern Conference Educational Fund, the most influential Communist organization currently operating in the South. Mr. Dobbs was a guest of honor at a 1957 meeting of the Emergency Civil Liberties Committee. He was also a signer of the brief *amici curiae* submitted to the U. S. Supreme Court on behalf of the Communist Party in the fall of 1955.

"It may be enlightening to give some totals which indicate the extent to which the top leadership of the NAACP has given aid and comfort to the Communist-front apparatus. Listed on the current letterheads of the NAACP are the names of 236 different national officers. One hundred forty-five (or more than 61 per cent) of these individuals have been involved, in one way or another, with Communist enterprises, for a grand total of 2,200 affiliations of public record. Forty-six of these NAACP national officers have had one or two Communist affiliations; 99 have had 3 or more such affiliations; 52 have had 10 or more; and 46 have had 15 or more."

Some of the national officers of the NAACP whose Communist affiliations number fifteen or more include Edward L. Parsons (Protestant Episcopal bishop); Guy Emery Shipler (Protestant Episcopal clergyman); Roger N. Baldwin (American Civil Liberties Union); Algernon D. Black (Society for Ethical Culture leader); Freda Kirchwey (editor of *The Nation*); Henry Hitt Crane (Methodist clergyman); Max Lerner (newspaper columnist and professor); Channing H. Tobias (Methodist clergyman); James H. Wolfe (Chief Justice of Utah

Supreme Court); Archibald MacLeish (poet and university professor); A. Philip Randolph (labor union president); Frank P. Graham (University president, ex-U.S. Senator); Reinhold Niebuhr (clergyman and theological professor); Roscoe Dunjee (Oklahoma newspaper editor); Benjamin E. Mays (college president and clergyman); Edwin McNeill Poteat (Baptist clergyman); Norman Thomas (socialist leader); Henry Smith Leiper (Presbyterian clergyman).

This, of course, is but a partial listing. Some of these above names have an extraordinarily large number of Communist affiliations. Bishop Edward L. Parsons has over 100; Guy Emerey Shipler, 76; Roger N. Baldwin, 64; Algernon D. Black, 60; Henry Hitt Crane, 46; Max Lerner, 43; Channing H. Tobias, 43; A. Philip Randolph, 38. (The Communist-front affiliations of these various NAACP national officers is according to the testimony of Dr. J. B. Matthews mentioned above.)

The assassin of John F. Kennedy, Lee Harvey Oswald, according to the FBI report, may have been acting on his own in the killing of the President. If he did it on his own, it does not alter the fact that Communism did it, for Oswald was an indoctrinated Communist. If he did it on his own, it was obviously not a snap judgment. The evidence indicates that he tried to assassinate General Edwin A. Walker on the previous April 10. His widow said that the night of April 10, her husband told her boastingly and excitedly that he had just made an attempt on the life of General Walker. Oswald apparently was an assassin who had plenty of time to think over the entire question of assassination. If Oswald did assassinate the President without outside instruction, what could have been the more immediate circumstance which led him to do it, other than the fact that he was a Communist? The President had made a speech the Monday before he was killed in which he indicated that if the Cubans would get rid of the Castro government, our nation would help them rebuild Cuba. Oswald had said publicly that he would fight to defend Castro. It may have been that he decided the U.S. was going to either invade or to assist in the assassination of Castro, or otherwise work to overthrow the Castro government. He may have then decided that now was the time to strike a blow for Castro and strike it in the high place. Whether he did it alone or under orders, we see in his terrible act the evil essence of Communism. Just as Oswald assassinated the President, so Communism aims to assassinate humanity, civilization, freedom, morality, and God.

The Soviet Union has given the United States Government its file on Lee Oswald. Now what does that prove? The obvious facts are that the Kremlin would withhold any information that would indict international Communism and, furthermore, by pretending to cooperate with the U.S. Government in this move, they proved that they do not want the United States in any way to stiffen its attitude toward Communism as a result of the fact that a Communist killed the President of the United States.

Some of the spokesmen of the far left insist that Oswald was insane. However, it is a fact that he was not a raving maniac, but a cruel, calculating killer, according to the evidence turned up by the police and also as indicated by his own conduct most of the time. He had eaten at least part of his lunch while waiting for the President's caravan to appear below him. He was seen sipping a Coca-Cola shortly after he shot the President. Police stated, according to *Newsweek* magazine, December 9, 1963, that Oswald was "in full possession of his mental powers." We are not denying that he was warped in his thinking. It may be that his hatred toward others helped condition his mind for the reception of Communism, and as a Marxist, he was certainly out of touch with reality, for Marxism as a philosophy of life is a perversion of reality.

Some have felt that since Oswald denied that he was guilty of the assassination that there is therefore grounds for doubt that he was guilty. Al Capone never pleaded guilty to being a gangster and he was not jailed for being one, but for evading income tax.

According to the police and the evidence which has been made public, Lee Oswald (one) was a *Communist*, (two) was an expert marksman in the Marines, (three) had lived in the Soviet Union and renounced his American citizenship, and (four) had applied at the American Embassy in Moscow for a passport to return home, being loaned money by Ambassador Llewellyn Thompson in the amount of $450 in order that he might come back to the United States with his Russian wife. (Llewellyn Thompson is now assistant to Dean Rusk, Secretary of State.)

The question in a lot of minds is "Did Castro ask Lee Oswald to assassinate President Kennedy?" According to the *New York Times*, November 25, 1963, Castro denied that he had anything to do with it. However, we know that the denial of a Communist is not sufficient grounds on which to base a conclusion. Gromyko lied to President Kennedy concerning missiles in Cuba, even though he must have known that Kennedy knew that Gromyko was lying. To the Communists, any lie is the truth if it helps Communism. Although we do not know at this point whether or not Castro ordered the assassination of President Kennedy, anyone who has studied Communism and also Castro, knows that he would not hesitate to do it if he thought he could get by with it and it would serve the cause of Communism.

Back on March 30, 1961, Senator Thomas J. Dodd (Democrat-Conneticut) spoke of the American newspapers and their determination to crush the John Birch Society. He said: "But for some reason which I cannot understand . . . (the press) . . . has not used this weapon anywhere near as effectively against the Fair Play for Cuba Committee, the various off-shoots of the 'Communist Peace Offensive' and the other Communist-front operations in this country." The former FBI undercover agent, Herbert A. Philbrick, said of the pseudo-liberals of the far left: "Show them a movement like the Fair Play for Cuba Committee organized under Communist direction and with Communist financial support, and these self same liberals are just not interested."

It was interesting to see the chairman of the Fair Play for Cuba Committee, Vincent Theodore Lee, trying to deny that Lee Harvey Oswald had the official sanction of the national office to set up the Fair Play for Cuba Committee in New Orleans. It is especially strange that the organization should have waited until after Oswald murdered the President to publicly disclaim Oswald. Why should we believe individuals and officials of this organization and what they say when not under oath since they invoke the Fifth Amendment when before Congressional Committees?

Congressman Cramer of Florida stated on the floor of Congress, March 5, 1962: "Beginning in April of 1960 and continuing for a period of some fourteen months, the Senate Internal Subcommittee held hearings to determine whether the Fair Play for Cuba Committee was a subversive organization and thus whether it should properly be placed on the Attorney General's subversive list. Imagine my continuing surprise and consternation to learn that the Attorney General has not yet seen fit to list the Fair Play for Cuba Committee as being subversive in spite of over-whelming evidence to the contrary produced at the several hearings by the Senate Subcommittee. Indeed, I ascertained a certain amount of misguided feeling that this group of rabble-rousers had gone underground after Fidel Castro made his open announcement that he had formally embraced Communism, and I seem to gain the impression that the Department of Justice might feel that there no longer remained any need for being apprehensive about what the Fair Play for Cuba Committee has recently been up to. I detect this feeling among those who should be chasing Communists instead of forgetting about them."

As a result of the hearings by Senator Eastland's Senate Internal Security Subcommittee, it was proven that the Fair Play for Cuba Committee was born in the spring of 1960. One of the top men of CBS news, Robert Taber, and another man named Waldo Frank put together the Fair Play for Cuba Committee. (Waldo Frank, incidentally, as far back as 1932, wrote an article for *New Masses* magazine entitled "How I Came To Communism: Symposium.")

Congressman Cramer said that Robert Taber "duped" the Columbia Broadcasting System and the network was used for Castro public relations in the United States, which resulted in picturing Fidel Castro as "a regular salt of the earth." Another CBS newsman also associated with this Communist front — Richard Gibson. After terminating his services with CBS news, CBS thought well enough of Gibson to send him to Columbia University in New York on what is known as a CBS Fellowship. Soon after he arrived on the campus, Columbia University found itself with an active full-fledged chapter of the Fair Play for Cuba Committee.

Soon after the committee had been formed in New York, Taber placed a full-page ad in the *New York Times*, headlined: "What Is Really Happening In Cuba," which, of course, supported the position of Fidel Castro. Some of the "best known" names in the far left camp were listed as sponsors of this organization, including Negro author James Baldwin, Rev. Donald Harrington, Rev. John Papandrew, Prof. Robert G. Colodny, Prof. Eugene Noble, and three well-known authors — Truman Capote, Norman Mailer, and Jean Paul Sartre. The ad listed Waldo Frank as chairman and Carleton Beals as co-chairman of the Fair Play for Cuba Committee.

The Senate Internal Security Subcommittee quizzed both Taber and a prominent New York City physician, Dr. Charles A. Santos-Buch, as to the cost of the ad and the source of the funds used to pay the bill of $4,725. Dr. Santos-Buch admitted that their efforts to raise money for the ad through private and voluntary subscriptions fell flat and aside from a few hundred dollars they managed to raise, the funds came to Taber and Santos-Buch from the Cuban Government, specifically from Raul Roa, Jr., the son of Castro's foreign minister and himself a member of the Cuban delegation to the United Nations. Santos-Buch, incidentally, is registered as a foreign agent and according to the latest count, is assistant pathologist at New York Hospital-Cornell Medical Center.

Congressman Cramer in his March 15, 1962, speech further stated: "The Attorney General's failure to place this group on the subversive list becomes all the more baffling when we consider that the annual FBI report for the fiscal year 1961 states, in part: 'FBI investigations also have shown that the Fair Play for Cuba Committee has been heavily infiltrated by the Communist Party and the Socialist Workers Party, and these parties have actually organized some chapters of the committee. Both organizations, of course, are on the Attorney General's subversive list.' "

The *Weekly Review*, published in London, issue of December 20, 1963, stated, concerning the Fair Play for Cuba Committee: "Organized in April 1960, the Fair Play for Cuba Committee represents a joint undertaking between the Communist Party and the Socialist Workers Party (Trotskyite Communist) to defend, support, and otherwise carry out the aims of Castro's Cuba. With four chapters in Canada and twenty-three chapters in the United States, this Communist organization is one of the most fanatical Red networks in existence. Lee Harvey Oswald, one of the chapter chairmen, played an important role in the 6,000-member organization. When he pulled the trigger to kill President Kennedy, the Fair Play for Cuba Committee symbolically stood behind the stock. The Fair Play for Cuba Committee network effectively covers the United States and Canada. Communist fanatics similar to assassin Lee Oswald can be found in any of its local chapters."

It is interesting to note in some areas the Fair Play for Cuba Committee holds its regular meetings in churches. For instance, in Los Angeles the committee held periodic meetings at the First Unitarian Church, 2936 West 8th Street. Its minister, Stephen H. Fritchman, is listed as honorary chairman of the committee.

FPFC Chairman Vincent T. Lee, thirty-five years of age, according to the Tampa, Florida *Tribune*, December 15, 1961, is actually the son of Mr. and Mrs. Charles Tappin of New York City. When appearing before the committee, Lee refused to answer whether or not he knew the Tappins, whether he was a member of the Communist Party or had ever received financial compensation from it, and all questions relating to his education, date and place of birth. The *Tampa Tribune* article declared that Lee was known to have been a member of the now-defunct Socialist Youth League.

It is interesting to note that according to the Senate Subcommittee report, Lee obtained a United States passport to visit Castro's Cuba in December 1962 as a radio reporter representing radio station WBAI, New York City. WBAI is affiliated with the Pacifica Foundation which controls two stations in additon to the New York station — KPFA, Berkeley, and KPFK, Los Angeles. Pacifica Foundation has recently been the object of hearings by the Senate Internal Security Subcommittee to determine possible Communist infiltration.

It is apparent that after Lee Harvey Oswald, Kennedy's assassin, returned to the United States from the Soviet Union, he immediately went to work for Fair Play for Cuba in New Orleans, Louisiana, where he was arrested for passing out anti-American literature on the streets of New Orleans.

On Thursday, November 28, 1963, the *Dallas Morning News* carried a story entitled "Evidence Points to Red Activity," which included the following: "A prosecutor has said that evidence found in the Oak Cliff room of Lee Harvey Oswald proves he was 'an active worker in the Communist cause.' Assistant District Attorney William F. Alexander said the evidence included letters in which a Communist leader thanked Oswald 'for past services.' Alexander said part of the letters were written on 'Communist Party of America' stationery while others carried a 'Fair Play for Cuba' letterhead. 'All of them were written in recent weeks and were signed by the same man,' the Assistant District Attorney said. 'He is a New Yorker who is an active Communist.'"

On Friday, December 20, 1963, Robert Beatty Fennell, 29, of San Francisco, California, was arrested by the United States Secret Service in nearby Berkeley. Fennell carried in his pockets notes exclaiming, "My immediate goal: The Assassination of President Johnson." Fennell admitted that he was a member of the Fair Play for Cuba Committee. When this story was reported in the far-left *Newsweek* magazine, December 30, 1963, page 15, the liberal editors conveniently neglected to point out that Fennell was a member of the Fair Play for Cuba Committee. In fact, only two short paragraphs were devoted to the story. On the other hand, a college student at Arlington, Texas, Russell W. Mc-Larry, 21, who had reportedly said prior to Kennedy's visit to Dallas that he would "be waiting with a gun to get the President," was arrested by the Secret Service, charged with making a threat against Mr. Kennedy and was released on a $2,500 bond. *Newsweek* magazine reproduced a picture of McLarry and devoted four long paragraphs to this story, but, as I said, there was no mention of the Fair Play for Cuba Committee membership of Mr. Fennell in the accompanying story.

Our Oklahoma Senator, Howard Edmondson, like many of the liberal crowd, hastened to blame the anti-Communist conservative community for the assassination of Mr. Kennedy. In fact Senator Edmondson was not even original in his attack. In his "Senator Edmondson Reports To The People" for December 1963, he reprinted in its entirety a column by Walter Lippmann which appeared in the *Washington Post,* in which the far-left columnist blames the conservatives for the assassination. In a letter to Senator Edmondson dated December 17, 1963, I stated: "It is strange to me that neither you nor Mr. Lippmann have had anything to say about the Fair Play for Cuba Committee and the American Civil Liberties Union, in both of which Lee Harvey Oswald, the President's assassin, was interested. In fact, in our *Tulsa Daily World,* Thursday, December 12, there was an Associated Press article saying that the Communist who assassinated Mr. Kennedy, Oswald, had attended a meeting of the American Civil Liberties

Union on the campus of the Southern Methodist University less than one month before the assassination. At that time he was shown a real hate film called 'Suspect' put out by the ACLU. The film is designed to turn the liberals against the anti-Communists and conservative opposition in the United States. So if Lee Oswald assassinated the President because of a hate climate, may I assure you, based on fact, Mr. Oswald's motivation was a hate film, put out by a hate organization called the American Civil Liberties Union. He was not influenced by, let's say, 'Operation Abolition' put out by the House Committee on Un-American Activities or by 'Communist Encirclement' put out by Harding College. It was not an anti-Communist film that angered Mr. Oswald. If, indeed, he plotted the assassination of the President because of the hate climate in Dallas it was a hate climate which had been created by the liberal leaders of the Dallas community."

An editorial on hatred appeared in the January 4-11, 1964, *Saturday Evening Post* which deserves consideration:

"Hatred knows no logic, whether it is from the left or the right. In the first hours after President Kennedy was assassinated, most people automatically blamed right-wing extremists. It turned out that the President's assassin was a mentally disturbed Marxist, but this did not stop many people who had deplored the 'hatred' that brought his death from continuing to vent *their* hatred upon the radical right.

"Conservative members of Congress were deluged with threats and abusive letters. Sen. John Tower, arch-conservative from Texas, was the outstanding example.

He was besieged with letters, telephone calls and wires charging him with responsibility for the President's death. The threats were so serious that the Senator's family had to move out of Washington temporarily for protection.

"The worst offender, oddly enough, was a minister from Waco, Texas. He wrote Senator Tower an abusive letter that said, 'I hope you're satisfied. If a few people could be charged with blame for death of our President, your name would be near the top.'

"We rarely agree with Senator Tower. To our way of thinking, his political philosophy belongs in another era. But he was elected to the Senate by his constituents; he is entitled to his views, and he expresses them fairly and politely. He bore about as much responsibility for the assassination of President Kennedy as a Fiji Islander. That point became clear when Lee Harvey Oswald's background was known, but unfortunately some people practice the very hatred that they deplore in others."

Of all of the movements of the far left, the American Civil Liberties Union (ACLU) is possibly the best known. It would take an entire book to even touch on the activities of this organization. The ACLU is an outgrowth of a pacifist organization called the American Union Against Militarism, formed in 1915. The notorious left-winger, Roger Baldwin, joined the staff early in 1917 and established a Civil Liberties Bureau. It soon became an independent organization with a board of its own which included the present head of the Socialist Party, Norman Thomas. In September, 1918, the United States Justice Department raided its offices and seized its files. Baldwin resigned as director when drafted for military service. He refused to serve in the military, was subjected to prosecution and was sentenced to one year in prison.

In January 1920 under the leadership of a New York lawyer, Albert DeSilver, the American Civil Liberties Union was born. The Communist clergyman, Rev. Harry F. Ward, was its chairman and Roger Baldwin and then-Communist Louis F. Budenz served on the National Committee. Other Communists, including A. J. Muste and Scott Nearing, also served on the original National Committee.

In order to understand the American Civil Liberties Union, we need to understand Roger Baldwin, its leading light, and for thirty years its director. He has remained an important member of the organization since stepping down as director. Baldwin went to prison for draft evasion in World War I. He was among the early Fabian socialists at Harvard University, which has been one of the chief centers from which socialistic poison has pervaded the American mind.

Roger Baldwin made his philosophy very clear in a statement he wrote in a Harvard reunion book at the 30th anniversary of his 1905 class. On page seven of this class book, Baldwin said: "My chief aversion is the system of greed, private profit, privilege and violence which makes up the control of the world today, and which has brought it to the tragic crisis of unprecedented hunger and unemployment ... therefore, I am for socialism, disarmament and ultimately for abolishing the state itself as an instrument of violence and compulsion. I seek social ownership of property, the abolition of the property class and sole control by those who produce wealth. Communism is the goal." He could hardly have made it clearer.

Testifying before a special House of Representatives committee investigating Communist propaganda in the U. S. during 1930-31, Mr. Baldwin upheld the "right" of a citizen to advocate murder, assassination or the violent overthrow of the government. The chairman asked Mr. Baldwin: "Does your organization uphold the right of citizen or alien ... to advocate murder or assassination?" Mr. Baldwin's answer to both was "Yes."

He was also asked: "Does your organization uphold the right of an American citizen to advocate force and violence for the overthrow of the government?" Mr. Baldwin answered: "Certainly; insofar as mere advocacy is concerned." Naturally, Baldwin has a very extensive Communist-front record.

The American Legion has repeatedly called for an investigation of the American Civil Liberties Union. Among the reasons given by the Legion are the following, which are quoted from the December 1, 1953, issue of the American Legion's *Firing Line* publication:

" ...In 1953 ...Baldwin, in his official capacity as director of the American Civil Liberties Union, appeared on American college campuses and led students in taking the 'Oxford' pledge not to bear arms in defense of the United States ... fully 90% of the American Civil Liberties Union's time, efforts, and funds have been expended in behalf of Communists, radicals, subversive aliens and other disloyal elements who have come into conflict with the law ... control of the American Civil Liberties Union

for many years has been in the hands — not of good
Americans, who subscribe to the avowed purposes of
this organization — but native or alien stooges in the
grand conspiracy to overthrow the American government
by force and violence."

At their 42nd Annual National Convention in Mi-
ami Beach, Florida, October 17-20, 1960, the American
Legion again called on Congress to make an official
investigation of the American Civil Liberties Union, together with its officers and directors.

House of Representatives Report No. 2290, of January 17, 1931, stated the following in regard to the
American Civil Liberties Union: "American Civil Liberties Union is closely affiliated with the Communist
movement in the United States, and fully 90% of its
efforts are on behalf of Communists who have come into
difficulty with the law. It claims to stand for free speech,
free press, and free assembly, but it is quite apparent
that the main function of the American Civil Liberties
Union is to attempt to protect the Communists in their
advocacy of force and violence to overthrow the government, replacing the American flag by a red flag."

Some of the famous liberals who were elected to the
board in the 1940's, include George S. Counts, Norman
Cousins of "World Government" fame, Elmer Davis,
Melvyn Douglas, Harry Emerson Fosdick, Robert M.
Hutchins of "Fund for the Republic" fame, Max Lerner
of the *New York Post*, Greenville Clark of "United
World Federalists" fame, Archibald MacLeish, A. Philip
Randolph, Will Rogers, Jr., Arthur Schlesinger, Jr., Ray-
mond Graham Swing, Roy Wilkins; in the 1950's, ad-
ditional liberals were placed on the board, including

publisher Palmer Hoyt of the far-left *Denver-Post*.

In addition to House Report No. 2290 quoted previously, the ACLU was cited by a California Committee. The California Senate Fact-Finding Committee on Un-American Activities in its 1943 and 1948 reports listed the American Civil Liberties Union as "a Communist front or transmission-belt organization. At least ninety per cent of its efforts are expended in behalf of Communists who come into conflict with the law."

A close look at the file of clippings from American newspapers on the ACLU reveals that it boasted in its monthly publication of May 1962 that the Peace Corps contained "a great number of volunteers who belong to the American Civil Liberties Union." That the ACLU claims strength in the Peace Corps is an interesting reality, especally when we consider that William A. Delano, a member of the American Civil Liberties Union National Board of Directors since 1957, was appointed in October 1961 as General Counsel to the Peace Corps.

Among the things that ACLU stands for and opposes are: (one) ACLU opposes universal military training (35th Annual Report of the ACLU, 1954-1955, Page 21); (two) ACLU protests military officers participating in anti-Communist seminars (41st Annual Report of the ACLU, 1960-61, page 43); (three) ACLU demanded that Defense Secretary McNamara halt the threat of censorship against publications on military newsstands such as the infamous *Overseas Weekly* ("*Civil Liberties*" No. 199, June 1962, page 2); (four) ACLU objects to "nativity scenes" on school premises and Good Friday observances in public schools (38th Annual Report, 1957-1958, pages 31-32); (five) ACLU claims compulsory saluting of United States flag is unconstitutional (Report of ACLU of Northern California, 1958-60, page 13); (six) ACLU believes our national motto, "In God We Trust," is unconstitutional (36th Annual Report, page 44); (seven) ACLU opposes investigation of Communism by Government Committees (Report of ACLU of Northern California, June 1958-June 1960); (eight) ACLU is against prayer recitation in public schools (38th Annual Report, 1957-58, page 27); (nine) ACLU opposes bill to forbid passports to Communists and Communist sympathizers (40th Annual Report ACLU 1959-1960, page 32-33). These are but a few of the pronouncements of the ACLU.

No organization in the United States warrants an investigation any more than the American Civil Liberties Union. Such an investigation of this particular powerful far-left group is long overdue.

In closing this book, reviewing what I have written, I realize that I have merely touched the surface of the Communist threat internally. However, I sincerely hope and pray that I have given enough insight into the ever-increasing threat of Communism *internally* that my readers will want to dedicate their lives to God through Jesus Christ, to preserve our Constitutional concepts of Government and New Testament Christianity in these days of crises. Let me challenge you with this thought. God hates a coward. This is no time to be fearful. We have a choice before us. We can be American or Communist. We can't be both. Whether we are bored by repetition or not, Communism is a fact that must be confronted; it is a menace not to be minimized; it is a force to be fought.

Communism is so insidiously clever that it has grown within our boundaries almost imperceptibly.

Communism, though a monster of gigantic proportions, is vulnerable. It can be attacked from many angles. Economically unsound; philosophically false; practically running counter to every human inclination and instinct; it can be refuted. To refute, however, is not to check it; to denounce it is not to destroy its power. Something must be done about it as well as something said about it. And remember, God hates a coward.

I consider General Carlos P. Romulo a friend. His article "America, Wake Up!" which appeared in the November 1960 issue of the *Reader's Digest* has been a source of inspiration to me. He said:

"... We can yet drive the Reds in their turn onto the defensive. There are plenty of weaknesses and vulnerable spots in the Communist camp — and we can exploit every one of them. We can turn the Communists' own weapons, including infiltration and subversion, against them. We can create 'crises' in *their* home territory, instead of waiting passively for crises in ours. We can train specialists in every branch of cold warfare instead of relying on amateurs. We can keep alive the hope of release from servitude among our enslaved brothers under the Communist yoke.

"Appeasement is as futile in a cold war as it has proved to be, throughout the ages, in hot war. Continued apathy, or half-measures, in the struggle now under way will only encourage the Communists to underrate our will to resist, thus eventually crowding us into a corner where we will have to choose between nuclear war and surrender.

"The only possible solution is to wage this protracted conflict twice as hard, twice as effectively, as the Communists are now waging it. We must embark on a massive offensive, turning every Communist trick and stratagem — from propaganda to infiltration — against our mortal enemy. This is the one and only way to win the struggle for survival."

The answer to the question, "How can we fight and win?", has also been answered well by Dr. J. B. Matthews in his book *Odyssey of a Fellow Traveler*. He wrote:

"I believe that stark tragedy for America lurks in any crusade to salvage civilization in other parts of the world, and that, if civilization is to be saved in this generation, there is plenty of work for every American at home.

"I *know* that conservatives who would oppose successfully the left-wing illusions of our time must drop their divisive interpretations of what lies back of the Communist and socialist movement.

"In opposing the collectivistic movements and tendencies of the day, I do not believe that misrepresentation can be successfully answered with misrepresentation, of hate with hate. Many years ago, I taught in a Chinese Confucianist school. I learned there something of the great Chinese conservative sage and his law of measure or balance. It was when I neglected this precept that I stumbled into the left-wing politics of this distraught age of ours, where men are in such frenzied haste to make the world better that they seize upon hatred, vulgarity, and immoderation as means toward their end. I marvel at the facility with which Communists have put forth mere hoodlumism as an ideal, have dressed the naked lust for unearned power in the garb of a utopian impulse; but for myself, I have confidence in the wisdom of the ages, and I must, therefore, put aside both haste and hate as the self-defeating urges of barbarians who have not shared in the cultural heritage of mankind.

"I do not propose either quietism or defeatism in the presence of the colossal conceit of Bolshevism. I wish only to express the belief that the advance of Communism can be stopped in this country before it reaches the stage of the barricades and civil war, and that our ability to accomplish this depends in large measure upon our own care for facts and our own coolheadedness in confronting a foe who is anything but collected, despite his philosophy of collectivism."

We must wake up or perish. The continually expanding power of the Communist conspiracy in our nation is frightening to any informed person. For America to be saved from this cruel conspiracy and its powerful allies there will have to be an awakening of the American people on an unheard-of scale. The help of God is essential and I feel that our nation can be spared from the iron heel of the Communist conspirators only if many more Americans turn to the Gospel of Jesus Christ and stop listening to and supporting the false prophets in those socialistically-inclined churches, many of whom participate in Communist-conspiracy front operations. You can surely find a "true to the Bible" church to attend in the city where you live.

Many of the informed American patriots who have been in this fight for America are getting tired. They are extremely discouraged at the apathy and complacency of fellow Americans. They are discouraged at the closed-mind attitude of many who persist in deluding themselves that they are being told the truth by their popular magazines and newspapers in spite of mountains of evidence to the contrary. Those of us in this fight for America need fresh help — help from those who have thus far sat out this struggle for America. Whether we like it or not, we are all in this struggle between the forces of Satan and truth. To refuse to fight back merely aids the enemy, who is moving ever closer to complete enslavement of us all. Let us all resolve to do our part in this all-important struggle for survival and never forget that to win we must remain loyal to our God and Saviour. On this crusade of the century, let's resolve to "Go with God!"

THE END